AUG 22 20

A NATION LIKE ALL OTHERS

WARREN I. COHEN

A NATION
LIKE ALL OTHERS

A Brief History of American Foreign Relations

Columbia University Press / New York

Columbia University Press
Publishers Since 1893
New York   Chichester, West Sussex
cup.columbia.edu

Library of Congress Cataloging-in-Publication Data

Names: Cohen, Warren I., author.
Title: A nation like all others : a brief history of American foreign
relations / Warren I. Cohen.
Description: New York : Columbia University Press, 2018. | Includes index.
Identifiers: LCCN 2017023267 | ISBN 9780231175661 (cloth : alk. paper) |
ISBN 9780231545952 (e-book)
Subjects: LCSH: United States—Foreign relations. | United States—
Foreign relations—1865–
Classification: LCC E183.7 .C625 2017 | DDC 327.73—dc23
LC record available at https://lccn.loc.gov/2017023267

∞

Columbia University Press books are printed on permanent
and durable acid-free paper.

Printed in the United States of America

Cover illustration: Joseph Ciardiello
Cover design: Chang Jae Lee

In memory of my beloved wife

Nancy Bernkopf Tucker

and

the wonderful life we shared

and

to three extraordinary young women

Kate Brown

Marjoleine Kars

Marianne Szegedy-Maszak

who accepted Nancy's assignment

to look after me in my dotage

CONTENTS

CONTENTS

CONTENTS

PREFACE

OR THE INTERESTED reader, there are two magnificent histories of American foreign relations, beginning to end: George Herring's *From Colony to Superpower* and the *New Cambridge History of American Foreign Relations*, which I edited and to which William Weeks, Walter LaFeber, Akira Iriye, and I contributed volumes. Both remain excellent sources, beautifully written, well documented, with superb bibliographies. They have one major drawback consistent with their quality: both run over a thousand pages.

Many years ago, Daniel Boorstin asked W. Stull Holt to write a *short* history of American foreign relations for a series he was editing (which included William Leuchtenburg's classic *Perils of Prosperity*). Stull kept waiting for the war in Vietnam to end, and when it finally did, the old World War I fighter pilot was too close to the end of his life to complete the task. As his student, I've long felt that the responsibility for picking up that challenge was mine. Stull, a die-hard supporter of the war in Vietnam, would not have liked this book, but he always tolerated my deviances— even my sympathetic treatment of the revisionist historians he despised.

Without apology, I offer herein an interpretive essay, minus the scholarly paraphernalia I've demanded from my students and of the authors whose books I've reviewed over the past fifty-odd years. The reader who wants more is advised to refer to the Herring and *Cambridge History* volumes.

In the course of writing this book, I happened to read David Bromwich's *Moral Imagination*—which he defines as "the power that compels us to grant the highest possible reality and the largest conceivable claim to a thought, action, or person that is not our own." Empathy for the Other is not commonly thought of as an essential element of foreign policy, a requirement for would-be policymakers, the men and women recruited to serve the national interest. My use of Bromwich's ideas is regrettably reductive, but they do help provide focus for my evaluation of the foreign policies of the United States and of its leaders. I, like Bromwich, am concerned with the relationship between power and conscience.

Like many—if not most—Americans, I grew up as a confirmed believer in American exceptionalism, in the United States as a force for good in the world. I felt that strongly when I enlisted in the U.S. Navy sixty-one years ago. And although I can think of no other nation with a role more exemplary, it has saddened me over the years to recognize the abuse of power of which our leaders have been guilty—the lack of moral imagination that has permeated American foreign policy from colonial times through these last years of my life, from the many years of aggression against Native Americans to the present mismanagement of affairs in the Muslim world. And, sadly, the fact that more than 40 percent of the American people would support the candidacy for president of a man like Donald Trump—*and* elect him—suggests that a nation like all others is composed of a people like all others.

In brief, I hope my readers will share in the exhilaration I still feel when I think of Europeans cheering when the Yanks came to liberate them in both World Wars—and the shame of being reminded of the mistreatment of Native Americans in the eighteenth and nineteenth centuries, of Vietnamese in the twentieth, and of prisoners at Abu Ghraib in the twenty-first. Ours is a nation with the power—and often the will—to do great good, and too often the power to do evil as well. I pray that President Trump will amaze the world with a hitherto hidden capacity for moral imagination.

Finally, had Nancy Bernkopf Tucker lived to read this manuscript, her challenges, as always, would have resulted in a better book.

ACKNOWLEDGMENTS

M Y THANKS GO first to Anne Routon, formerly with Columbia University Press, who encouraged me to write this book as I was emerging from the self-inflicted paralysis that followed the death of my wife. Kate Brown, Marjoleine Kars, and Marianne Szegedy-Maszak were the friends who got me that far.

For the most part I spared knowledgeable friends the task of reading the manuscript, with two important exceptions: John Jeffries and Jim Mann. Both of them read the Obama chapter and my "Last Thoughts." Neither was satisfied with what they read, but I did make *some* of the changes they suggested.

I was fortunate to receive two remarkable readers' reports obtained by the Press, remarkable for both their insight and their depth. One reader was easily identifiable as George Herring. I think I made almost all the corrections both George and the anonymous reader requested and added a few pages both thought necessary. They respected my desire to write a *short* history of America's foreign affairs but seemed to think my product might be a little too short.

I am also grateful to Stephen Wesley of Columbia University Press, who stepped in when Anne left. He not only managed the progress of this book but also took on oversight of the Press's Nancy Bernkopf Tucker and

Warren I. Cohen series in American–East Asian Relations. Anita O'Brien, a colleague of long standing, did a magnificent job of copyediting my manuscript. And Katie Benton-Cohen rode to the rescue when I had no idea how to work with the copy Anita sent.

A NATION LIKE ALL OTHERS

1

TO CREATE A NATION

OUT OF THIRTEEN disparate, often unruly British colonies lining the Atlantic coast of North America in the mid-eighteenth century, there was to emerge a great and powerful nation. That outcome, believed by some to have been ordained by God, was apparent to few mortals at the time.

On the eve of what the American colonists called the French and Indian War (the Seven Years War of 1756–1763), they perceived themselves surrounded by hostile Indians and French and Spanish colonists—all engaged in a struggle for land. The war began as the Americans pressed westward from the coastal regions, contesting control of areas once dominated by Indians and now equally desired by the French. Soon the British military was drawn into what became the fifth Anglo-French war since 1689, a long-standing competition for dominance in Europe and North America.

In addition to lusting for land, the American colonists, specifically the merchants among them, craved greater opportunities for trade, circumventing the restrictions of British mercantilism whenever they could. But much of their freedom of action, whether to expand their landholdings or their trade, came under pressure after 1763. The British were exhausted financially by the war and found it necessary to impose new taxes on the colonies, enforce their navigation laws more rigorously, and restrict

American settlers from crossing the Appalachians to provoke Indian uprisings or other European settlers.

The colonial elite was outraged by each perceived interference with its liberty, its freedom to speculate in western lands, its freedom to smuggle goods into and out of Dutch, French, or Spanish possessions. For generations the colonists had brought the blessings of civilization to the West, replacing heathen Indians with Christian settlers. For decades the colonies had been part of the Atlantic trading community, aspiring to free trade while ignoring the dictates of British mercantilism. Now London was tightening the reins, attacking what the colonists imagined to be their rights as Englishmen.

In the late 1760s and early 1770s, few of the men and women who occupied Britain's American colonies thought to create an independent state. The prevailing demand was for autonomy, a continuation of the salutary neglect the colonies had enjoyed before the French and Indian War, those glorious days when there was minimal interference with westward expansion and illicit commerce. Parliament, however, was adamant: the colonies had to contribute financially to their own protection, fit snugly into the British mercantilist system, and stay east of the Appalachians where there would be fewer confrontations with Indians and other European settlers.

Gradually London and its American colonists became alienated and drifted toward forceful resistance by the colonists and a military response ordered by London. In 1774 a "Continental Congress" assembled to discuss means of achieving relief from Britain's oppressive new rules. There was little talk of independence: the participants demanded the restoration of their rights as Englishmen. Neither king nor Parliament offered solace. By the time the second Congress met, in May 1775, tensions were great. British troops assembled in Massachusetts, under orders to tolerate no colonial impudence. In April they had marched on Concord and Lexington, where armed colonists awaited them. Scores died on both sides in the ensuing skirmishes.

It was obvious to the members of the Congress that a war had begun—a war the colonies could not win without outside assistance. They created a Committee of Secret Correspondence for negotiations with foreign countries, hoping to obtain aid with minimal involvement in the sordid affairs of Europe. They understood they were edging toward independence—that they could expect little if any support abroad if their aim was merely better treatment within the British Empire. Nonetheless, they were willing, initially, to countenance only commercial ties with their potential benefactors in Paris and Madrid. They imagined that by opening their ports to all, by substituting free trade for mercantilism, others in the Atlantic trading community would be willing to provide the needed support.

Ultimately, a Declaration of Independence proved necessary—if not sufficient—to alert foreign capitals to the imminent creation of a new republican state, a redeemer state, dedicated to changing the existing international order. Presented to the world on July 4, 1776, at a time when George Washington's disheveled forces had yet to win a battle, the Declaration gained little attention; nor would its republican principles have won much favor in the courts of European monarchs. Given the existence of slavery in the colonies and the brutality with which the colonists treated Indians who posed obstacles to their land grabs, the Declaration's insistence that "all men are created equal" could not have been viewed as more than gross hypocrisy. No one could conceivably imagine how subsequent generations of Americans would struggle for centuries to turn that vision to reality.

They were not yet representatives of a country; nonetheless colonial leaders saw themselves and their people as a breed apart from Europeans. They were the occupants of the "city on the hill"; theirs was a model society, guided by God's hand. And yet they feared negotiations with European diplomats they perceived as unscrupulous, ever-ready to take advantage of American innocence and commitment to principle. Fortunately, they had Benjamin Franklin on their side.

Franklin was enormously successful in manipulating a willing French court. Count Vergennes, the French foreign minister, was eager to weaken the British Empire in any way he could—short of going to war. No supporter of the republican principles that the Americans espoused, by no means eager to see an American nation arise that would challenge French interests in North America, he was nonetheless willing to proffer loans sufficient to keep the Americans in the field. Not until the colonists won their first major victory, at Saratoga in October 1777, was he willing to ally France openly with them.

In the Franco-American treaty of alliance in 1778, Franklin gained the essential American goal: France would fight until the Americans gained their independence. Military supplies, French troops, and French ships would be forthcoming. Virtually all the munitions with which Washington's men were armed came from France. The critical battle of Yorktown, the surrender of Lord Cornwallis in 1781, was achieved only because of the participation of French troops and the presence of the French fleet in Chesapeake Bay. Without the role of France, the colonists could not have won their freedom from the British Empire.

It must be noted, however, that in accepting the terms of the treaty, the Americans capitulated to the norms of eighteenth-century world politics. They promised not to sign a separate peace with Great Britain, committing themselves to fight alongside their French ally—which in turn had committed itself to fight alongside Spain until the Spanish regained Gibraltar. What would have happened had the Americans honored the treaty, had they stood by their alleged principles as the Spanish continue to struggle to regain Gibraltar into the twenty-first century?

Fortunately for the soon to be independent country, its negotiators abandoned principle and violated the first treaty ever signed on its behalf— as well as their instructions from a Congress bribed and manipulated by the French. Franklin and his obstreperous and mistrustful colleagues John Adams and John Jay chose to meet with London's envoy and, in due course, to sign a separate peace. The British terms were generous, astonishing Vergennes, who, steeped in Realpolitik, did not fault the Americans for abandoning their ally—especially when it gave him an excuse to renege on his promise to fight until Spain regained Gibraltar.

Thus in 1783 the thirteen colonies achieved independence, only to learn that the great empire their diplomats had won, westward to the Mississippi, northward to Canada, and south to the border of Spanish Florida, would be theirs only if they were willing to fight for it. Indians, most of whom had fought alongside the British, were no more willing to vacate their lands than they had been before the war. The British showed little inclination to leave their forts in the Northwest, and the Spanish and French plotted to thwart the imperial dreams of the Americans.

Jealous of their liberties, the Americans had intentionally created a government too weak to oppress them. It was also too weak to defend them and their interests. The government under the Articles of Confederation, conceived in 1777 but ratified only in 1781, lacked the power to tax, to regulate commerce, to provide for national defense. The states, though nominally united, pursued their disparate interests, often to the detriment of the nation. The economy was depressed, and no country anywhere in the world was volunteering assistance. Free from the monopoly of the British East India Company, American merchants immediately entered the China trade, but it was not nearly sufficient to compensate for the losses sustained by exclusion from historic markets within the British Empire. It was evident to European leaders that this new nation, conceived in liberty, would not survive for very long.

It was apparent to the American political elite as well that its vision for the republic was in danger, and that the central government had to be given greater authority—at minimum to regulate commerce, domestic and foreign. Gradually in the course of 1786, a consensus grew to call a convention to amend the articles, and a Constitutional Convention opened in May 1787, with Washington chosen unanimously to preside. Any thought of merely amending the Articles of Confederation vanished quickly, and the men assembled began work on a new constitution.

Obviously, the Constitutional Convention was necessitated by the exigencies of foreign affairs, by an existential threat to the United States of America. It remained to be seen whether the participants could produce a document that would both provide a foundation for a strong government and win the acceptance of states jealous of their powers and in conflict with one another over issues as vital as land borders and slavery.

2

A NOT QUITE PERFECT UNION

T HE GOVERNMENT CREATED by the Articles of Confederation had
proved inadequate to meet the needs of the new nation, primarily
in its foreign affairs. The men who inspired the Constitutional Convention were determined to remedy this and other deficiencies. The constitution they constructed gave the central government the powers they
thought it required to control commerce and other relations with an indifferent, often hostile world. Where authority to determine foreign policy
would rest within the new government, the balance between executive and
legislative power, was left ambiguous. The certainty that George Washington would be the first president mitigated fears that republican ideals
would be subverted by a monarchial figure.

The country Washington came forward to lead was in serious trouble. It
was threatened on all sides by nations that had no interest in seeing it pros-
per. The British had failed to honor the peace treaty of 1783, continuing to
operate their forts in the northwestern territories and to support Indian
nations struggling to hold on to lands coveted by American settlers. In the
South, Spanish authorities hemmed in other settlers as best they could and
fostered separatist movements to deny American access to the Mississippi.
And trade had suffered significantly as a result of lost access to the British
West Indies and restrictive mercantilist practices against which government under the Articles of Confederation lacked recourse.

With Thomas Jefferson and Alexander Hamilton at his side, Washington perceived three goals: the expansion of commerce, the expansion of territory under the control of his government, and the respect of the Western world. His first success came in the confrontation with the Indians who fought to protect their homes, with British support, in the Ohio territory. After several disastrous expeditions, decimated by the Indians, General "Mad Anthony" Wayne drove them out of their lands, razing their villages as his men moved forward in late 1790 and early 1791. Sensibly, Wayne and his British counterparts avoided direct conflict.

Success in getting the British to withdraw from their forts, as pledged in 1783, came later. Progress in expanding trade was slower yet—enormously important not only for the economy generally but because customs duties were usually the federal government's primary source of income before the twentieth century. And respect was a long way off.

The French Revolution, to which most Americans appear to have been sympathetic initially, imagining France would pursue their model of democratic republicanism, soon divided the country. Jefferson and his followers remained supportive of France, despite abuses by the revolutionaries. Washington, Hamilton, and others, appalled by the chaos and violence, turned against the revolution. When the wars provoked by the revolutionaries erupted in 1792, Washington, despite the alliance of 1778 with France, proclaimed American neutrality. Neither he nor Hamilton was unaware of the extent to which the American economic system was tied to Britain. He never doubted the need to avoid being dragged into a war, the need to give the new nation time to strengthen.

The outbreak of war in Europe intensified partisanship in the United States. Those who would tilt toward France, led by Jefferson, perceived Hamilton and the president, who appeared to follow his lead, to be Anglophiles, despite the contempt with which London treated their country. This, indeed, was the context in which the first political parties emerged.

The British navy refused to respect American neutrality and the American contention that "free ships make free goods." It seized American merchant ships and impressed seamen from those ships, many of whom were deserters from the Royal Navy. Control of the seas—the ability to deny resources to France—was central to British strategy. London was also inciting Indians in the Northwest as insurance against American inroads into Canada. By 1794 an Anglo-American war seemed likely.

Determined to avert war, believing his country needed another generation of peace to assure its security, Washington sent John Jay to London to seek a compromise. The British, too, were eager to avoid war but not so eager that they were willing to ease restrictions on American trade with France. They did end the seizure of American shipping in the British West Indies and evacuated their forts in the Northwest, nothing more than what they had agreed to do in 1783, but Jay could get no further concessions. The treaty he signed in 1794 disappointed Washington and outraged Jefferson and others who sympathized with France. Washington understood, however, that the United States lacked the power to exact more from the British and signed the treaty into law after the Senate ratified it in secret.

Remarkably, in the years that followed, arguably as a result of Jay's treaty, the United States prospered. Betrayed by the British, the Indians of the Northwest were driven back and brutalized by the American army, opening their land for further settlement. American exports soared, bringing great wealth to the port cities. And the South and Southwest gained as well: Spain, fearing an Anglo-American rapprochement, yielded to demands of the frontiersmen for access to the Mississippi and the use of New Orleans as a depot. Madrid even yielded to the Americans in the Florida border dispute.

None of this, however, prevented the country's political elite from dividing into a Federalist Party dominated by Hamilton and commercial interests in the Northeast and a Republican Party led by Jefferson and James Madison with support primarily from agricultural interests in the South and West. The Federalists tilted toward Great Britain and the Republicans toward France.

In 1796 Washington prepared to step down as his countrymen narrowly selected John Adams to succeed him. In his Farewell Address, fully aware of French efforts to interfere in the election on behalf of Jefferson and troubled by partisanship, he warned against the dangers of foreign influence. He argued that permanent alliances, such as Americans had signed with France in 1778, were a mistake. Given that the nation's prosperity depended on international trade, isolation was impossible, but it was essential for the United States to maintain its freedom of action.

British pressures on American trade continued, but it was the French depredations that most troubled the Adams administration. Angered by French efforts to intimidate the United States, Adams built up the American navy. When the French negotiators demanded bribes, he responded with force. From 1798 to 1800 the United States and France fought an undeclared naval war in which American forces performed magnificently. To add to France's woes, the Adams administration offered support to the slave rebellion in Santo Domingo, despite fears it might spread to the American South. The French chose to negotiate and in the Convention of 1800 tacitly conceded the end of the alliance and reduced their interference with American shipping.

At the close of the eighteenth century, on the eve of the peaceful transfer of power from Adams to Jefferson, from Federalists to Republicans, the American people had much with which to be pleased. In the decade of the 1790s, their new government had functioned well. It had succeeded in avoiding any major military confrontations, allowing the nation time to build its strength and consolidate its hold on its western territories. It had gained British withdrawal from the northwestern forts, driven back the Indians, and won significant territorial concessions from Spain. Its economy, thanks to enormous profits from international trade, despite British and French interference, was thriving. Jefferson inherited a vibrant nation, a successful experiment in republicanism.

In his inaugural address, Jefferson echoed George Washington, promising there would be trade with all, "entangling alliances with none." In fact, he never overcame his ambivalence about trade—to the extent of admiring China's attempts at commercial isolation. He never doubted his country's exceptionalism; that its policies would reflect high moral purpose; that it would be an "empire of liberty." His sympathies for France had faded with the rise of Napoleon, but his enmity toward Great Britain had not. He was determined to force the British to respect the American interpretation of neutral rights. And in other respects, most notably in his approach to the Barbary pirates, he proved more belligerent than his predecessors. Most striking, perhaps, was his determination to increase his nation's territory. He proved to be a more aggressive expansionist than his Federalist predecessors.

Although philosophically committed to limiting the power of the central government and of the executive, as president Jefferson did not hesitate to take actions that exceeded the powers granted by the Constitution. Washington and Adams had paid tribute and ransoms to the Barbary pirates, but Jefferson sent the U.S. Navy into the Mediterranean to do battle from 1801 to 1805. In effect, he granted himself the power to make war. At considerable cost, the Americans prevailed briefly, but a permanent end to Barbary piracy had to wait until after the War of 1812.

Similarly, as Jefferson knew, purchase of the Louisiana Territory exceeded his authority, but he never hesitated to overlook his principles when convinced he was acting in the national interest. As he observed Napoleon's efforts to subdue the revolt in Santo Domingo, he feared the French would attempt to establish themselves in New Orleans and cut off American access to the Mississippi. On the one hand, he resumed assistance to the rebels on the island; on the other, he warned France that the United States was prepared to support Great Britain should its interests in Louisiana be threatened. When the Spanish denied Americans use of New Orleans as a depot, Jefferson assumed Napoleon was behind the action and sent a mission to Paris to do what was necessary to reopen the port. He began to prepare for war, presumably to seize New Orleans. To his astonishment, Napoleon, whose forces had been decimated in Santo Domingo, offered to sell the entire Louisiana Territory to the United States. Jefferson seized the opportunity, thus more than doubling the size of his country. He now presided over a vast empire that included tens of thousands of French Creoles and more than a hundred thousand Indians—and control of the Mississippi. Yet his vision for his country was unfulfilled as he tried unsuccessfully to add the Floridas and then sent Meriwether Lewis and William Clark off to establish claim to the Pacific Northwest.

War resumed in Europe in 1803, and gradually British pressures on American commerce intensified. After 1805 the Royal Navy seized almost a fourth of the ships it stopped in the Atlantic. The French seized others when they reached ports under French control. Once again, Jefferson stretched the powers of the president. This time, his enforcement of an embargo on shipping had a disastrous impact on the American economy without gaining any concessions from the British or the French. In New England, hostility toward his administration, stoked by Federalist politicians, brought forth thoughts of secession.

In addition, the impressment issue was inflamed in 1807 when the British stopped an American warship, the USS *Chesapeake*, an unquestionable violation of international law, and impressed four men. Contemptuous of the American government, London waited four years to apologize, ignoring Jefferson's demands.

Jefferson's greatest—and accidental—accomplishment was the purchase of the Louisiana Territory. His efforts to force Great Britain and France to respect America's neutral rights were an utter failure, inflicting more damage on his own country than on the combatants. To his protégé and successor, James Madison, he passed on a failed foreign policy that had made a shambles of the economy and brought the nation to the verge of disunity. He had overestimated American power greatly.

Blindly, Madison continued Jefferson's approach, apparently unable to realize that the embargo, destructive to the United States, was little more than a nuisance to Britain and France. The European powers were confident the Americans would not go to war, aware of the trend toward disunity in the country, and unable to conceive of any reason to save Jefferson or Madison from the dilemma they had created for themselves.

In addition to the self-inflicted wounds to the economy, the Americans were confronted by a major Indian uprising in the Northwest. Quite naturally they deflected blame from the provocations of their own settlers, who took Indian lands by force, and held the British responsible. It was a problem that some thought could be eliminated by invading Canada and driving the British out. Violations of neutral rights, affronts to national honor, and Indian troubles all led the hapless Madison to ask Congress for a declaration of war against Great Britain in 1812.

The nation went to war with considerable ambivalence—just as the British were preparing to offer concessions. Westerners, expansionists generally, were eager, assuming Canada could be taken easily, and Florida as well. Shipping interests, especially those in the Northeast, voiced reluctance— an end to the embargo would have served their interests better. Madison and his supporters overestimated their nation's readiness to confront British power.

The Americans were battered and humiliated in the war. The invasion of Canada was repelled easily. In August 1814 British troops marched through Washington and burned the city to the ground. Fortunately, they were halted in their attack on the important port city of Baltimore, a defensive victory celebrated by Francis Scott Key's "Star-Spangled Banner." The U.S. Navy, on the other hand, fared surprisingly well, defeating the British in battles on Lake Erie and Lake Champlain. But the end of the war in Europe in 1814 allowed the British to shift resources to North America, and London demanded that the Americans surrender the gains of the Treaty of 1783 as the price of peace.

The Americans were saved by the British realization that the anticipated collapse of the American government was not likely, by London's desire to focus on continental affairs—the scheduled Congress of Vienna and the possible resumption of war—and by the brilliance of the American negotiators, Albert Gallatin, Henry Clay, and John Quincy Adams. Grudgingly, despite the havoc they had wrought in the United States, the British agreed to the Treaty of Ghent, which allowed for a return to conditions that existed before the war. Given the poorly planned war and the disastrous results on the ground, to have escaped with their nation intact seemed to renew the confidence of Americans that God was on their side. When the news of General Andrew Jackson's victory over British forces at New Orleans—after the treaty had been signed—spread across the land, they deluded themselves into believing they had won the war, a second war for independence. Theirs was a great nation, ready to expand to the Pacific, unwilling to tolerate any European interference on *their* continent.

Although battered by the British during the war, the American military, at its conclusion, was stronger than it had been at the outset, partly because Madison raised defense spending above prewar levels. The navy, which had acquitted itself well during the war, was prepared to protect shipping against piracy and to fight for freedom of the seas. The army, buoyed by Jackson's victory, was eager to challenge hostile Indians, especially after the British had abandoned those of the Northwest. Spanish authorities in Florida had reason to be uneasy about American intentions. Indeed, in 1817 Jackson, ostensibly acting to suppress Seminole transgressions emanating from Florida, seized control of the entire territory. No apology was forthcoming from Washington, and Spain eventually found it expedient to surrender Florida and its claims to the Pacific Northwest, hanging on to Texas and California.

James Monroe, who succeeded Madison in 1817, and John Quincy Adams, his secretary of state, remained apprehensive about threats from Europe, where friendly governments did not exist. There were credible rumors that Spain, eager to suppress revolution in its American colonies, would receive support from other European powers hostile to republicanism. In fact, Great Britain, perceiving that a Latin America free of Spanish rule would be a commercial boon, was determined to thwart any such intervention on Spain's behalf.

Adams in particular, but Monroe as well, was a committed expansionist who foresaw a transcontinental republican empire and was not shy about proclaiming his vision. He told a British diplomat that the United States would leave Canada—which it had coveted but failed to conquer in the War of 1812—to Great Britain but claimed the rest of the continent for itself. And the nation's power grew, propelled by its booming trade and soaring population.

Most Americans, not least Monroe and Adams, were sympathetic to the revolutions sweeping Latin America, but the government remained officially neutral while it maneuvered to relieve Spain of the territories it coveted. Moreover, there was little expectation that the peoples freeing themselves of colonial rule were ready for democracy. Indeed, few were either white or Protestant, widely perceived preconditions for that exalted state. Nonetheless, any restoration of European monarchial rule in the Americas was viewed as a threat to the security of the United States.

A more remote threat was posed by Russian pretensions on the Pacific coast of North America. The Russians were troubled by American commercial activities in the area and in 1821 drew the line at the 51st parallel, declaring all waters north of that line off-limits to foreign ships. The tsar's ukase would deny Americans access to a region Adams and Monroe foresaw as part of the United States. It was unacceptable.

Confronted by Russian dictates on the Pacific coast and the possibility of Europeans crossing the Atlantic to intervene in Latin America, Adams and Monroe chose to warn them off, to declare the American continents off-limits to the Europeans. The British proposed a joint statement against any effort to restore Spanish rule over its colonies, but Adams demurred—not least because the British proposal would have had both parties renounce any intention to take the territories for themselves. He wanted to deliver an independent statement of policy that preserved American freedom of action. The United States, standing alone, would challenge all the great powers.

Monroe ultimately proclaimed the position of the United States in a message to Congress in December 1823 that came to be known as the Monroe Doctrine. A key part of the message was the concept of two spheres, the Old World and the New, each to stay out of the affairs of the other. The American continents were not to be subject to any new colonization—there could be no new imperial adventures in the Western Hemisphere.

The country lacked the power to enforce its dictate, but Monroe and Adams knew the British would preserve the freedom of Latin America. Indeed, Adams had rejected the British proposal for a joint statement, knowing full well that British opposition made European intervention in Latin America highly unlikely. The Russians, for reasons of their own, backed off their more extreme position and in 1824 signed a convention drawing a compromise line above the 54th parallel. The rising American power had staked out its claim to dominance in the New World.

For Adams, arguably the most skilled diplomat ever to serve as secretary of state, commercial expansion was paramount. Years later, when other Americans were criticizing the British for attacking China in what came to be known as the Opium War, Adams praised the British and condemned the Chinese for their refusal to open their country to unrestricted trade, perceiving such a policy to be a cultural flaw.

Adams took one position that would underlie debates over American foreign policy throughout the country's history. On July 4, 1821, in response to a request for support from Greek revolutionaries fighting for independence from the Ottoman Empire, he declared that his nation would serve as the "beacon" of democracy. It would not go abroad "in search of monsters to destroy." It wished well to all who sought freedom and independence but was the "champion and vindicator" only of its own. Wise as this was for a relatively weak, rising power, would his thoughts be consistent with the responsibilities of a great power—of the greatest power on earth?

3

A RISING IMPERIAL POWER

THE YEARS BETWEEN the presidencies of James Monroe and Abraham Lincoln were marked by the massive expansion of American territory. Old Glory came to fly over more than a million additional square miles. Most of that land was taken by force—much from Mexico, more from Native Americans. Few Americans had difficulty justifying the seizures, given their contempt for both Mexicans and Indians, largely on racial grounds. It was, many Americans came to believe, their Manifest Destiny to create a republican empire that would spread over the whole of North America.

The term "Manifest Destiny," usually attributed to John L. O'Sullivan, a journalist, was an expression of romantic nationalism, part of the enduring sense of American exceptionalism. From its origin, the United States was carrying out God's will, reshaping the world in its own image, bringing liberty and republicanism to all. Manifest Destiny also reflected attitudes later described as taking on the "white man's burden," bringing civilization to the less fortunate—usually people of color, pagan, or Catholic. Always used to legitimize the taking of other people's land, the justification varied. The original residents were perceived as shiftless (Mexicans) or accused of not using the land as God had intended (Indians, peons, trappers). This ideology, elements of which persist into the twenty-first century, appears to have been widely and genuinely accepted in the decades of the 1830s, 1840s, and 1850s. But greed, the lust for land, resources, and commercial opportunities, as much as ideology, drove Americans westward toward the Pacific.

The several decades prior to the Civil War constituted an era in which the nation's soaring power was readily apparent. Technological advances, most notably the railroad and the telegraph, seemed steel bands holding the nation together, enabling its leaders to govern a burgeoning empire. In the 1840s American clipper ships dominated oceanic commerce, joined in the 1850s by steamboats. American whalers provided most of the whale oil that lit the world's lamps. The great powers of Europe had no choice but to consider the United States as a factor in their calculations. Chinese and Japanese elites may have been slower to recognize this new force in world affairs, but American warships soon won their attention—most obviously Commodore Matthew Perry's "Black Ships," which provided the wedge ending Japan's relative isolation.

On the other hand, one great issue that divided and might yet destroy the country, slavery, was never far from the surface. Compromised by the Founding Fathers in the Constitutional Convention, it reemerged ominously in 1820, tied inevitably to the modalities of expansion.

In 1817 the Missouri Territorial Assembly petitioned for statehood. Immediately, the question arose as to the legal status of slavery in Missouri. When Congress considered the Missouri petition, a New York congressman proposed an amendment aimed at ending slavery in the would-be state. A similar effort was made to exclude slavery from the Arkansas Territory. Both efforts failed, but antislavery forces persisted in their efforts. To maintain the sectional balance in the Senate, Maine was admitted first as a "free state" and Missouri as a slave state with slavery prohibited in the Louisiana Territory north of 36°30', the so-called Missouri Compromise of 1820.

Hopes that slavery would cease to be economical and allow the issue to disappear quietly were thwarted by the enormous importance of the cotton crop after the invention of the cotton gin. Cotton became the greatest source of national wealth, enhancing the value of the slaves who picked it. The institution gained rather than declined in importance.

Fear that the addition of another slave state would shatter the façade of national unity led John Quincy Adams and Andrew Jackson, both ardent expansionists, to resist efforts to bring Texas under the American flag. But the Americans who migrated to Texas at the invitation of the Mexican government soon chafed under laws that prohibited slavery and the further influx of U.S. citizens. In 1836 they revolted successfully, established the Republic of Texas, and maneuvered toward admission as one of the United States. Neither Jackson nor Martin Van Buren, who succeeded him in 1837, was willing to risk near certain war with Mexico and the explosion of sectional tensions in the existing states. Texas remained outside the Union until 1845.

Other than his caution regarding Texas, Jackson's foreign policy was consistent with the aggressive practices that had characterized his military career. He demanded respect for the United States and built up the navy to project power as well as defend American interests at sea. He promoted international trade, succeeded in opening the British West Indies, and sought trade agreements and treaties in the Middle East and East Asia. Probably the earliest example of American "gunboat diplomacy" in Asia, the leveling of an offending town in modern Indonesia, occurred during his presidency.

Jackson's continued contempt for Indians was evident. His administration ignored treaties preserving land for various tribes, and he signed the Indian Removal Act of 1830, providing for the forcible removal of those Indians who could not be persuaded to abandon their lands "voluntarily." Eventually, under the presidency of Martin Van Buren, this provided the context for the horrific saga of the "Trail of Tears," as the largely assimilated Cherokees were driven out of their homes.

There were also territorial issues between the United States and Britain. One relatively minor border dispute between the state of Maine and Canada erupted into the brief Aroostook War of 1838–1839, quickly tamped down by the Van Buren administration. Of greater significance and potential for confrontation was the delineation of the border between Canada and the United States in the Pacific Northwest. In addition, there was a pair of incidents involving American ships that offended the national ego. The *Caroline* was set afire by Canadian troops in U.S. waters in 1837, and the slaves who had mutinied aboard the *Creole*, en route from one American port to another, were freed when they brought the ship into Nassau in 1841.

Some of these concerns that challenged a fragile Anglo-American amity were glossed over in the Webster-Ashburton Treaty of 1842. The Maine–New Brunswick border was set, a division of the disputed land favoring the Americans, and acceptance of the compromise bought from Maine and Massachusetts by Washington for a mere $150,000 apiece. Secretary of State Daniel Webster accepted Lord Ashburton's unofficial apology for the *Caroline* incident. Although the *Creole* case and questions about division of the Oregon Territory remained, John Tyler, the president Webster served, focused his ambitions for his country on Texas, Hawaii, and China.

Tyler happily submitted a treaty with the Texas Republic, allowing it to enter the Union, but the Senate voted against ratification. The Texans flirted with Britain, largely as a means of arousing American ardor, and there was strong support for annexation in the slaveholding South, but Tyler could not find a way around northern opposition until the closing days of his presidency. Before he left office, he succeeding in getting Congress to pass a joint resolution to admit Texas, a procedure of dubious constitutionality. James Polk, who succeeded him in the White House, was no less eager to annex Texas, and a few months later Texas became an American state, virtually ensuring war with Mexico and national divisions that required civil war to resolve.

Tyler was also active in promoting the expansion of American interests in and across the Pacific. With missionaries spearheading the drive, Hawaii became an American protectorate. In 1842, when it seemed possible that France would act against the Hawaiian kingdom, Tyler issued a warning, dubbed the Tyler Doctrine, that Hawaiian sovereignty had to be respected, and that Hawaii was not open to colonization. The islands were perceived as being within the sphere of influence of the United States.

The principal target of Tyler's Pacific policy was China, a potentially vast market for American exports. When Tyler inherited the presidency from William Henry Harrison, who died shortly after being elected, the Opium War was raging in China. In 1842 the British forced the Chinese to sign the Treaty of Nanjing, which opened several ports to trade, gained control of Hong Kong, a highly valuable entrepot, and exempted British subjects from Chinese law. Thus began what the Chinese came to call their "Hundred Years of Humiliation."

The Chinese government was amenable to extending the same privileges to Americans and other foreigners, but some Americans insisted that the United States should have a treaty of its own. Tyler was persuaded and sent Caleb Cushing, a former congressman, to Macau to conduct the necessary negotiations. Despite Chinese suspicions, agreement was reached in July 1844. It was hardly more than a summary of China's treaties with Great Britain, gaining little not already granted by Peking, but it was an *American* treaty.

Enter James Polk, who proved to be a yet more aggressive expansionist—bluffing a war, provoking a war, and acquiring enormous tracts of land during his presidency. He presided over the process of annexing Texas that Tyler had begun, threatened war with Britain if the British did not accept his outrageous claims to the Oregon territory (54 40 or fight), and happily went to war with Mexico in support of the excessive border claims of the Texans—and to seize California and the rest of what became the American Southwest. He was not averse to annexing yet more Mexican territory, and he even tried to buy Cuba.

There was considerable opposition in New England to expansion, to the anticipated extension of slavery into the new territories. Polk, untroubled, did not share fears that the expansion of slavery would shatter the Union and outmaneuvered his opponents. His demands for the Oregon territory pacified some northerners—no one feared the extension of cotton culture to that region.

Polk went through the motions of seeking a peaceful settlement with Mexico while building up the military for war. He sent troops to the Rio Grande, the border claimed by Texans, well beyond the Nueces, the historic limit of their territory—a deliberate provocation. When negotiations failed and shots were fired at the Rio Grande, Polk's request for a declaration of war won support in Congress and among the American people. The war's popularity declined in the North as evidence mounted of Polk's deviousness. Eventually the House of Representatives passed a resolution declaring the war unnecessary and charging Polk with acting contrary to the Constitution in starting it. But once American troops were in battle, most Americans saw no alternative to pressing on to Mexico's surrender.

Despite their weakness, the Mexicans fought on, shifting to guerrilla warfare when overwhelmed in direct confrontation with superior American forces. As their army drove deep into Mexico, some Americans called for taking all of Mexico. Racism played a major part in deflating the All Mexico movement. Mexicans were perceived as racially and religiously inferior, and there was no desire to bring many into the Union. The goal was to seize as much land with as few Mexican residents as possible. A peace treaty was eventually negotiated in February 1848 by Nicholas Trist, a State Department official who had ignored his recall. Having obtained most of what he wanted and faced with growing opposition to the war, Polk accepted the Treaty of Guadalupe-Hidalgo.

The threat to the nation posed by the fruits of its aggression against Mexico were underscored by the introduction of the Wilmot Proviso in August 1846. David Wilmot, a congressman from Pennsylvania, proposed that slavery be prohibited in any territory obtained from Mexico. Although the proviso never became law, and although southern leaders doubted that slavery would be viable west of Texas, they opposed any prohibition of the "peculiar institution." In the North, many who supported Wilmot's idea did so less out of concern for the enslaved blacks than because of a disinclination to live beside them. No matter how they reasoned, for the men and women concerned the issue became irreconcilable. In the years that followed, compromises were sought in vain. Certainly for abolitionists, for those who saw slavery in moral terms as an unmitigated evil, compromise was impossible.

The other major goal of the expansionists—the Oregon territory, "54 40 or fight"—was quietly settled during the war with Mexico. The British had no desire to fight, and Polk was embattled in Mexico. A sensible division was reached, with the Americans gaining all they really wanted—full control of the Columbia River and Puget Sound. The main outlines of the continental United States had been drawn. Now some way would have to be found to hold the Union together.

Some of the more extreme expansionists continued to look for ways to seize parts of Central America and Cuba. These were the men who came to be known as "filibusters," adventurers who led invasions of Nicaragua and Cuba in particular. None succeeded; none had the support of the U.S. government—which might have done more to restrain them.

The acquisition of California also stimulated interest in a trans-isthmian route to the West Coast from the East, not least after the discovery of gold in the new territory. Disturbed by British machinations in Nicaragua, Polk looked further south, where an arrangement with New Granada (Colombia) provided the United States with a protectorate over Panama in 1848. The rivalry between London and Washington was resolved amicably in the Clayton-Bulwer Treaty of 1850, in which both parties agreed there would be no exclusive control over any canal that was built and that it would not be fortified. The agreement, unpopular with more assertive American nationalists, held until the 1890s, when, under pressure, the British yielded their claim.

Further evidence of the rising power of the United States was provided by Commodore Perry's adventures in East Asia in the 1850s. Japan lay athwart the Great Circle route between America's new West Coast and China. The Japanese had proven inhospitable to foreign mariners, often American whalers, who entered their waters. After unsatisfactory contacts with European traders and Jesuit missionaries in the sixteenth and seventeenth centuries, Japan's rulers were determined to limit and control contacts with the West, permitting only the Dutch to maintain a small station in Nagasaki harbor. Americans had experienced Japan's reserve during the Napoleonic wars, when the Dutch commissioned American merchantmen to undertake the allowed annual voyage. U.S. Navy attempts to establish official contacts in the 1840s had been repulsed. The British and the Russians also maneuvered to force Japan to admit their traders, but it was Perry to whom the Japanese yielded.

In 1851 President Millard Fillmore was persuaded to send a naval force to impress on Japan the importance of treating shipwrecked sailors humanely and the potential value of trade with the United States. Washington was also interested in obtaining coaling stations for the steamships that were now crossing the Pacific to China. American success in opening Japan would likely increase the nation's standing internationally. Once assigned to command the expedition, Perry perceived an opportunity to extend American power to East Asia. His goals were more expansive than

Fillmore's, and he utilized his discretionary powers to the maximum, seeking strategic outposts for the navy.

Perry's "Black Ships" reached Japan in July 1853. Imperiously, he delivered Fillmore's request to Japanese authorities and left, warning that he would return the following year with a larger force. After an intense internal debate, the Japanese government determined to appease him by granting some American demands. In particular, with the Treaty of Kanagawa in 1854, they opened two ports and agreed to permit a resident American consul. The United States gained little but glory for Perry, but the concessions led to years of civil strife in Japan.

Neither Perry nor Peter Parker, a missionary doctor in China who shared his aspirations for a major American presence in East Asia, lived to see one. The interests of the United States in the region, commercial and strategic, remained marginal until the final years of the nineteenth century. For the remainder of the decade, the slavery issue dominated political discourse—and ultimately led to the temporary destruction of the Union.

4

CIVIL WAR

F ORESHADOWED IN THE late 1840s in the debates over the acquisition of
Texas and the spoils of the war with Mexico, the national consensus
on expansion fractured in the 1850s. The Damoclean sword was, of
course, the slavery issue: would the "peculiar institution" be allowed to
spread into the new territories? Southerners demanded that they be free to
bring their slaves wherever they chose to settle. Increasingly, Northerners
objected, some because they were intent on abolishing slavery, an affront
to the ideals of the Declaration of Independence; others because they preferred not to live in proximity to Negroes.

In 1850 Henry Clay brokered a compromise that admitted California to
the Union as a free state while leaving the status of the remaining territories obtained from Mexico to be determined at some later date by those
who lived in them. For the moment, no additional slave states were admitted, but the Fugitive Slave Law, requiring escaped slaves to be returned to
their owners, was strengthened, to the horror of the abolitionists.

But especially in the South, the drive to expand the empire persisted,
most notably in the efforts to acquire Cuba. President Franklin Pierce,
responsive to such pressures, ordered the American minister to Spain to
buy Cuba. When that effort failed, the American ministers to Britain,
France, and Spain met in Ostend, Belgium, and issued a manifesto calling
for the seizure of Cuba, deemed essential to the security of the United

States and the preservation of the institution of slavery. Confronted by the outrage of men and women opposed to slavery, Pierce retreated, and Cuba remained a Spanish colony until 1898.

Whatever faint hope remained that the Compromise of 1850 would still the forces of division within the nation was shattered following the Kansas-Nebraska Act of 1854. The act embodied the principle of "popular sovereignty," meaning that the people of a given territory could choose for themselves whether they would enter the Union as citizens of free or slave states. In practice, it meant that advocates of each side armed their supporters, who then fought mini–civil wars throughout the territory. There could be no doubt that irreconcilable differences existed between North and South.

In the months that followed, the Whig Party, failing in its effort to straddle the sectional divide, collapsed. In its place, the Republican Party, a narrowly Northern party, emerged to contest the presidential election in 1856. The Democrats, still a national organization despite defections in the North, prevailed with the election of James Buchanan—one of the signatories of the Ostend Manifesto—as president. Although an accomplished diplomatist, Buchanan maintained Southern sympathies that guaranteed failure in his timid efforts to preserve the Union. It is difficult to imagine that anyone could have succeeded.

The election in 1860 of Abraham Lincoln, the Republican candidate, eliminated any doubt among Southerners of the need to secede from the Union and create an independent state. Lincoln and the Republicans were rightly perceived as a threat to the Southern way of life. Many feared a slave uprising, supported by the federal government, a danger to the families and property of slaveholders.

William Seward, Lincoln's secretary of state, immediately offered the president a classic plan for preserving the Union. As Shakespeare's Henry IV, on his deathbed, advised his son and heir, "Be it thy course to busy giddy minds with foreign quarrels," so Seward proposed declaring war on one or more European countries as a means of uniting the country, of transcending sectional divisions. Lincoln chose not to pursue that course and instead constantly evolved tactics designed to keep Europe out of what became the American Civil War.

It was widely understood—in the North, the South, and Europe—that the outcome of the secession crisis would likely be determined by the actions or inactions of the European powers. Britain, France, and Spain had ample reason to enjoy the prospect of an independent Southern state, of a balance of power in North America that would sharply reduce the threat the United States posed to their interests in the Western Hemisphere. The Lincoln administration's most urgent foreign policy objective was to prevent European intervention on behalf of the South.

Lincoln never doubted that he would have to resort to force to prevent the breakup of the nation. With an eye to public opinion at home and abroad, he waited, however, for the secessionists to fire the first shot. When Confederate forces attacked Fort Sumter, he had the necessary provocation. The "insurrection" could not be tolerated.

Although Lincoln chose not to call the ensuing battles a war, he ordered actions—most notably a blockade of Southern ports—that were considered acts of war under international law. He was disappointed, angered by European decisions to recognize a state of belligerency, fearful that recognition of the Confederacy would follow. Seward quickly warned the European powers that they risked war with the United States if they took any further actions deemed supportive of the South.

Confederate leaders were confident they could win assistance from Great Britain, which would likely be followed by aid from France and Spain. Their optimism was based on the assumption that the mills of England were dependent on cotton. They were unconcerned about the possible effectiveness of the blockade because they intended to withhold cotton exports, to force London to confront the likelihood of massive unemployment. In time, they assumed, the British navy would put an end to the blockade.

British and other European leaders considered the Union cause hopeless but had no desire to become involved in a war with the North that might prove more harmful to their interests than a lack of American cotton. They chose to wait patiently, intending to intervene, to recognize the Confederacy, when the succession of Southern victories on the battlefield left little doubt of the outcome even to Lincoln. They could afford to wait because they were initially well stocked with cotton after the bumper crop of 1860. But the moment for which they waited never came. A cotton shortage did occur—and did hurt—but was mitigated as sources other than the American South were developed. And if King Cotton did not prevail, the South had little else to offer. Its diplomats proved incompetent, and British leaders, at least, were always uncomfortable about lending support to a regime that espoused slavery.

Nonetheless, as the battle progressed at Antietam in 1862, the British were prepared to respond to a Confederate victory by intervening on humanitarian grounds—to stop the bloodshed and force the North to accept the obvious outcome of the struggle. But Confederate troops withdrew when the fighting ended, allowing Lincoln to claim victory. A few days later he issued his Emancipation Proclamation. The British held off, and soon it was the Union army that appeared unstoppable as it forced its way through the South. Subsequent Confederate victories kept open the possibility that London would intervene, but the North's victories at Gettysburg and Vicksburg in the summer of 1863 virtually ended such thoughts among British leaders, if not those in Paris.

There were several other reasons for British restraint. Probably the most important was a grain shortage in the early 1860s that forced dependence on corn and wheat from the American North. In this instance, grain outweighed cotton. Second was instability in Europe, with crises that erupted in Italy and Poland and demanded London's (and Paris's) attention. In East Asia, Seward ordered the U.S. Navy to cooperate with the Europeans, and American ships joined British, French, and Dutch ships in bombarding the capital of a powerful antiforeign Japanese clan. And perhaps not least was the role of Russia, the only strong supporter the Union had. The tsar had no fondness for democracy, but he had freed the serfs and saw in Lincoln's concern for the plight of slaves a kindred spirit. The fact that Americans had supported Russia during the Crimean War and appeared to be a useful balance to British power in the Atlantic and the Americas was not lost on the tsar's advisers. The appearance of a Russian fleet in New York harbor created a sensation in the North, pained the South, and at least annoyed British leaders.

There were, of course, several issues that might have provoked an Anglo-American confrontation. The blockade was technically illegal; the Union lacked a sufficient number of ships to meet existing international norms for effectiveness. But the British Admiralty, looking to the future, perceived an advantage to respecting it. It would be difficult for the United States to protest British practices in the future. A more dangerous moment occurred in November 1861 when an American ship stopped a British vessel in international waters and removed two Confederate diplomats without observing the rules for search and seizure. The Americans had committed a violation of neutral rights, akin to the impressment Washington raged against during the Napoleonic wars. The seizure of the two men, John Slidell and James Mason, delighted Northerners but evoked calls for war in London. Seward wisely chose to declare the U.S. action an error and ordered the men released. And there were other incidents in which the fight to preserve the Union outweighed traditional American efforts to protect and expand neutral rights. When survival was at stake, principles such as freedom of the seas could be—and were—compromised.

Although the Confederacy failed to gain the support it had anticipated from Great Britain, it did succeed in having commerce raiders built in British shipyards and outfitted elsewhere as warships. These ships inflicted enormous damage on the U.S. merchant marine. Toward the end of the war, Confederate agents almost succeeded in a plan to purchase two ironclad vessels to be outfitted as rams—the "Laird Rams"—to destroy the wooden warships on which the U.S. Navy was still largely dependent. Although London had no intention of allowing the ships to be sold to the South, warnings from Charles Francis Adams, American minister to Britain, left no doubt Washington would consider such a sale an act of war.

Lincoln's initial framing of the battle as a fight to preserve the Union warmed few hearts in Europe. Desperately trying to preserve the loyalty of border states and Northerners indifferent to slavery, he initially chose not to seize the moral high ground. His determination to end slavery would not be voiced until a more propitious time. But in 1862, in addition to the Emancipation Proclamation, he took several steps that indicated his commitment to black freedom at home and abroad. The United States at long last recognized the Republic of Haiti and posted a minister there. Washington also joined London in a pact to cooperate in the suppression of the African slave trade. Perhaps most significant was Lincoln's decision to enlist former slaves in the Union army. Over 200,000 blacks served in the U.S.

military in a war that was as much for their freedom as for the preservation of the Union. Could Great Britain intervene to preserve slavery in the American South?

Confederate troops won several major battles in the closing years of the war, and on each occasion, especially during the summer of 1864, opposition to the war mounted in the North and the specter of European intervention loomed. But in the late summer and on into 1865, Generals Ulysses S. Grant, William Tecumseh Sherman, and their colleagues led Northern troops on a relentless march through the South, until Robert E. Lee surrendered at Appomattox Courthouse in April 1865.

Lincoln and Seward succeeded in achieving their most important foreign policy goal: nonintervention in the American Civil War by any European power. Obviously, success on the battlefield was essential in deterring British and French aid to the Confederate cause. Perhaps equally as important was Lincoln's management of the slavery issue—the exquisite skill with which he balanced the need to rally the border states and racist Northerners to the cause of preservation of the Union with his own conviction, shared by British leaders, of the moral necessity of ending slavery.

5

THE NEW EMPIRE

I N THE SEVERAL decades following Lee's surrender, foreign affairs were less important to the men who led the U.S. government than they had been during the Civil War. There were no foreign threats, and the domestic agenda was overwhelming. First and foremost was the need to reintegrate the former Confederate states into the Union. Equally challenging was the task of coping with enormous economic growth, rapid industrialization, urbanization, and a population whose increase was accelerated by massive immigration.

On the other hand, the postwar years were marked by an intense surge of nationalism and expansionist visions comparable to the 1840s, the era of Manifest Destiny. Having reunited their country, Americans were ready to take on the world. William Seward, who remained secretary of state after the assassination of Lincoln, had to settle for the acquisition of Alaska, but his successors gradually realized much of his ambition to extend the empire across the Pacific. And the lust for Cuba and other parts of the Caribbean never faded. For these reasons and because of the importance of foreign markets to the economy, the nation became deeply involved in world affairs.

"Seward's Folly," the purchase of Alaska from Russia, was accomplished with relative ease. Observing the relentless American drive toward continental expansion, Russian leaders feared their Alaskan possession might someday just be taken over by American settlers. Surely it would be better to sell, and Seward was willing to pay $7.2 million, which, ignorant of the gold eventually discovered there, they perceived as a good price. Moreover, they were focused increasingly on developing Russian interests in East and Central Asia. The Russian minister to the United States bribed recalcitrant members of Congress and the deal was done. Seward had taken one important step toward realization of his goal. It was also during his time in office that the United States claimed Midway, a Pacific island inhabited only by goony birds.

Of course, Seward wanted much more. He wanted an isthmian canal, a base at Samana Bay in the Dominican Republic, the Virgin Islands, the Danish West Indies—domination of the eastern approaches to a canal he would have built across Panama. He actually negotiated treaties to acquire all these, but none was ratified. On the Pacific approach to the canal he envisioned, he thought it best to annex Hawaii. All came to naught in his lifetime, not least because his president, then Andrew Johnson, was fighting impeachment and the country was overwhelmed by domestic concerns.

Among the internal affairs that occupied the nation in the postwar era was the disposition of Native Americans. The Founding Fathers had conceived of Indian tribes as nations and negotiated treaties with them—treaties that the settlers persistently violated as they pushed westward across the continent. In 1871 the Supreme Court validated further violations of Indian rights by granting Congress the right to override existing treaties. Inexorably, the Indians were forcibly, brutally, driven off their homelands onto reservations. Most appalling was the massacre U.S. troops carried out in 1890 against an Indian encampment at Wounded Knee. The rationale was a familiar racist ideology, frequently voiced when taking territory from Mexicans: Native Americans were uncivilized; they were not utilizing the land adequately. Only white Americans, preferably Protestants, could civilize them; only white Americans would use the land as God intended. By the 1890s few Indians remained outside the reservations.

A major obstacle to domination of the Western Hemisphere by the United States was British power. In addition to Canada, Britain had colonial possessions in the Caribbean and extensive economic ties in Latin America. In the late 1860s Anglo-American relations were roiled by Fenian raids into Canada and Washington's demand for reparations for the damage done to its commerce by the *Alabama*, built in England for the Confederacy. The Fenians were Irish immigrants, some of whom were Civil War veterans, trying a new tack in the fight for Ireland's independence. Not until the administration of Ulysses S. Grant did the U.S. government make a serious effort to stop the raids.

Tensions between Britain and the United States were greatly alleviated by the Treaty of Washington in 1871. In the negotiations, both sides demonstrated remarkable prudence, removing most of the sources of confrontation. The British apologized for their contribution to the depredations of the *Alabama* and other commerce raiders launched from their territory and agreed to arbitration of the claims issue. The Americans dropped their claims for indirect damages attributed to British actions during the Civil War. Long-standing differences over the U.S. border with Canada and fishing rights were resolved. And negotiations included representatives of the *Dominion* of Canada (a status granted in 1867 to lessen the likelihood of Canadians acquiescing in American efforts to annex the territory). Implicitly, Washington was recognizing Canada's new status—without surrendering hopes it would someday be part of the United States.

The British remained an obstacle to American domination of the Western Hemisphere but perceived little benefit in contesting the United States in that arena. The two countries sparred over their conflicting interests in Costa Rica, Nicaragua, Brazil, and Venezuela and the question of who would control the inevitable trans-isthmian canal. In each instance, London chose to appease the Americans, paving the way for a rapprochement of extraordinary value to both for most of the twentieth century.

Seward's successors retained his interest in Cuba, Santo Domingo, and the Caribbean generally. By 1880 they had determined that any canal across the isthmus would have to be American, regardless of the Clayton-Bulwer Treaty of 1850. Looking to the future, they sought to acquire bases to protect that canal—with no more luck than Seward had.

While serving as secretary of state, James Blaine, the "Plumed Knight" and presidential aspirant, was probably the most aggressive of them, primarily in the Caribbean but also throughout the hemisphere in his quest for a Pan-American customs union. He was the convener of the first

Pan-American Conference, staged in 1889. Blaine perceived an urgent need for the United States to provide leadership for the Americas. Sharing the usual racist biases of most of his countrymen, he viewed Latin Americans as uncivilized, requiring the moral influence of their northern neighbors. It was important to teach them to behave to prevent them from giving Europeans cause to intervene in their affairs—a fear that remained a concern in Washington for another hundred years.

On one occasion, suspecting British inspiration for Chile's claims in its fight against Peru in the War of the Pacific, Blaine attempted to provide political support to Peru. His representatives failed to do anything useful, alienating Peruvians who had anticipated meaningful assistance and Chileans who recognized Washington's efforts to deny them. Chilean antipathy toward the United States may have contributed to a barroom brawl in which several American sailors were killed or injured. Blaine's mishandling of the ensuing diplomatic brouhaha came close to resulting in a military confrontation. There was little evidence that his assertive policies won any friends for the United States in Latin America.

In the Pacific, Blaine and Benjamin Harrison, the president he served, very nearly succeeded in annexing Hawaii. A reciprocity treaty ratified in 1875 had tied the Hawaiian economy, dominated by American businessmen, to the United States. In the late 1880s Washington won an agreement to give the United States the exclusive right to build a naval base at Pearl Harbor. An attempt by Queen Liliuokalani to retrieve power from American planters led to a coup supported by sailors from an American warship. The administration invited a request for annexation that was duly negotiated on the eve of Harrison's departure from the White House. The incoming administration of Grover Cleveland allowed the treaty to die, but it was inevitable that the Americans who had seized control of the islands would eventually bring them under Washington's aegis.

Another European country, Germany, about whom Americans were less apprehensive than they were of Britain, emerged as a new concern in the final decades of the nineteenth century. Otto von Bismarck had created a great power, and its rise led to differences with the United States in the Western Hemisphere, the Pacific, and Africa. The Germans were active in the 1870s and 1880s in several Central American countries. They did not hesitate to use gunboat diplomacy to protect their investments. Bismarck was interested in obtaining colonies or at least bases in the region but, confronted by strong opposition from Washington, found less threatening means of developing German economic interests across the Atlantic.

A second area of potential German-American friction, in which American interests were markedly less significant, was Africa—particularly the Congo. American merchants were always looking for markets, and the U.S. Navy was always seeking coaling stations and bases—by no means averse to advertising their potential commercial value. The discovery of the Congo's mineral wealth had awakened the interest of several European states, then competing for colonies and protectorates in Africa and Asia. No one in Washington had any interest in controlling the Congo, but the possibilities for trade and investment were not lost on a handful of diplomats, politicians, and speculators. Those most involved chose to support the claims of King Leopold of Belgium, believing he would ensure American access to an imagined market in the Congo. In 1884 Bismarck, less desirous of a Congolese colony than Americans may have imagined, convened a conference on the Congo. Perhaps to his surprise, the United States, despite its fear of entanglement in European affairs, sent a representative, but the treaty endorsing Leopold's claims failed to be ratified by a U.S. Senate still suspicious of any links to Europe. Leopold went on to establish one of the most brutal colonial regimes the world was ever to see.

Considerably more dangerous was an actual confrontation between American and German warships in Samoa. American businessmen had found their way to these South Pacific islands, and in 1872, spurred by these commercial interests and the navy's own quest for bases, an American naval officer negotiated a treaty with Samoan leaders. The principal U.S. objective was control of Pago Pago, a superb harbor. The Samoans willingly granted control of the harbor in exchange for a promise of American assistance in their efforts to ward off British and German pressures. In 1879 the American, British, and German consuls in Samoa signed a tripartite agreement on the governing of the islands, a modest exercise in multilateral imperialism. The British seemed satisfied, but the Germans were not. In 1885 the German Navy began military action aimed at taking control of all of Samoa—in response to which the American consul, without authorization, declared Samoa to be an American protectorate. Neither Washington nor Berlin was prepared to support its men in the field, and conditions on the islands approached the status quo ante.

In 1887, encouraged by a diplomatic deal with the British, German warships sailed to Samoa, deposed the king, and demonstrated Germany's intent to seize the islands. President Cleveland responded by sending American warships to defend American interests. As the navies faced off against each other, any overzealous gunnery officer could have precipitated a war—which neither Bismarck nor Cleveland desired. Bismarck called for a conference in Berlin. In March 1889, before the conference could convene, a devastating hurricane struck the harbor, wiping out both fleets and eliminating the possibility of a naval battle. Later that year, American, British, and German representatives met in Berlin and worked out another tripartite power-sharing agreement, leaving Samoa nominally independent—and preserving American control of Pago Pago.

The economic, strategic—and missionary—interests of the United States were propelling the American flag across the Pacific, involving the country in complicated relationships with Asian and European states. The Aleutians, Hawaii, Midway, and Samoa were way stations to East Asia where Americans eager for commercial opportunities, bases, and souls to save encountered European imperialists as well as the region's native peoples.

Active in China since the birth of the nation, Americans became enmeshed in the British-led multilateral imperial system imposed on the Chinese by the treaties of the decades following the Opium War. A most-favored-nation clause inserted in the Treaty of Wangxia in 1844 guaranteed Americans all the privileges the Europeans exacted from China by force. American goods flowed into China under the terms of a treaty tariff that precluded protectionism. Thanks to the provision for extraterritoriality, Americans lived and worked in China subject to American law, with minimal concern for Chinese laws. American Protestant missionaries roamed the country, disrupting Chinese society, often protected by American gunboats. At the same time, Chinese immigrants, most recruited to work in the United States, were harassed and discriminated against, sometimes murdered, and ultimately excluded in violation of their rights under a treaty ratified in the Seward era. Treatment of Chinese in the United

States strained relations between Beijing and Washington, especially in the 1890s.

Japan, in the decades after Perry accelerated its opening to the West, was also forced to accept humiliating treaties similar to those imposed on China. Although antiforeignism remained powerful, Japanese leaders after the Meiji Restoration of 1868 recognized the need to modernize their country if they were to achieve equality with the world's major powers. Westerners in Japan never achieved the degree of dominance they enjoyed in China. American educators, missionary and secular, played an important part in Japan's transformation, but the Japanese looked primarily to European countries for models. When writing their constitution, the Meiji elite found German writings most compatible. They turned to Britain for help in building a modern navy and to France to train their army.

Perceiving colonies and protectorates—imperialism generally—to be the source of Western power, Japan moved against its neighbors, China and Korea, to demonstrate its strength and its claim to be treated as an equal. Few Americans were troubled by Japan's aggressive actions, not even by its routing of China in the Sino-Japanese War of 1894–1895. In Washington and among Americans in China, there was a sense that the Chinese needed to be taught a lesson, to awaken them to the need for reforms that would allow them to join the modern world. And some Americans, with an exaggerated sense of the importance of their countrymen's contribution to the opening and modernization of Japan, took pride in the accomplishments of their presumed protégé.

On the other hand, Americans in Korea, especially the missionary doctor Horace Allen, soon to be appointed minister to Seoul, were dismayed by Japanese actions. The perennial quest for markets had led to efforts to obtain a treaty with Korea as early as 1867. Driven off by the Koreans time and again, the U.S. Navy achieved success—with Chinese support—in 1882, winning a treaty similar to those with China and Japan. The two countries established diplomatic relations, and Korea granted the Americans most-favored-nation status, allowing Americans to reside in the treaty ports it opened, largely exempt from Korean law. Politically, the Americans were in over their heads. They never understood Korea's status as a Chinese tributary or the fact that the Chinese were trying to use them to protect their interests on the peninsula from Japanese efforts to gain control. Trade proved to be negligible. In all, the United States was a minor player in Korean affairs, lacking the strategic stake the Chinese, the Japanese, and the Russians had in the region.

At home, Americans were suffering from the chaos that came from revolutionary developments in industry, transportation, and communications. Unregulated, the business cycle, an integral part of capitalism, wreaked occasional havoc with the economy, creating widespread misery for small businesses and the industrial labor force. With unemployment came hostility to immigrants who vied for available jobs and often worked for lower wages. And farmers faced little understood competition from abroad that forced down the value of their crops.

After several years of rapid economic growth, the initial collapse occurred in 1873. The "Panic of 1873" was a major depression that lasted until 1879, although the suffering continued for many sectors of society. Banks failed, railroads failed, factories laid off workers. In addition to a sharp drop in wages, unemployment soared into double digits. Labor unrest shook the country, most notably in the railroad strike of 1877, to which the government responded with lethal force.

As always, low wages, a weakening of purchasing power, led to underconsumption, a weakening of the domestic market. Producers of both agricultural and manufactured goods looked to exports, to foreign markets for relief. Competition for markets overseas often required price cuts, necessitating further wage reductions. And then in 1893 came another great "Panic," another major depression that devastated the country through the mid-1890s. The prevailing explanation focused on excess production—a glut of goods unabsorbable at home—intensifying an obsession with expanding exports.

American naval officers, always seeking more ships, more bases, and a larger budget for the navy, eager to drum up support from the business community, were quick to call attention to the need for a powerful navy to protect the nation's merchant fleet. The most successful lobbyist for the navy was Captain Alfred Thayer Mahan, whose book *The Influence of Seapower Upon History* (1890) won admirers among influential politicians at home and abroad, as well as among leading businessmen. The lessons of the past, Mahan argued, demonstrated the potential value of the U.S. Navy to the American economy: give it enough ships, especially a significant battle fleet, and it could protect commerce from competitors and create new opportunities abroad. And, of course, it would need bases around the world from which to operate. In the 1890s the United States began production of a first-class fleet, as befit a nation eager to become a world power.

Little of the outward thrust of American influence in the 1880s and early 1890s originated in Washington, despite the efforts of men like Blaine. It was the seekers of markets and investment opportunities, the wielders of economic power, who developed the interests of the United States across the globe. The American public and its elected leaders had minimal desire to acquire territory populated by alien races, but investors bought huge tracts of land in Hawaii, Mexico, Cuba, and various parts of Central America. They took over sugar plantations, grew bananas and pineapples, opened mines, explored for oil, built railroads. In some instances, they created the earliest multinational corporations. Familiar names such as Carnegie, Dole, Morgan, and Rockefeller were involved, but so were many less prominent. And the agricultural sector was heavily represented in the export market, relying on foreign purchases of corn and wheat, textiles and tobacco. This was the era in which the myth of the China market loomed large, the vision that hundreds of millions of Chinese would consume American surpluses (in fact it was Japan, not China, that could afford to become a major importer of American goods). Washington did its part by expanding and improving the consular service.

Missionaries and tourists also spearheaded the nation's engagement with the world. Missionary activity was most marked in East Asia, especially China, in part because Europeans had staked out most of the rest of the pagan world. Much of what Americans learned about China in the final third of the nineteenth century and the first half of the twentieth came from the missionaries and their offspring. Europe, on the other hand, provided few opportunities to spread the gospel but wonderful vistas for tourists, whose travelogues informed American opinion about the Old World.

Another issue that emerged in this era was that of human rights. At home, Americans tormented—even murdered—Native Americans, African Americans, and Chinese immigrants. Problems arose with the mistreatment of other immigrants—Italians, for example. Nonetheless, concern was shown for the British treatment of Ireland and Russian pogroms against Jews. Irish Americans had given up raiding Canada, but without significant government interference they armed terrorists in the motherland—and continued to do so through much of the twentieth century. Troubled by the flow of poverty-stricken, hapless Jews into the United States, Washington protested against the Russian policies that drove them to emigrate—a problem more easily resolved eventually by passing new immigration laws that reduced opportunities for European immigrants to enter the United States.

And so, in 1896, on the eve of a presidential election, only a few years away from a new century, the nation was uneasy. The effects of the Panic of 1893 lingered. There was substantial labor unrest, generally suppressed by force—usually company hired thugs but sometimes government troops. Unrest in agricultural regions was evidenced by the rise of the Populist Party and the presidential candidacy of William Jennings Bryan. The powers that prevailed, the Republican representatives of the business community, focused on increasing exports to reinvigorate the economy. Bryan's call for "Free Silver," an inflationary monetary policy, failed to resonate with a majority of voters.

Thirty years after the American people had fought a civil war over the issue of slavery, freeing African Americans from bondage, the free men and women were subjected to Jim Crow laws and the brutality of the Ku Klux Klan. Racism, north as well as south, prevailed in the treatment of Native Americans and immigrants from China and eastern and southern Europe as well. Racism ran so deep in the national ethic that it inevitably carried over into the conduct of foreign affairs.

Throughout the post–Civil War era, there had been a widespread desire, especially evident among elites, for the country to take its place among the great powers. By the 1890s the economic and population bases were there. The United States verged on being the world's leading industrial power. Among the powers, its population was second only to Russia's. A naval buildup was underway. As men like Mahan, Theodore Roosevelt, Brooks Adams, and Henry Cabot Lodge looked abroad, they were aware of the new explosion of imperialism. The European powers were seeking once again to exploit weaker nations and the Japanese were following suit, perceiving imperialism as the route to national power and respect. The United States had been conceived in opposition to imperialism and had avoided overseas empire while building its continental imperium. But it was inching in the same direction other rising powers had throughout history—toward domination of weak neighbors such as Mexico and the several states of the Caribbean and Central America. It had established protectorates in Hawaii and Samoa. It participated in and benefited from the multilateral imperialism that had controlled China since midcentury. As the nation's ability to extend its power outward increased, there was little to prevent its activities from mirroring those of the other great imperial powers.

The Republican Party platform of 1896 called for protective tariffs to preserve American markets for American products and reciprocity treaties to provide markets abroad for the surplus, for whatever manufactured goods or crops could not be consumed at home. It insisted that Hawaii be controlled by the United States, that a trans-isthmian canal be built across Nicaragua and operated by the United States unilaterally, and that the Danish West Indies be purchased to provide a base to protect the canal. Noting the brutal insurgency in Cuba, the foreign policy plank called for the United States to work peacefully for the island's independence. It was a platform appropriate for a rising power anticipating a larger role in international economic, political, and strategic affairs. And when the American people elected William McKinley, the Republican candidate, they gained a president with the skill and ambition necessary to conduct an expansionist foreign policy.

The point of no return in American foreign policy was the Spanish-American War of 1898. Although the pretense to exceptionalism lived on in the nation's self-image, the United States had openly surrendered its claim to moral imagination: its leaders unapologetically chose to compete for world primacy on the backs of subject peoples. They never ceased voicing their faith in the ideals on which the nation had been founded—and on occasion served them—but after strenuous debate and with full understanding of the road being taken, they chose to make America just another imperialist power.

In retrospect the war seems to have been inevitable. Presidents, diplomats, businessmen, and slaveholders had lusted after Cuba throughout the nineteenth century. American economic interests on the island were enormous, and its strategic value had long been recognized. One day Cuba would be a part of the United States. In 1898 Spanish efforts to crush the insurgency raging there troubled many Americans. Various suggestions to Madrid that it was time to accept Cuban independence were ignored. McKinley was among those who were determined to see the United States gain control of the island, peacefully if possible, by other means if not. There was also a feeling spreading in the country that the United States had a responsibility to end the suffering of the Cuban people. With great power came great responsibility—a theme to be repeated throughout the rest of the nation's history. Yes, the continued unrest in Cuba threatened American economic interests, but Washington could easily perceive of intervention on humanitarian grounds, in service of the nation's ideals as well as its self-interest.

Peaceful resolution of the Cuban fight for independence proved beyond reach. An uneasy Spanish queen feared that to surrender the island would undermine the monarchy. Her advisers knew war with the United States would be likely—and few in Spain or elsewhere in Europe believed the decrepit Spanish military had any chance of prevailing in such a conflict— but defeat in war was more honorable than craven surrender. And so the two countries were doomed to a senseless military confrontation.

For the only time in American history, it was Congress rather than the president that introduced the declaration of war, in April 1898. Two incidents in February had brought war fever to a peak. First was publication of a letter written by the Spanish minister in Washington disparaging McKinley and indicating that Spain had no intention to carry out genuine reforms in Cuba. Second was the explosion of the USS *Maine* while docked in Havana, a probable accident widely blamed on Spain. To the disgust of an aroused American public, McKinley continued to work unsuccessfully for a peaceful solution. He was not troubled, however, when Congress moved ahead.

The U.S. Navy's plans in the event of war with Spain called for destruction of the Spanish fleet in Manila Bay. Theodore Roosevelt, assistant secretary of the navy, sent the attack orders to Admiral George Dewey, commander of the Asiatic Fleet, whose ships easily defeated the hapless Spaniards.

The fight against the Spanish in Cuba also resulted in an overwhelming victory for marginally competent American forces. Most American casualties came from disease. McKinley was prevented from annexing the island, however, by the Teller Amendment to the war resolution. The amendment precluded any declaration of American sovereignty over the island—a self-denying statement that was finessed a few years later by the Platt amendment to the Cuban constitution giving the United States the right to intervene to ensure order and the reciprocal trade agreement of 1903, which tied the Cuban economy to that of the United States.

The issue of what to do with the Philippine Islands proved much more complicated. There, too, was a major anticolonial insurgency, eager for American support but not American control. The insurgents and American forces fought together against the Spanish, but once Spain surrendered, the victors had very different agendas. McKinley never intended to give up the harbor at Manila. For him and his advisers, the question was how much more of the Philippines the United States would have to take to ensure the security of a naval base in Manila Bay. There was no doubt of German interest in the islands and perhaps Japanese as well. The island of Luzon would probably have to be American controlled to protect Manila—and eventually McKinley concluded the United States would have to take all the other islands to protect Luzon.

The American decision to replace the Spanish colonizers was not acceptable to the Filipinos who were fighting for their independence. They were unwilling to exchange one set of masters for another. By 1900 a full-scale war erupted between the forces of the United States and the Filipinos to whom Washington sought to extend the blessings of American civilization. The war lasted approximately three years, during which both sides were guilty of atrocities. One technique the Americans introduced to the benighted natives was the "water cure," forcing contaminated water down the mouths of captives in an attempt to acquire information. Led by hardened veterans of the Indian Wars, shouting racist epithets at the "goo-goos" and "niggers" they were fighting, American troops prevailed. More than 4,000 Americans were killed in action. About 20,000 Filipino combatants were killed, and over 200,000 Filipino civilians died as a result of the war.

At home there was intense but narrow opposition to the idea of the United States blatantly seizing the imperialist mantle, of choosing to impose its rule on an alien people of color, never destined for citizenship. But the sense of national pride at taking on what Rudyard Kipling had called "the white man's burden," of carrying abroad the long-standing mission to bring Christianity and democracy to the heathen, prevailed. Imperialism was supposed to be the critical issue in the presidential election campaign of 1900. It was not: Bryan's efforts were pathetic, and McKinley easily won reelection. America had an empire and prosperity returned.

That empire extended beyond Cuba and the Philippines. In the Caribbean, the United States also took Puerto Rico from Spain. In the Pacific, the importance of Hawaii on the route to East Asia could not have been more evident. McKinley ordered its annexation. Moreover, he and his advisers perceived a need for bases in the Western Pacific, taking Guam in the Marianas and Wake Island for a possible cable station. The sun did not yet shine on Old Glory all over the world, but as the United States entered the twentieth century the flag was on the move.

The war and the new empire seemed to bring the country together, uniting North and South together in the fight to liberate Cuba. Differences over principles, over whether American values were compromised by becoming a colonial power, faded, blurred by the conviction that as an exceptional nation, the United States, unlike other imperial powers, would be a force for good in the lives of its subject people. Perhaps the Cubans and Filipinos, denied their independence, were wrong to see things differently.

There was also a broad range of pressures on the McKinley administration to play a larger role in Chinese affairs. Some in the business community lusted after the China market. After China's defeat in its war with Japan in 1895, there were fears that it would be carved up by Japanese and European imperialists, ceasing to exist as a sovereign nation. Opportunities for American business might disappear. Others concerned, missionaries and romantic nationalists, also urged McKinley to be more assertive in protecting American interests in China. Neither the president nor John Hay, his secretary of state, perceived those interests to be significant. Eventually, in 1899, Hay responded to the pressures by sending the first of his "Open Door" notes to the powers active in China, asking them not to discriminate against American business in the spheres of interest they were establishing for themselves. He also asked them not to interfere with the operations of the Imperial Maritime Customs Service in those spheres. The responses were largely evasive, but none flatly rejected Hay's requests.

In 1900, during the Boxer War, a Chinese effort to free their country of foreigners, American troops from the Philippines were involved in liberating foreigners under siege in Beijing. In that context, Hay sent another circular note, asking that China's sovereignty and territorial integrity be respected. He did not request a response. For reasons of their own, the other powers chose not to dismember China. Had they decided otherwise, the United States asked that Samsah Bay in Fujian be awarded to it. Spared a sphere of influence in China, Hay and McKinley were content to pose as China's champions, the men who had saved China from the predators. Regrettably, Chinese leaders had no such illusions, engaged at the time in an unsuccessful effort to stop discrimination against Chinese immigrants in America's newly acquired territories across the Pacific.

6

TEDDY ROOSEVELT AND THE GREAT POWER GAME

T HE ASSASSINATION OF William McKinley in September 1901 brought Theodore Roosevelt to the White House. He was the perfect president for the era, the quintessential romantic nationalist. He was a leading member of the so-called Large Policy group, along with Mahan, Brooks Adams, and Henry Cabot Lodge. These were men who exulted in the rise of the United States to world power and were eager to see it play a more assertive role in international affairs. Perhaps more than any of the others, Roosevelt glorified power and was contemptuous of weakness. And he was an unabashed racist.

From McKinley he inherited the war with the Filipinos that he proceeded to prosecute brutally. Before long, however, he envisioned the distant Philippine Islands as America's Achilles heel in its efforts to expand its interests and influence in East Asia. If a confrontation ever came with Japan, he perceived the Philippines as indefensible—and that perception left him determined to avoid such a confrontation, to appease Japan.

Closer to home and of more immediate concern was his country's posture in the Caribbean. McKinley had included Puerto Rico as part of the booty taken from Spain in 1898. Valuable because of its location, the island, unfortunately, was densely populated by a Spanish-speaking people who had never known the blessings of democracy. They were deemed unsuitable for either American citizenship or self-government. The Foraker

Act of 1900 attempted to finesse the problem by declaring Puerto Rico an American possession but not part of the United States—not slated for statehood nor protected by the Constitution of the United States. Challenged by anti-imperialists, who insisted that the Constitution followed the flag, the issue was decided in 1901 by the Supreme Court ruling in the Insular Cases: Washington could govern its newly acquired possessions without the consent of the people. Roosevelt was not discomforted by the treatment of Puerto Ricans who quickly lost what little autonomy Spain had granted them. He was contemptuous of them, the Filipinos, Native Americans—non-Anglo-Saxons generally—as uncivilized peoples prone to misusing the land they inhabited, requiring tutelage from Americans such as himself. Respect for the Other was not part of his character.

One striking demonstration of Roosevelt's approach came in 1903 with his shameless seizure of the Isthmus of Panama. John Hay had succeeded in 1901 in winning for the United States the right to build, operate, and fortify a trans-isthmian canal. The British, eager to win the friendship of the newly emergent great power, had gradually surrendered the rights to which they were entitled by the Clayton-Bulwer Treaty of 1850. An American agreement with Colombia in 1836 authorized Washington to act as necessary to keep the peace in Panama, then part of Colombia. By the time of Roosevelt's presidency, there was no doubt that the United States was the dominant power in the region. This time, when the Panamanians began one of their frequent revolts against Colombian rule, Roosevelt, contrary to the terms of the 1836 accord guaranteeing Colombian sovereignty, sent ships to *prevent* Colombia from suppressing the rebels. Hastily, Hay and Philippe Bunau-Varilla, a Frenchman and erstwhile failed canal builder, negotiated an arrangement that gave the United States control of a zone across the isthmus. Panama received financial compensation, but Bunau-Varilla's authority to represent the Panamanians was dubious. Roosevelt simply saw an opportunity to further the interests of the United States and seized it—in blatant disregard of international law. Washington's representatives in the Canal Zone controlled an ostensibly independent Panama for many decades afterward. On the positive side, the Americans did succeed where Bunau-Varilla had not: they built the canal and eradicated malaria and yellow fever on the isthmus in the process.

Perhaps most striking, and most indicative of Roosevelt's sense of America's place in the world, was his claim of police powers in the Western Hemisphere—the famed Roosevelt Corollary to the Monroe Doctrine. He had initially accepted intervention in Venezuela by European states determined to protect the interests of their citizens—bad behavior had to be punished. The reaction among Americans, however, was strongly negative. He concluded that the United States had a responsibility, therefore, to assure that the nations of its hemisphere did not behave in any manner that might prompt European intervention. Disorder in the Dominican Republic in 1904 that threatened American commercial interests and stimulated unwarranted fear of German intervention provided the occasion for American action. American forces moved in and took control of Dominican finances through control of its customs houses—a practice repeated elsewhere in the Caribbean and Central America in the years that followed. Although the Monroe Doctrine had evolved with the ostensible purpose of protecting the states of the Western Hemisphere from foreign interventions, in Roosevelt's hands it was a justification for intervention by the United States.

To several of his friends associated with the Large Policy group, especially Brooks Adams, Mahan, and William Rockhill, Asia appeared especially important in America's future. They were eager to see their country exploit economic opportunities there, and Rockhill foresaw the United States as the balancer of power in the region. Roosevelt made several efforts to support American economic interests in China but quickly learned there was minimal interest among the business community at home. The first major issue to which he addressed himself was the Russo-Japanese War of 1904–1905. He was contemptuous of the tsarist regime, was irritated by Russian-imposed obstacles to American opportunities in Manchuria, and tilted toward the Japanese, who, he wrote, were playing "our game." Jacob Schiff, an American banker outraged by Russian treatment of Jews, worked assiduously to deny the Russians loans to facilitate their war effort and arranged loans to sustain Japan's efforts. But as the war progressed and the Russians suffered one major defeat after another, Roosevelt concluded that an overwhelming Japanese victory would pose a serious threat to American interests. The Russians had vital interests in

Europe and the Levant while Japan could focus all its power in East Asia. He then offered his services to mediate an end to the war, an effort that succeeded with the Treaty of Portsmouth in 1905 and won him the Nobel Peace Prize in 1906. At the same time he worked to end the war, he reached out to the Japanese in an effort to protect the Philippines, resulting in the Taft-Katsura Agreement of 1905. The United States acquiesced in Japanese imperialism in Korea, and the Japanese accepted the American role in the Philippines and Hawaii.

Another issue that roiled American relations with China and Japan was the treatment of Asian immigrants in the United States. When not excluded, they were subjected to harassment, segregation, humiliation, and occasionally violence. In 1905 Chinese, angered by the treatment of their compatriots in America, organized a boycott of American goods, an early expression of burgeoning Chinese nationalism. Roosevelt recognized the justice of their cause but had little authority to intervene in the states to ameliorate the condition of the immigrants. When, however, Tokyo expressed anger at the treatment of Japanese, he perceived a need to do something. Angry Chinese posed a minimal threat to the United States; Japan had become a great power with the means to damage American interests across the Pacific: its complaints could not be ignored. After several stumbles, he reached a "Gentlemen's Agreement" with the Japanese whereby Japan slowed the flow of immigrants to the United States—mostly from Hawaii—and Roosevelt succeeded in curbing some of the anti-Japanese actions by California officials. Aware of the potential threat from Japan, he stepped up building of his beloved battle fleet and instructed the navy to develop what became War Plan Orange, preparation for a military confrontation. To demonstrate American strength, he sent the Great White Fleet on a cruise that included a visit to Yokohama.

Further evidence of Roosevelt's respect for Japan was apparent in the Root-Takahira Agreement of 1908. He had recognized and praised the rise of nationalism in China. When a Chinese official met with him in November of that year to request assistance with modernization efforts in Manchuria, an attempt to counter Japanese influence there, Roosevelt spoke fulsomely of his desire for a strong China. But he offered only verbal support, while Secretary of State Elihu Root, at approximately the same time, assured Takahira Kogoro, the Japanese ambassador, of American acceptance of the status quo in Asia—which included Japanese dominance of southern Manchuria. Again, Roosevelt respected power: Japan had it, China did not. A few years later, when William Howard Taft, his successor in the White House, challenged Japan's role in Manchuria, Roosevelt warned him to desist, arguing the United States would need the equivalent of the British navy and the German army to counter Japan there. He reminded Taft of the volatile immigration issue and warned him about the vulnerability of American possessions in the Pacific.

Roosevelt was a shameless advocate of imperialism; nonetheless, his interest in world politics and understanding of the role of power in international relations generally served the interests of his country well. He and Root worked assiduously to modernize the nation's foreign policy apparatus. For better or worse, he demonstrated how executive agreements, sometimes secret agreements, could enable the president to accomplish ends that might otherwise be unachievable because of public or congressional ignorance, indifference, or hostility. He did not hesitate to become involved in affairs that many of his fellow citizens would have considered violations of American traditions, most obviously his mediation of the Russo-Japanese War and his intervention in the Franco-German Moroccan crisis of 1905–1906. Fearing an influx of impoverished Jews, he pressed (unsuccessfully) for more humane treatment of them by the Russians. Perhaps most important for the years that followed were his efforts to strengthen Anglo-American relations, his perception in 1902 that the United States might be a quiet third party to the Anglo-Japanese alliance, and his role in what the historian Bradford Perkins called the "Great Rapprochement" with Great Britain.

Taft was Roosevelt's chosen successor, but his approach to world affairs differed greatly from that of his erstwhile mentor. He was less of a romantic than Roosevelt, much more focused on acquiring economic opportunities, overseas markets, and investments, much less intimidated by appearances of power—such as demonstrated by the Japanese—perhaps more moralistic. Neither he nor his secretary of state, Philander Knox, had the understanding of international politics that Roosevelt and Root evinced.

Taft and Knox were known for what was labeled "dollar diplomacy." It was their intent to use American economic rather than military power to serve the national interest. Their chosen instrument was the banker, but on occasion they sent in the marines, as in the Dominican Republic and Nicaragua. Concerned primarily with Central America, they attempted to work with native elites there whose goals—political stability and economic development—were congruent with those of the Americans. Their efforts met with minimal success, and the instability that prevailed led to further military interventions and occupations.

When Taft and Knox attempted dollar diplomacy in China, they became involved in affairs they never fully understood and failed miserably, but at minimal cost to the United States. Taft, when he served as governor of the Philippines, had developed an obsessive hostility to Japan. He was determined to use American investment bankers to promote opportunities for American businesses in China—and, in the process, thwart Japanese efforts to dominate China. His reversal of Roosevelt's approach to Japan was striking, eliciting Roosevelt's warning about the disparity of power between Japan and the United States in East Asia. The Chinese welcomed Taft's efforts but no longer had much control over their affairs.

Taft personally requested Chinese support for American involvement in railroad construction in southern China, but the decision rested with European bankers and their home governments rather than Chinese officials. By the time the Europeans accepted the American group, the project had collapsed. Taft and Knox then turned to railroad construction in Manchuria. They believed that they could thereby preserve China's sovereignty over its northeastern provinces, to the benefit of American investors and merchants. Their attempt to isolate Japan failed, as did their effort to drive a wedge between Japan and Russia. Anticipated support from Great Britain never came. London had no interest in antagonizing its Japanese allies. Similarly, the French supported their Russian allies and the Germans had no interest in taking on the Russians and Japanese on behalf of Chinese sovereignty or American economic opportunity. Taft and Knox had much to learn about world politics. Knox's appeals to China's "moral right" to control its own territory or the "right" of the United States, under the Open Door policy, to trade and invest in Manchuria carried little weight with the practitioners of Realpolitik.

Disgust with Taft's foreign policies added to other grievances that propelled Roosevelt into the fight for the presidency against his protégé in 1912. His candidacy on the Bull Moose ticket paved the way for a Democrat, Woodrow Wilson, to win the presidency—and to pursue different policies that proved no less offensive to Roosevelt.

7

TO MAKE THE WORLD SAFE
FOR DEMOCRACY

A S THE UNITED States became more deeply involved in world affairs in the early years of the twentieth century, the Department of State was enlarged and reorganized to serve the nation's new role. Examinations were required for admission to the Foreign Service, and those admitted underwent rigorous training. Geographic divisions were created. Congress funded the purchase of embassies and legations overseas. The paraphernalia for functioning as a great power was put into place. In 1903 the Department of Commerce was created to meet the concerns of businessmen eager to compete with Britain and Germany in world markets. These were critical parts of the legacies of Theodore Roosevelt and William Howard Taft.

Woodrow Wilson had no intention of following in the footsteps of Roosevelt—or Taft. Roosevelt's militarism and Taft's economic imperialism troubled him. He mistrusted the State Department and many of the corporate leaders the Commerce Department served. The idea of America as the world's leading nation did appeal to him, but his conception of that leadership differed significantly. His vision was of a foreign policy less narrowly self-interested. He perceived his country's interests as being promoted best in a peaceful, democratic world—and he would use its power to create a new order, to achieve that end, to serve mankind as well as the United States. His vision came to be known as Wilsonian internationalism, and it had a major impact on his country and the world long after his death, on into the twenty-first century.

Shortly after beginning his presidency, Wilson left no doubt that he did not approve of Roosevelt's methods by apologizing to Colombia and offering compensation for Roosevelt's actions in facilitating Panamanian independence. Appalled by Taft's forcing an American group of bankers into the China consortium—which he believed to be an imperialist construct obstructing the development of the newly created Republic of China—he withdrew support from the American Group and recognized the government of President Yuan Shikai. Another revealing action was his decision to withhold recognition of the regime of General Victoriano Huerta in Mexico. Huerta had seized power and had his predecessor murdered in the course of the Mexican Revolution. Traditional practice had been to recognize any government that held power and met its international obligations. Wilson, ever the moralist, considered Huerta evil and would withhold recognition until a government of which he approved, presumably a democratic regime, was installed.

Along with most others in the United States throughout the history of the nation, Wilson believed in American exceptionalism. He was convinced that the country had a unique contribution to make to the world. He took great pride in American democracy and never hesitated to call to account foreign leaders who strayed from the American model and, when he deemed appropriate, to intervene in their affairs—to set them on the true course, to teach their people to elect good leaders. Unfortunately, his vision was clouded by racism and insensitivity to the nationalism of others. He was always surprised, disappointed, in the failure of those he would instruct to follow his lead. Despite his profound commitment to liberal internationalism, he, like his predecessors, demonstrated a lack of moral imagination.

Wilson had been appalled by military interventions in the Caribbean ordered by previous administrations. Certainly he intended to treat Latin Americans as equals—even though he believed them to be racially inferior and backward in their comprehension of what constituted good governance. Regrettably, he found it necessary, again and again, to send American troops to restore order, supervise elections, and prepare these benighted peoples for democracy. Cuba once, Panama twice, and Honduras on five occasions were subjected to American military discipline. Nicaragua, the Dominican Republic, and Haiti required far more than brief incursions. Nicaragua became an American protectorate with an American troop presence well into the 1920s. The people of the Dominican Republic did not respond adequately to military intervention in 1915, requiring Wilson to order the occupation of that country in 1916. It took the marines five years to still resistance, and the occupation lasted until the mid-1920s. The Haitians, too, resisted American instruction and did not regain their freedom until 1934. There can be no doubt that Wilson was well intentioned, but the peoples of these countries preferred the freedom to manage their own affairs in ways of their own choosing—a lesson neither Wilson nor many of his successors ever learned.

The challenge the United States faced in Mexico was far greater and included a high risk of a major war. It began with the revolution of 1910–1911, when the Mexican people rose against the long-standing dictatorship of Porfirio Díaz. Díaz's approach to modernization had been to welcome enormous foreign investment, allowing foreigners to control and exploit his country's natural resources, own and operate its railroads, and purchase huge tracts of land. His own people benefited little from the wealth thus acquired and deposed him in 1911. The leader of the revolution, Francisco Madero, established democratic political institutions but alienated American businesses—and the American ambassador—who perceived him as too supportive of European influence. They facilitated the overthrow of his government by Huerta, on the eve of Wilson's inauguration.

Wilson's moralistic approach to world affairs manifested itself immediately. Huerta was evil, responsible for Madero's murder, beholden to foreign businesses to the detriment of the Mexican people. Departing from traditional practice, Wilson withheld diplomatic recognition, hoping to set in motion a process that would lead to Huerta's departure and the election of respectable men. He imagined that his action would also signal the importance of good government to other nations in the region. The results were considerably less promising than he anticipated.

Wilson's agents demanded that Huerta step aside and order free elections. Instead, the Mexican leader took steps to strengthen his dictatorial rule.

And perhaps most disappointing was the response of the leader of the opposition to Huerta, who denounced American interference in Mexico's affairs. Wilson, however, was not deterred. He increased military pressure on Huerta and allowed the opposition to obtain arms. In April 1914, perceiving an opportunity to undermine Huerta, he took advantage of a minor incident involving the arrest of American sailors in Tampico to order the invasion of Vera Cruz. The United States would help Mexico create a stable democratic government—another early effort at nation building. Once again, Wilson proved oblivious to Mexican nationalism. Expecting to be welcomed, his troops had to overcome intense local resistance. The invasion was condemned throughout Mexico. U.S. Marines occupied the city for seven months, and Huerta was ultimately driven from power by opposition troops led by Venustiano Carranza—who also had little love for the North Americans.

Eventually, despite Carranza's refusal to imbibe the wisdom that flowed from Washington, Wilson extended recognition to his government. But problems with Mexico persisted as rebel leaders Pancho Villa and Emiliano Zapata stirred unrest. Wilson's offer to mediate was rejected, and eventually Villa launched attacks on U.S. border towns. Wilson sent a punitive expedition of ten thousand men into Mexico in a fruitless hunt for Villa, but the American troops managed to clash with Mexican troops, inciting calls across the United States for war, especially from business leaders whose Mexican holdings were threatened by the Carranza regime and the Catholic Church, troubled by Carranza's anticlericalism and confiscation of church property. Wilson mobilized the National Guard, sent thirty thousand troops to the border, and contemplated occupying all of Mexico. He quickly realized it would be a fool's errand—that occupying Mexico might require many hundreds of thousands of troops—and dishonor the United States in world public opinion. A negotiated peace brought the troops home in January 1917.

And in January 1917 Germany announced it would resume unrestricted submarine warfare. The Great War had begun with the "Guns of August" in 1914. Most Americans were only vaguely aware of the international political machinations, the alliance politics that had led to the war. Wilson declared American neutrality and asked his people to be neutral in thought as well as deed, no easy task given the ethnic diversity of the population. Wilson himself and many of the eastern elite were Anglophiles. Britain and France were democracies winning substantial sympathy for the Entente powers—even if they included tsarist Russia, anathema to American Jews. German and Irish Americans leaned the other way, but few tilting in either direction foresaw intervention by the United States. And as the war proceeded, enormous advantages accrued to the neutral United States: its merchant marine took much of the world's carrying trade, its factories and farms prospered from overseas sales, and its financial sector profited enormously from loans, mostly to Britain. Indeed, the United States was transformed in the course of the war from a debtor nation to the world's largest creditor.

The British effort to prevent trade with Germany through a blockade of continental ports to which the Germans had access constituted a major annoyance to the United States, and the Americans complained constantly, demanding respect for international law governing neutral rights. The British did not hesitate to point to precedents established by Lincoln's administration during the American Civil War but were careful not to be too provocative: a hostile United States would be devastating to their prospects for victory. In an effort to win American sympathies, they also mounted a major propaganda effort designed to portray the Germans as bloodthirsty monsters. German submarine warfare contributed greatly to the success of the British campaign, most notably with the sinking of the *Lusitania*, a British passenger liner, in May 1915. The presence of 128 Americans among the nearly 1,200 civilians killed horrified their compatriots, awakening them to the dangers the war posed. Responding to Wilson's admonitions, the Germans agreed not to attack passenger ships without warning. They, too, had to avoid provoking the Americans to intervene. Both the Entente and the Central Powers understood that hostile actions by the United States would likely tip the balance against them.

Wilson was angered by both the Germans and the British, but the booming American economy was becoming dependent on British purchases and the loans to Britain by American bankers that made those purchases possible. He tried unsuccessfully to mediate between the belligerents and bring the war to an end. But even as he campaigned for reelection in 1916 with the slogan "He kept us out of war," he began to prepare for the moment when the United States might have to fight—almost certainly against the Germans and their allies. The army and National Guard were strengthened and a major shipbuilding program, designed to give his country the world's most powerful navy, was launched.

Several events in the early months of 1917 led to Wilson's decision to call for war. Most important of these was the German conclusion that by resuming unrestricted submarine warfare, they could achieve victory before the United States could respond effectively. Although he broke diplomatic relations with Berlin, Wilson continued to hesitate, still hoping to broker a compromise peace. German U-boats began sinking American merchant ships without warning, and in late February the "Zimmermann Telegram" revealed that Germany had offered Mexico an alliance against the United States, proposing to help Mexico regain some of the territories taken from it by Americans in the nineteenth century. Publication of the telegram served British propaganda well, and Wilson concluded it was time for America to go to war, to stop the transgressions of German militarists and to have a place from which to lead at the peace table. The outbreak of revolution in Russia in March, the overthrow of the tsar, and apparent establishment of a democratic regime supported his idea that the United States would fight to make the world safe for democracy. There was also much talk in Washington of the creation of an international organization to replace alliances and preserve peace. Even pacifists such as the philosopher John Dewey could support a war effort, a crusade, with such magnanimous goals.

Wilson was aware that the Entente powers had negotiated a number of secret treaties to divide the spoils of war—most notably German colonies and chunks of the Ottoman Empire. Their plans were not consistent with the generous peace he was prepared to offer the Central Powers. To finesse this problem, he had the United States intervene as an "Associated" power rather than as a member of the alliance and, as such, not committed to the terms of the secret treaties.

To prevail, Germany had to defeat the Entente before American troops reached Europe. They sent Vladimir Lenin, the Bolshevik leader, back to Russia, understanding correctly that if he seized power, he would withdraw Russia from the war. Lenin revealed and denounced the secret treaties, dismissed Wilsonianism as bourgeois liberalism, and called the war a struggle between rival imperialisms. In March 1918 his regime signed the Treaty of Brest-Litovsk, a separate peace with Germany, freeing the Germans from having to fight a two-front war. The German Army launched an offensive that routed the Italians and came within a few miles of Paris. There the Entente lines held until hundreds of thousands of fresh American troops arrived in June. The Yanks had come—and they played the key role in driving the Germans back, ultimately in winning the war for the Entente.

Months before the first American soldiers reached Europe, Wilson perceived a need to respond to Lenin's challenge, to outline what he believed to be the requirements for a just and enduring peace. In January 1918 he announced his "fourteen points." He understood that he and Lenin were competing for the favor of world public opinion, and he outlined the formation of a liberal capitalist world order in which peace would be preserved by an international organization. He called for freedom of the seas and free trade. Even as he accelerated the growth of American military power, he expressed the hope that the peace agreement would include arrangements for major arms reductions, a critical part of his vision for a world without war. His demand for self-determination for all peoples, pointing to Poles and the various ethnicities of the Austro-Hungarian and Ottoman Empires, seemed ambiguous in its reference to colonies: their postwar distribution was to take into account the well-being of the indigenous populations. He did not call for an end to colonialism.

When the Germans agreed to a cease-fire in November 1918, they did so with the expectation that the peace terms would be generous, in the spirit of Wilson's words. But they—and Wilson—were quickly disabused of such notions. The Entente powers, specifically Britain, France, and Italy, were determined to punish their enemies, annex some of their territory and their colonies, wreck their economies, force them to pay reparations, and disarm them. There was nothing generous about the intentions with which their leaders attended the Paris Peace Conference in 1919. Moreover, at home, Republicans, having gained control of the Senate in the elections of 1918, left little doubt that Wilson's support at home was limited.

Wilson sailed to Europe in January 1919 and stayed at the peace conference for more than six months—with one brief return to the United States. He learned he had considerably less leverage than he had imagined. His principal antagonist was Georges Clemenceau, the French prime minister. Clemenceau had experienced two German invasions of his homeland. To guarantee that it would never happen again, he demanded the dismemberment and occupation of Germany. Only slightly less difficult was David Lloyd George, Britain's leader. Wilson held them off on the German question, but only after compromises that undermined the spirit of his stated war aims. Germany was not dismembered, and the French gained only temporary occupation of the strategically important Rhineland and the economically valuable Saar Basin. To get Clemenceau to back off that much, Wilson had to agree to limits on the German military and to join Britain in a promise to aid France should Germany ever attack it again. Lloyd George joined the French leader in insisting on the need for reparations from Germany to restore their national economies, ravaged by the war. The necessary funding could come from only one other source, the United States, which was not prepared to provide it. Wilson's plan for a generous peace in which Germany would be quickly reintegrated into the liberal capitalist world order was trashed.

Representatives of several colonial peoples came to Paris to gain Wilson's support for their independence. Their quest for racial equality was supported by China and Japan—and by a delegation of African Americans. Wilson was sympathetic to their desire for independence and fought to keep territories of the defeated powers from being annexed by the victors, but given his own racism and the racial attitudes of his fellow citizens, racial equality was not a cause for which he was willing to use his limited capital. Failure to gain a statement on racial equality led to a Japanese threat to withdraw from the conference. To keep them in the postwar system he envisioned, he was forced to yield to their demand to retain Germany's sphere of influence in Shandong—which the Japanese had occupied as soon as they entered the war on the side of the Entente and was promised to them in the secret treaties. China's intervention on the same side offered no protection against Japanese imperialism.

Wilson succeeded in preventing outright annexations with the creation of a "mandate system." Theoretically, the victors were awarded mandates over the various parts of the empires of the Central Powers with an obligation to oversee their governance. The results were not readily distinguishable from annexations, but the system provided the proverbial fig leaf. At one point the United States was offered a mandate over Palestine, which it chose not to accept.

Much of the Treaty of Versailles was controversial in the United States. There was little understanding of Wilson's need to compromise the lofty aims with which he had set out for Paris and widespread overestimation of the leverage he had possessed. Ultimately, however, it was the Covenant of the League of Nations that proved to be the principal obstacle to ratification of the treaty by the U.S. Senate.

Others, including prominent Republican leaders such as Taft, Elihu Root, and Henry Cabot Lodge, had envisioned the creation of an international organization, a "League to Enforce Peace," before Wilson. Wilson's initial forays into foreign policy had demonstrated his moralism, his assumption that when he declared the policies of other leaders to be wrong, they would change course, do the right thing. He was quickly disabused of that notion, not least in his efforts to rein in Japanese imperialism in China. He tried economic pressures without notable success. Military force was an option with the weak countries of Central America and the Caribbean, but even this approach failed to bring satisfactory results, and it was not conceivable against Japan, certainly not given the limited interests of the United States in China. He concluded that an international organization could provide China and the rest of the world with the freedom from aggression that the United States could not provide alone.

Wilson conceived of the League of Nations as an organization whose central principle would be the idea of collective security: an attack on any member would be considered an attack on all—and all would be obligated to ride to the rescue of a nation threatened by aggression. The instrument for activating collective security was embedded in article 10 of the League covenant, part of the Treaty of Versailles. It was this article, this proposed obligation, that ultimately prevented ratification and left the United States out of the League, rendering it ineffectual.

An overwhelming majority of American senators favored membership in the League and ratification of the treaty, but many had reservations and insisted on changes. There were a dozen or so, labeled "irreconcilables," who were adamantly opposed to having the nation join the League, primarily because of perceived limits on American freedom of action, but they lacked sufficient numbers to block ratification. Management of the ratification process rested with Henry Cabot Lodge, who detested Wilson on personal as well as political grounds. He insisted on gutting article 10, laying down the gauntlet for Wilson. The president refused to accept Lodge's reservations. The treaty came up for a vote three times, with a majority opposing on the first two occasions. Republicans would not vote for ratification without reservations, and a number of Democrats, who favored ratification, supporting their leader, would not vote for it with reservations. In the final vote, taken in 1920, a majority voted for ratification with reservations, but the treaty failed to achieve the two-thirds majority required by the Constitution.

No one can resolve the debate over who was responsible for the failure of the United States to join the League of Nations. Lodge's partisanship, his determination to destroy Wilson, allows for easy vilification. Wilson's stubborn refusal to compromise on article 10 cannot be ignored—although there is little doubt that he was correct in his insistence that undermining the collective security clause would limit the effectiveness of the organization severely. But on the issue of collective security, Wilson appears to have been too far out in front of the American people, asking them to play a role in world affairs for which they were not yet prepared. Perhaps the question of whether the United States should have joined the League of Nations is less important than it seemed at the time—and for a generation afterward.

Of greater consequence than it appeared at the time was the American response to the communist takeover of the Russian Revolution. Wilson had been delighted by the fall of the tsarist regime but appalled by the Bolshevik seizure of power. Lenin's call for worldwide revolution to overthrow capitalism ran counter to Wilson's vision. Wilson was further angered by Lenin's separate peace with Germany. He refused to recognize the Bolshevik government and continued modest support to the Provisional government that the Bolsheviks had shoved aside. Nonetheless, he resisted intense pressure from Britain and France to intervene in Russia—until July 1918, when he decided to be a good ally. American troops intervened in both northern Russia, at Murmansk and Archangel, and Siberia. In both instances, the initial impetus was to attempt to salvage an eastern front in the war against

Germany. Much had been made of a Czech legion, eager to fight the Germans but trapped in Russia. There was concern about Russian arms depots that the Germans might capture. And in Siberia, Wilson realized, the Japanese were intent on seizing territory and might be deterred if joined on the ground by American forces. Whatever his intent, American interventions served the opposition to bolshevism—and Wilson was not much troubled, although he came to regret his decisions. He also made an effort to meet with Lenin during the peace conference, but the two men could never agree on terms. Forever after, the communist regime in Russia could point to the fact of American forces on Russian soil from 1918 to 1920 as evidence of American hostility.

Fighting to arouse public support for the League of Nations and the Treaty of Versailles, Wilson suffered a severe stroke in September 1919. He never recovered the ability to provide the leadership his cause required. His country declined the role he had cast for it: it was not ready for primacy in world affairs, not yet willing to be the decisive force in international politics. But he left his successor a powerful military, the world's dominant economy, and a nation more deeply involved abroad than it had ever been—and from which there could be no retreat. Others at home, in Europe, and in Asia were enamored of his vision and continued to hope that the League would be able to maintain world peace, that would-be aggressors could be deterred, that peoples everywhere could live under governments of their own choosing. His crusade to make the world safe for democracy did not end with his presidency or his death.

8

WORLD LEADERSHIP

THE UNITED STATES that Warren Harding inherited in March 1921 was involved in world affairs to an extent unprecedented in its history. To be sure, it was not engaged in any major military action and had failed to join the League of Nations. It had emerged from the war in Europe, however, with enormous economic power and with an extraordinary stake in the new world order. The Republican leadership of the 1920s was no less internationalist than Woodrow Wilson had been. Moreover, the business community with which it was closely allied and the broader public demonstrated more intense interest in world affairs than ever before. Americans traveled abroad in huge numbers, contributing mightily to the economies of the regions they visited. American movies were watched throughout Europe and much of the rest of the world. The United States became the center of mass culture. This was the decade in which the foreign policy "establishment," symbolized by the creation of the Council on Foreign Relations, emerged as a major force influencing government actions. It was also the period in which the universities, most notably Georgetown and Johns Hopkins, began to train students to play a role in the Americanization of the world. And not least, these were the years when the American peace movement proved extraordinarily important in channeling national energy away from imperialism and toward disarmament and the hope of outlawing war.

In retrospect, it was the expansion of American economic power that was most striking. A nation already the world's leading industrial power at the beginning of the decade increased production by a nearly incredible 70 percent between 1922 and 1928. In the same period, its gross national product (GNP) increased 40 percent and per capita income rose 30 percent. But the strong international demand for American machinery, automobiles, and other industrial products required other countries to obtain dollars. When U.S. protective tariffs prevented would-be purchasers from acquiring those dollars through exports, they were forced to borrow. In the course of the war, the United States had ceased to be a debtor nation and became a creditor nation, the world's dominant lender, the principal source of capital to fuel the global economy in the 1920s. All the world lined up on Wall Street, the new center of international finance. Between 1919 and 1929 approximately $12 billion went abroad, mostly in the form of loans—without which the postwar economic order could not be sustained. The power thus acquired by American bankers gave them tremendous influence abroad, and the men in Washington did not hesitate to exploit that influence.

Harding allowed the issue of American membership in the League to die. He and Charles Evans Hughes, his secretary of state, did not, however, shrink from the idea of world leadership by other means. They were responsive to demands from the burgeoning peace movement for naval disarmament, a cause championed vigorously by Senator William Borah (R-Idaho), a forceful voice on Capitol Hill and a major figure in opposition to the League. Hughes understood that the powerful navy planned by Wilson posed a threat to Britain's historic domination of the oceans and to Japanese pretensions in the Pacific. A naval arms race loomed—which the United States would doubtless win, but at great cost. Shrewdly, in 1921 he chose to invite the British and the Japanese to a conference in Washington at which he devised a formula for reducing the size of all three nations' battle fleets. In accepting the invitation, the British enlarged the conference agenda to enable it to deal with related concerns in East Asia. Key Japanese civilian leaders were eager to demonstrate that they were prepared to accept Wilson's new world order. They were embarrassed by army excesses in China and had the support of the navy for an effort to reach agreement with the Americans and British.

When the conference opened in November 1921, Hughes immediately offered a plan to limit the battle fleets of each of the major naval powers— even naming specific ships to be scrapped. He gained the attention of the world and delighted the peace movement, at home and abroad. He understood that before any of the participants would agree to limit naval building, let alone to decommissioning existing battleships, each required assurances that its security and that of its empire would not be compromised. The greatest tensions were between the United States and Japan in the western Pacific. Hughes demanded abrogation of the Anglo-Japanese alliance.

While world public attention focused on navies and efforts to internationalize America's Open Door policy toward China, Hughes secretly negotiated an agreement with Britain and Japan to abrogate the alliance— which both did grudgingly. Rejecting the alternative of a trilateral alliance, Hughes accepted a four-power nonaggression pact to which France was invited as the fourth. In sum, he won elimination of the alliance at no cost to the United States.

The Five-Power Naval Arms Limitation Treaty between the United States, Great Britain, Japan, France, and Italy constituted the first time in recorded history that the great powers voluntarily surrendered their freedom to arm as they pleased. The treaty focused on capital ships (battleships and aircraft carriers) and provided for a 5:5:3 tonnage allowance for the capital ships of the three major navies. There was also a clause in which they agreed not to build new bases or fortify existing bases in the Pacific. The American and British fleets would be roughly equal. Japan accepted the inferior position but was left dominant in the western Pacific. Not least, Tokyo and Washington had reduced the tension between them and established a basis for further cooperation.

The third major agreement to come out of the conference was the Nine-Power Treaty relating to China. Its primary purpose was to stabilize competition among the powers to preclude rivalry in China from erupting into war. The signatories agreed not to seek new privileges in China and to respect China's sovereignty and territorial integrity and the principle of equal commercial opportunity there—language similar to that used by John Hay in his Open Door notes. The Chinese failed to achieve an end to the "unequal treaties," but thanks to Hughes they regained partial control of Shandong. They were not satisfied, but in the United States there was great satisfaction at international acceptance of the American formula.

The conference was a triumph for Wilson's vision. Great Britain, Japan, and the United States would cooperate in a peaceful rivalry without further harm to weaker countries such as China. The Pacific treaty system, designed primarily by Hughes and his staff and accepted by London and Tokyo, envisioned a future in which none of the powers would attempt to maximize its advantage. Assured by the Americans that its "special interests" in Manchuria and Inner Mongolia would not be threatened, the Japanese government proved eager to adopt the system. Unfortunately, the nascent Japanese-American friendship was undermined in 1924 by racist legislative action excluding Japanese immigrants from the United States.

Within the peace movement there remained strong interest in the League of Nations and growing support for the idea of outlawing war as means of strengthening the world's peace machinery. Hughes seemed more responsive to the League, and the United States was an active participant in its International Labor Organization (ILO) and Health Organization. At Geneva, where the League's headquarters were located, Hughes posted some of his ablest diplomats, who observed League activities carefully and met quietly with the organization's officials to discuss all the major issues of world politics. By 1925 there was an official representative of the United States at League meetings.

The force behind the outlawry of war movement was Salmon O. Levinson, a Chicago lawyer convinced that international law could prevent war. The principal catalyst for the realization of his dream was James T. Shotwell, a Columbia University professor and director of the Carnegie Foundation, a strong supporter of the League who contended that American cooperation with Britain and France was essential to world peace. In 1927 Shotwell met with Aristide Briand, the French foreign minister, and persuaded him to send an open letter, drafted by Shotwell, to the American people. In it, Briand proposed a bilateral treaty to outlaw war, in effect a negative alliance that would involve the United States in the French security system—for Shotwell a step toward further collective action by the United States.

Frank B. Kellogg, the American secretary of state, and Calvin Coolidge, the president he served, were not interested in being part of the French security system and intended to ignore the letter. The peace movement mobilized, however, and hundreds of thousands of Americans wrote letters or signed petitions supporting Briand's proposal. Forced to act, Kellogg came up with a clever ploy: he proposed a multilateral treaty to be signed by all nations. Every nation would promise not to go to war with every other nation.

The great powers signed the pact in August 1928 in Paris. Germany, Japan, Italy, the United States, France, and Great Britain undertook a solemn obligation to renounce war as an instrument of national policy. Ultimately sixty-four nations signed the pact, and Kellogg was awarded the Nobel Peace Prize.

The Kellogg-Briand Pact confirmed the power of the peace movement as a force in the shaping of American foreign policy. Illusory as its vision of having ensured perpetual peace obviously was, it had created a milieu in the United States in the 1920s that greatly restricted the freedom of the executive to take military action in the Caribbean and China or to coerce Mexico. The American quest for wealth and power would be pursued peacefully, and the United States had established itself as an important architect of the world's structure for peace.

Its expanded global interests involved the United States in efforts to cope with revolution and instability in Russia, China, Mexico, and Germany—as well as in its Caribbean protectorates. Closest to home was the Mexican Revolution to which successive administrations had failed to adjust since the overthrow of Porfirio Díaz in 1911. At the conclusion of the world war, tensions between Mexico City and Washington signaled the possibility of renewed armed conflict. Central to the dispute was article 27 of the Mexican Constitution of 1917 through which Mexico tried to reclaim land and resources sold to foreigners by Díaz. The article declared that the land and subsoil rights belonged to the Mexican people—at a time when more than 40 percent of the land and 60 percent of the oil industry was owned and controlled by citizens of the United States.

At issue was not a question of right or wrong but of conflicting rights. Historically, conflicts of this sort are resolved in favor of the contestant able to muster superior force. Moral imagination does not come into play. In this instance a weak state was challenging the world's most powerful nation, which had demonstrated its willingness to use force against Mexico on several previous occasions. President Álvaro Obregón, desperate for foreign capital, was willing to offer private assurances that his government would not enforce article 27 stringently, but Hughes demanded a treaty. Such a treaty would have cost Obregón his presidency, perhaps his life—and there was no movement until Thomas Lamont of J. P. Morgan rode to the rescue.

Lamont's principal concern was the collection of Mexico's debt to American bondholders, requiring a political settlement. The bondholders, unlike the oil and mining interests, were indifferent to article 27 and favored recognition. Obregón needed a development loan that only Lamont could deliver. They devised an agreement, and, ignoring the outrage of the National Association for the Protection of American Rights in Mexico, Lamont persuaded Hughes that Obregón was a man with whom the United States could deal. With Lamont as broker, the United States and Mexico held talks in 1923 in which they reached a modus vivendi. The United States dropped its demand for a treaty and accepted the Doctrine of Positive Acts, an interpretation of article 27 by Mexican courts that excluded land developed prior to the coming into force of the constitution. Shortly afterward, Calvin Coolidge, the new American president, recognized the Obregón government and the crisis was over—for the moment.

As usual in world affairs, the 1923 settlement did not prove to be a permanent solution. In 1924 Obregón was succeeded by Plutarco Elías Calles. The oil and mine owners insisted he was a Bolshevik, and he provided grist for their mill with attacks on the Catholic Church and a new law limiting to fifty years possession of oil lands acquired before 1917.

When Calles ignored warnings from Kellogg, the new secretary of state, calls for intervention sounded in Washington. Throughout 1926 the threat of war between the United States and Mexico intensified. Kellogg's staff perceived a Mexican plot to dominate Central America by supporting rebels in Nicaragua against the Washington-backed regime. His assistant secretary of state orchestrated a campaign to prepare the American people for war with Mexico.

Lamont was among the few Americans who had good relations with Calles, but Kellogg, a Minnesota politician, mistrusted eastern bankers. As the war scare intensified, Lamont found formidable allies in the press, the peace movement, and the Senate. Quickly they mobilized public opinion against war and the Senate called unanimously for arbitration, for the peaceful solution of Mexican-American differences. Lamont convinced Coolidge that a mutually beneficial agreement was possible and volunteered another Morgan partner (and college friend of the president), Dwight Morrow, to serve as ambassador to Mexico.

Morrow proved to be a superb choice. He developed an excellent personal relationship with Calles, easing tensions. Soon Mexican courts and, at Calles's direction, the legislature reaffirmed the doctrine of positive acts. It took Morrow a little longer to get Calles out of the mess into which his anticlericalism had gotten him, but by mid-1929 mass could be heard again in Mexico.

The postwar milieu in which the Harding and Coolidge administrations addressed tensions with Mexico also affected the way in which the United States managed its empire in the Caribbean. Anti-imperialist sentiment was strong, and much of it focused on the activities of American marines in the Dominican Republic, Haiti, and Nicaragua. The public was warned of the danger of marines being used to protect investments.

With Germany's defeat in the world war, there were no longer any security concerns to justify "protectorates" in the Caribbean. There was little interest in controlling any Latin American countries, and there was little in the American experience to suggest that intervention ensured stability.

In 1924 the marines were finally withdrawn from the Dominican Republic, and political power shifted from the U.S. Navy to Dominican leaders. Washington, however, retained significant influence over Dominican finances by continuing the customs receivership Roosevelt had established nearly twenty years before. When stability came to the Dominican Republic, it was provided by Rafael Trujillo, one of the more vicious dictators in the region. How Dominicans treated one another was a different issue. The U.S. government had begun its retreat from imperialism in the Caribbean.

Nicaragua posed a more complicated set of problems, providing the quintessential example of the perils of intervention. No policymaker cognizant of events there would ever send American troops into another nation's civil war without raising serious questions as to the person's sanity.

In August 1925 the marines were brought home from Nicaragua. Almost immediately, the newly elected Nicaraguan government was overthrown and civil war ensued. By May 1926 the marines had begun to trickle back, and a major force landed in December. The United States backed one side and Mexico the other. Despite tough talk by the Coolidge administration, it was evident that the public support necessary to sustain military intervention did not exist, and Washington had to back down.

The United States could not impose on Nicaragua a government chosen by Americans. To do so would require destruction of opposition forces and occupation of the country. But the sensible course—to let Nicaraguans resolve the Nicaraguan civil war—was deemed inconceivable. Washington leaders feared surrendering American influence to Mexico. Coolidge sent Henry L. Stimson, a lawyer with a distinguished career in public service, to Nicaragua to end the civil war and bring into existence a government able to sustain itself and protect American interests without U.S. Marines.

Stimson concluded, much as Wilson might have, that Nicaraguans had to be educated to appreciate the value of free elections. Although both major parties considered elections supervised by Americans in 1928, 1930, and 1932 to be fair, a split in the Liberal Party prevented internal peace. One Liberal general, Anastasio Somoza, became commander of the Guardia National. Another, Augusto Sandino, refused to accept an agreement Stimson negotiated in 1928, took to the hills, and vowed to rid Nicaragua of Yankee invaders. Somoza became the hated dictator whose family maintained order for more than forty years. Sandino, an American-killing bandit to Washington, became a folk hero, not only in Nicaragua but in much of Latin America. U.S. Marines chased him for years, but he always slipped away—only to be betrayed and murdered at Somoza's direction. It was January 1933 before the last of the marines came home.

Stimson learned a valuable lesson: it was relatively easy to involve American forces in the civil strife of another country and virtually impossible to create in another country conditions under which the troops could be withdrawn with a sense of mission accomplished. American ideas about the value of free elections for Nicaragua or any other country were doubtless salutary, but if important sectors in the other country chose other means, the price of imposing the American solution was too high. Never again—at least not for anyone aware of the American experience in Nicaragua in the 1920s.

The wellspring of anti-Americanism that Sandino had tapped in Latin America had to be diverted. Hughes, Kellogg, Stimson, and the presidents they served all came to understand the need to divest the Monroe Doctrine of the blatantly imperialist overtones that Theodore Roosevelt had contributed in 1904 when his notorious corollary claimed for the United States the right to exercise police power to prevent "wrong doing" in the hemisphere.

In the 1920s Washington perceived itself to be retreating from the imperialism of Roosevelt, Taft, and Wilson, but the rest of the world was unconvinced. An American military presence remained in Cuba, Haiti, and Panama. Puerto Rico was still an American possession with no prospect of statehood. Nonetheless, sensitivity to Latin American fears had penetrated the thinking of elites in the United States, and policymakers were ready to negotiate the terms under which the United States might be both hegemon and Good Neighbor.

Revolution in China ran roughly parallel to revolution in Mexico. The Qing dynasty had collapsed in 1911. The Chinese revolutionaries promised social reforms that threatened the interests and privileges of foreigners. Once successful against the Qing, factionalism prevailed among the revolutionaries and strongmen emerged. The death in 1916 of Yuan Shikai, the first president of the Republic of China and would-be emperor, removed the last semblance of unity. Civil strife intensified, and various regions of China came under the control of warlords. When the Harding administration arrived in Washington, the Beijing government controlled only parts of North China, its leadership constantly changing, reflecting shifting coalitions among northern warlords.

Amid the chaos in their country, Chinese intellectuals were unified in their anti-imperialism, in their determination to rid the country of the hated "unequal treaties" imposed by foreign powers in the nineteenth century. Other nations controlled parts of their country in so-called spheres of influence. Demand for revision of the treaties became the symbol of Chinese national aspirations, but China's disunity allowed the great powers to ignore Chinese demands.

Gradually, Sun Yat-sen, nominally father of the revolution, and his Kuomintang (Nationalist Party) provided a rallying point. The American government had lost interest in Sun, viewed in Washington as an irresponsible visionary and inveterate conspirator. Sun had once courted the Japanese, but their assistance was no longer feasible. If foreign assistance would be necessary for Sun's new dream of uniting China by force, to whom could he turn?

It was Soviet Russia that came to Sun's aid. Soviet agents had combed China looking for potential allies, and Sun proved receptive. The Soviets helped him reorganize the Kuomintang along the lines of the Soviet Communist Party—designed to seize and control power in a one-party state. They persuaded Sun to ally with the nascent Chinese Communist Party, and they brought Sun's top military aide and ultimate successor, Chiang Kai-shek, to Moscow for training. Perhaps most important, the Comintern sent Michael Borodin, a brilliant political organizer, to work with Sun. To all these developments, the American government responded with indifference at best and occasional hostility—as when it sent warships to prevent Sun from seizing the customs surplus at Canton.

The United States and the other Washington Conference signatories clung to the hated symbols of imperialism, the privileges exacted by force in the nineteenth century. There was little public sense of Americans enjoying imperial privilege in China—or that these privileges might prove costly to retain. The explosion came in May 1925. A strike at a Japanese-owned textile factory in Shanghai led to a spontaneous outburst of anti-imperialist rage throughout China. And this time there were trained agitators serving the Kuomintang-Communist alliance to fan the flames and give focus to Chinese demands.

The American minister to China argued against any concessions and the American business community in Shanghai called for a show of force, but that was not an option available to Kellogg and Coolidge. Neither Congress nor public opinion would tolerate old-fashioned gunboat diplomacy, as events in Central American and Mexico were revealing. There already had been calls for the withdrawal of American gunboats and troops from China. Early in 1927 the U.S. House of Representatives overwhelmingly passed a resolution calling for negotiations to give the Chinese the treaty revisions they demanded. Once again the scene was set for a retreat from imperialism. There would be no war to retain the privileges of empire.

As Chiang attempted to consolidate his hold on the country, the Kuomintang and Communists split and the White Terror swept those parts he controlled. The Communists, Borodin, and the rest of the Soviet advisers fled. Without illusions as to the real as opposed to nominal authority of Chiang's government, Kellogg chose to treat it as the de facto government of all China. Coolidge declared the Chinese Revolution to be a worthy imitation of the American Revolution, a praiseworthy effort by the Chinese to free themselves from foreign control. In July 1928 the United States and China signed a treaty granting China tariff autonomy. The treaty constituted recognition of Chiang's government.

Americans had enjoyed imperial privileges in China since the mid-nineteenth century. They had worked in collusion with more aggressive powers to obtain these privileges through the treaty system, and few were eager to surrender them. The government of the United States was slow to respond to Chinese nationalism. When the violence in China finally impinged on the consciousness of American leaders, they understood the United States would have to yield. The ability of the revolutionaries to mobilize the masses meant that retention of the privileges of empire would require the sustained use of force, would mean American casualties. That was not a price the American people or their leaders were willing to pay. Instead they retreated and imagined themselves as "champions of the sovereign rights of China."

Even more remote from immediate American interests was the revolution in Russia. There was widespread support for the men and women who overthrew the tsar, but after the Bolshevik seizure of power, Vladimir Lenin quickly alienated Washington—not least by signing a separate peace with Germany. Wilson had withheld recognition and had sent American troops on expeditions to northern Russia where they remained until June 1919 and to Siberia where they remained until April 1920. His reasons had been complex, and American forces were instructed not to interfere in the Russian civil war, but their presence was disadvantageous to the Bolsheviks.

The Harding administration also chose to withhold recognition of Lenin's government, troubled by Moscow's repudiation of debts incurred by its predecessors—and by its confiscation of American-owned property. Hughes seemed offended especially by Soviet support for an American Communist Party dedicated to the overthrow of the American government. Soviet expressions of bewilderment at Washington's hostility were ingenuous.

Nonetheless, the Soviet government had considerable success reaching out to American businessmen. The consistent inability of the U.S. government to harness foreign economic policy to political policy worked to Soviet advantage. American financing and technology contributed enormously to the modernization of the Soviet economy in the 1920s. By 1928 a fourth of all foreign investment in Soviet Russia was American. By 1930 Americans led all exporters to the Soviet state with 25 percent of the market.

The limits of American hostility to the Bolshevik state were apparent also in the response to the famine that struck Russia at the conclusion of its civil war in 1921. Herbert Hoover orchestrated a magnificent relief effort providing food, clothing, and medicine for an estimated ten million Russians. His extraordinary performance strengthened the Soviet government—may even have saved it—and won for him its "deepest gratitude," however short-lived.

Most elements of the peace movement favored recognition of the Soviet regime, but specialists in Russian affairs in the State and Commerce Departments were hostile. They received powerful support from the Catholic Church and American Federation of Labor. The church, intensely anti-communist, was outraged by the execution of its vicar general in Russia, and labor leaders had few illusions about the well-being of the proletariat in the Soviet state. All American leaders would have liked to see the Bolshevik regime disappear; none feared it enough to advocate action to eliminate it. The larger role of the United States in world affairs in the 1920s was as evident in the Soviet Union as anywhere in the world, and in few places was it more benign.

The greatest concern of Wilson and Allied leaders in 1919 had been the containment of German power. Wilson also understood the need to reintegrate Germany into a stable Europe, but he failed. The peace terms imposed on Germany, especially the reparations on which France and Great Britain insisted, were harsher than he had wished and resented bitterly by most Germans. When Harding and Hughes took charge, however, they saw a demilitarized Weimar Republic that threatened no one. They did not perceive Germany as a major concern.

In 1922 the Germans failed to make reparations payments they considered an injustice. Every German leader, including the highly respected Gustav Stresemann, sought revision of the Treaty of Versailles to relieve their country of the price of defeat. The Americans were indifferent; the British were eager to improve relations with Germany. The French, virtually alone, were determined to force the issue.

In January 1923 French and Belgian troops occupied the Ruhr, the heart of the German coal and steel industry. The idea was to operate Ruhr industry in lieu of reparations—to force the Germans to pay. In response the German government organized passive resistance throughout the region. The French action was condemned widely in the United States, arousing sympathy for the defeated enemy and a sense that France was the greatest threat to the peace of Europe.

Harding and the Coolidge were unwilling to get involved, fearing they might be maneuvered into accepting the connection between reparations and allied war debts to the United States. The British and French made no secret of their inability to ease their demands for reparations unless the United States, "Uncle Shylock," would forgive at least some of their war debts—an idea unpopular with the American public. Instead, the administration pushed American bankers forward, working from behind them to impose an American solution.

The occupation and the resistance weakened the French economy and undermined the German mark, which soon collapsed, setting off devastating hyperinflation. Both sides were ready to retreat by the end of the year. The United States, the dominant financial power in the world, held the key hand. The French and Germans were forced to play by American rules. An experts committee assembled in Paris in January 1924, chaired by Charles G. Dawes, an American banker.

The French were forced to seek a loan to stabilize their currency and had to turn to J. P. Morgan and Company, specifically to Dwight Morrow. Morrow and Lamont were sympathetic to France's plight, but banking is never a nonprofit operation. Investors had to be assured of a favorable business climate. Lamont insisted on guarantees that France would not resort to force again. Only a peaceful Germany and a stable Europe would provide the desired climate.

Once France capitulated, Lamont cleared the loan with Hughes. A few weeks later the Dawes committee reported its plan. Germany would resume small-scale reparations payments immediately, increasing them as its economy improved. Money for the payments would come in part from loans floated by J. P. Morgan—from which France also could anticipate loans so long as it renounced sanctions against Germany. The French had lost leverage over Germany but had no choice given the attitude of leaders in Washington and on Wall Street.

Clearly, the United States, working outside the League of Nations, uncommitted to any security arrangements with the European powers, nonetheless played the central role in stabilizing Europe in the mid-1920s. Conscious of American financial dominance, the Harding and Coolidge administrations, using American bankers, were able to call the tune. American loans enabled Germany to rebuild its economy and required France to back away from the threat of force to preserve its security. Tensions between Washington and Paris over war debts, the invasion of the Ruhr, and France's obstructive policies in East Asia declined. Relations with Great Britain and Germany prospered as well. In Europe, the American approach to world affairs was manifestly successful.

Fueled by American loans, Europe experienced a spurt of economic growth and prosperity, but the world economic system remained seriously flawed. Too much American money flowed into Germany, and too much of it was used for nonproductive purposes, paying off reparations and earlier loans. The Germans were not taking the burden of reparations payments on themselves, and the United States was not importing anywhere near what the Germans had to sell to repay what they borrowed. The system depended on the continued flow of dollars across the Atlantic. Should American loans to Germany stop, the system was likely to collapse.

A second problem was the German desire for revision of the Versailles treaty—to be relieved of reparations payments and the presence of occupying forces on German territory. Germany joined the League in 1926, signed the Kellogg-Briand Pact in 1928, and pressed for revision. In 1929 another committee of experts, again led by an American, Owen Young, lowered Germany's reparations bill and called for the evacuation of all foreign troops from the Rhineland. The Young Plan was quickly approved, and the last of the occupying forces left Germany in June 1930. German good behavior had won renewed respect in Washington and European capitals, and the world might look forward to enduring peace and prosperity. Americans could be proud of their government—and their bankers.

Most striking was the technique evolved for using nongovernmental leaders such as Lamont, Morrow, and Young to serve the ends of American foreign policy. In theory, these men functioned as private citizens. Generally, however, the government could direct their efforts—select them, inform them, instruct them—almost as easily as if they had been on payroll. The waters out there were mined, and shrewdly, while the government and people of the United States gained an education in the use and responsibilities of power, Washington sent the businessmen ahead to clear the way.

The virtues of the system of reliance on the private sector for conducting public policy were balanced, however, by a flaw most evident in East Asia. However public spirited the Morgan partners may have been, their interests and those of the American government did not always coincide. In such circumstances, patriotism gave way to self-interest. In East Asia, the State Department was eager for Lamont to arrange loans for the Chinese government. The government of the United States did not want Morgan financing Japanese imperialism in China, facilitating exclusion of American business interests. But Lamont had no interest in lending money to a succession of shaky Chinese regimes and was delighted to lend to Japan, surely a safer investment. He used his considerable genius to circumvent all efforts by his friends in Washington to prevent loans to Tokyo. Obviously, private citizens, however gifted, are imperfect instruments of national policy.

In March 1929 Herbert Hoover was inaugurated as the thirty-first president of the United States. As secretary of commerce for the previous eight years, he had been a major force in shaping domestic and foreign policy, one of the principal architects of the cooperative association of government and the private sector. A Quaker, reluctant to use force as an instrument of power, he was the ideal choice to maintain the American empire—and the world—peacefully.

On October 23, 1929, the stock market—which had responded favorably to Hoover's election—fell sharply. On October 24 the market collapsed in the face of panic selling. The Great Depression had begun its withering course. As the economy stumbled, the American presence around the globe began to contract. Over the next several years, the Depression dominated every aspect of American life. Nothing that occurred anywhere in the world could compete for the attention of the nation's leaders and their people. No foreign threat could compare with the danger the Depression posed to the survival of American institutions and values—to democracy in America. The nation turned inward to concentrate on the suffering of its own people.

The most obvious impact of the Great Depression on American foreign policy came in economic affairs. The bankers stopped lending money to foreign governments in 1929. Congress closed the door to foreign imports by passing the Smoot-Hawley tariff in 1930. By 1931 American tourists had all but disappeared from the world's grand hotels, spas, casinos, and exotic sites. Corporate investment abroad ended. The result was a 68 percent decline in the dollars available abroad—the dollars whose circulation had kept the international economic system afloat in the 1920s. Much of what was left was consumed by fixed obligations such as war debts. Virtually nothing was available for the purchase of American goods, and the whole system collapsed.

As the woes of the Depression multiplied at home, little thought was given to East Asia—not even to warnings that the Japanese military was growing restive. In the summer of 1931 Shidehara Kijuro was the Japanese foreign minister, a man admired and respected by Western diplomats who had worked with him since the Washington Conference. His policies were restrained, threatened no American interests, and suggested that he had the Japanese military under control. Hoover and his advisers were persuaded that rivalry with Japan was not going to be a concern.

The Japanese had established their presence in Manchuria in the course of defeating Russia in 1905. China retained but nominal control over the region, its three northeastern provinces. Military or civilian, moderate or extremist, all Japanese leaders—including Shidehara—viewed Manchuria as a vital interest and were committed to keeping it under Japanese control. Perceiving a threat from Chiang's recently created Nanjing government, Shidehara attempted to negotiate with the Chinese. The Japanese Army despaired of his efforts and on September 18, 1931, sprang into action. To allege Chinese provocation, the Japanese set off an explosion in the vicinity of the Japanese-owned and -operated South Manchuria Railroad. Responding to the "provocation," Japanese troops drove Chinese authorities out of Mukden and began the military conquest of all of Manchuria.

Chiang, mired in struggles against Communist rebels and secessionists from his own party, appealed to the League of Nations, to Great Britain, and to the United States. Deep in the throes of the Depression, nations of the West were in no hurry to rally to China's support. American leaders prayed the incident would be an isolated matter, and, Stimson, now Hoover's secretary of state, having little choice, put his faith in Shidehara. But Shidehara had lost control; the Japanese Army continued its advance, intent on driving all Chinese forces out of Manchuria.

In Washington, Hoover's cabinet was forced to focus on the issue, to put aside the economic crisis for the moment. Hoover considered the actions of the Japanese Army to be outrageous and immoral, violations of Japan's pledges. On the other hand, no one in the cabinet argued that important American interests were threatened. And the secretary of war declared that the military was not strong enough to confront Japan.

The strongest pressure on the administration to act came from the peace movement. Although the movement was divided over the importance of disarmament, outlawry of war, and membership in the League, all activists agreed Japan posed a serious threat to the peace system constructed after the world war. If Japan could violate its commitments, the system would collapse. The United States had to act to stop Japan.

Stimson, much like Wilson, perceived a need for the United States, the world's greatest power, to maintain a world order in which there would be no place for aggression. Japan had to be stopped, the peace system, the new world order, had to be preserved—but how? Neither Hoover nor most of leaders of the peace organizations contemplated force. And the military left no doubt that the means to use force were not available. Hoover and Stimson chose to cooperate with the League in a campaign of moral suasion.

The United States and the League proved impotent. In desperation, Stimson turned to a refusal to recognize the fruits of Japan's aggression. He sent notes to both China and Japan rejecting the legality of the situation in Manchuria and refused to accept any arrangements there that affected its treaty rights, including those pertaining to China's sovereignty and territorial integrity. The United States would not recognize any situation brought about in violation of the Kellogg-Briand Pact. The Japanese were unaffected by what came to be known as the "Stimson Doctrine," attacking Shanghai soon afterward.

Within the American peace movement, demand for economic sanctions boiled. The president of Harvard attempted to organize a nationwide boycott of Japanese goods. Leaders of the peace movement were driven by a greater sense of urgency than Hoover and Stimson. Their fears for the survival of the peace system intensified. And they feared the growth of influence of organizations such as the Navy League that insisted military force alone would stop Japan.

Hoover was persuaded to move U.S. naval and marine units to Shanghai to protect Americans there and to signal that the United States was not surrendering its pretensions to power in East Asia. But the Japanese military was not intimidated by American gestures or moved by American protests. Japan in 1932 was in the hands of military and civilian extremists, men very different from those with whom the West had cooperated in the 1920s. A League commission to investigate the events of September 1931 in Manchuria began its work in May 1931, but its efforts were futile. The

Japanese did finally terminate hostilities in Shanghai, not under duress from the West but because they never intended more than to bloody the Chinese for daring to harass Japan's interests in the city.

Having established control over Manchuria, most Japanese were satisfied. The empire was secure, and Japan had stood up to the Western nations, especially the United States, which persistently denied Japan's demand for equality.

In January 1933 Adolf Hitler became chancellor and eliminated the remnants of Weimar democracy in Germany. In February Japan withdrew from the League of Nations. The peace movement had failed. In the era of Adolf Hitler and Japanese militarism, a more apocalyptic vision would prevail. And Hoover, determined not to use force in support of policy, not to waste taxpayers' money on military expenditures, was the wrong man to lead the United States on a world stage that would have to be shared with Nazi Germany and the Japanese generals.

Washington's vision during the presidencies of Harding, Coolidge, and Hoover had been of a world in which American influence, based on American financial power, spread quietly and benignly. And the power and influence of the United States did grow throughout the world. Directly or indirectly, Washington participated in nearly every important international meeting of the era. The Great Depression changed all that. Income from international trade and investments dropped sharply. The informal empire built on American investments was jeopardized as capital flowed back to the United States. A new system of international trade and finance would have to be erected on the wreckage of the old, but by the time Hoover left office, it seemed clear any new system would be based on economic nationalism and warfare.

Politically, the world scene was no less grim. Hitler's determination to overthrow the Versailles settlement and resurrect German power was evident. War might be the outcome. In East Asia, no one could be sure when the appetite of Japanese imperialists would be whetted again. The breakdown of the peace system threatened the formal American empire. The Philippines were at Japan's mercy, and the American navy was no match for the Japanese in the western Pacific. Would the Japanese come after

Guam, Wake, Tutuila, Midway? And what of the Hawaiian Islands they had long coveted? Would the Third Reich seek an empire in the Caribbean threatening American hegemony, as had Kaiser Wilhelm?

Finally, American military forces were not adequate to protect the empire. Throughout the 1920s, in the absence of any serious threats to U.S. interests, military power seemed superfluous. The 1930s had begun on a darker note. The United States could no longer preserve its security and broader interests without the willingness to enter into collective security agreements, without creating and using military power. This was the reality Franklin Roosevelt inherited.

9

FRANKLIN ROOSEVELT LEADS
THE NATION TO WAR

F RANKLIN D. ROOSEVELT'S immediate concern when he took office in March 1933 was to find a way to relieve the misery of millions of Americans who were without work, many without the basic necessities of life. The world order was collapsing around them, but the greatest threat to the United States was internal, the effects of the Great Depression. Totalitarian movements arose in the United States as well as in Europe and Asia. Could a democracy cope with the crisis? Roosevelt had no more idea of how to rescue the nation's economy than had Hoover. The principal difference between the men was revealed by Roosevelt's intellectual flexibility, the optimism inherent in his personality, and his willingness to try almost anything, as demonstrated by the programs of his New Deal—not all of which proved useful. And, ultimately, it was a war economy that put everyone back to work.

Roosevelt had served in a minor post in the Wilson administration and had run as the Democrats' candidate for vice president in the campaign of 1920, won by the Republican Warren Harding. He had campaigned as an ardent supporter of American participation in the League of Nations and as a Wilsonian internationalist in general. But foreign policy was not an important concern in 1933. America had to save itself before it could venture out to save the world. Membership in the League was for most a forgotten issue. International cooperation had to be subordinated to the plans for national recovery. Roosevelt demonstrated this a few months after he became president when he undermined the World Economic Conference in London, refusing to accept European programs for currency stability that he feared might be detrimental to his domestic policies. His first term in the White House, 1933–1937, is the only period in American history when the country might fairly be labeled isolationist.

Elsewhere the destruction of the peace system of the 1920s was demonstrated again and again. The Japanese had seized control of all of Manchuria, withdrawn from the League of Nations in 1933, and were pressing into North China. In Europe, Adolf Hitler had come to power in Germany, and in 1935 he renounced the disarmament terms of the Treaty of Versailles. In 1936 he sent troops in to reoccupy the Rhineland. Italy, led by Il Duce, Benito Mussolini, attacked Ethiopia in 1935. In 1936 civil war roiled Spain, with fascists backed by Hitler and Mussolini eventually overthrowing a democratic government. And in July 1937 full-scale war erupted between China and Japan.

In the United States there was little inclination to risk involvement in these events overseas. There was a widespread feeling, shared to some extent by Roosevelt, that it had been a mistake to intervene in the world war in 1917. The result had not been as glorious as Wilson had promised, and the nations the Yanks had saved from the Hun had shown little gratitude. In the mid-1930s an overwhelming majority of the American people were determined to stay out of any foreign war. Congress, examining the policies that revisionist historians deemed responsible for drawing the country into war, passed legislation to prevent a recurrence. Invoking the lessons of the past, the first of these "Neutrality" laws (1935) surrendered the nation's right to sell arms or lend money to belligerents—steps that might have avoided being drawn into war in 1917. Remembering the response to the sinking of the *Lusitania*, Congress also demanded that Roosevelt warn travelers that they sailed on belligerent ships at their own risk. Roosevelt would have liked discretion to apply the law in such a way as to favor victims of aggression but was denied by Congress.

The trigger for the 1935 law was Italy's attack on Ethiopia. Roosevelt could find no way to punish Italy, as demanded by African Americans to the dismay of Italian Americans. He called for a "moral embargo" on trade and hoped the warning against traveling on belligerent ships would hurt tourism in Italy, but these moves were ineffectual. Although the League had declared Italy an aggressor and imposed sanctions, it restricted nothing of importance. Italy conquered Ethiopia quickly and withdrew from the League.

The Spanish Civil War divided Americans. Liberals and the country's few leftists supported the democratic government. Indeed, several hundred formed the Abraham Lincoln Brigade and went off to Spain to fight fascism. American Catholics, disturbed by the anticlericalism of that government, favored the fascists, led by Francisco Franco. Joseph Stalin provided the government with a modicum of aid, stirring fears of bolshevism, but neither the League nor the United States offered the least counterweight to German and Italian support for Franco's rebellion. Most infamous was the vicious bombing of Guernica by German and Italian planes, immortalized in Pablo Picasso's painting. Franco prevailed and ruled Spain harshly for decades.

In July 1937 a minor incident in North China led to full-scale war as the Japanese drove deep into China, forcing the Chinese government to retreat to the interior of the country, to Chongqing in Sichuan Province. As the invaders entered Nanjing, erstwhile capital of the Republic of China, they carried out unspeakable atrocities—rapes and murders that took an estimated 300,000 civilian lives, some of it documented by American missionaries in the city. Public opinion in the United States was never neutral, not divided as with Spain, and the horrifying accounts of the "Rape of Nanjing" intensified sympathy for China. But sympathy was not going to stop the Japanese militarists, and Americans remained unwilling to act on behalf of China. The shocking Japanese attack on the USS *Panay* in the Yangzi in December 1937 brought calls to pull American forces out of China rather than a demand for action against Japan. In the absence of a declaration of war, Roosevelt did not invoke the neutrality legislation, hoping thus to permit the Chinese to obtain aid. It proved to be a futile gesture. With its ports all controlled by the Japanese, getting arms or other supplies to the Chinese was difficult if not impossible. The "cash–and–carry" provisions of the Neutrality Act of 1937 were useless to the Chinese, who had neither the fleet nor the cash. The act allowed the United States to sell anything but arms to any nation that could pay cash for the goods and transport them on its own ships. Roosevelt and others who feared Hitler saw this as a way to help Great Britain and France if war came to Europe. China was not a primary consideration.

There was a modicum of hope on the European scene in October 1938. British and French leaders, desperate to avoid war, met with Hitler in Munich to discuss his intentions overall, but specifically toward Czechoslovakia. To Roosevelt's relief, the negotiations led to what British prime minister Neville Chamberlain called "peace in our time," bought by the British and French at the expense of the Czechs, who lost part of their country. Hitler soon violated the agreement, seizing the rest of Czechoslovakia—and giving appeasement, a frequently sensible diplomatic option, a bad name forever.

By 1938 there were stirrings among the American people that suggested a trend away from isolation and toward cooperation with the victims of aggression. An early indication came with the creation of the American Committee for Non-Participation in Japanese Aggression, driven by men who had missionary connections to China, including Henry Luce of *Time* magazine, and other friends of China. Henry Stimson, still seeking a way to counter Japanese imperialism, served as honorary chairman until he returned to government service. Their task was to find a way to help China without provoking war. Cleverly, the organization sought an embargo on sales to Japan, arguing these materials made the United States a participant in Japanese aggression. Famously, it produced a photograph of a crying Chinese baby sitting at a devastated railway with a bomb fragment labeled "Made in America." Americans may have hesitated to act on behalf of China, but they certainly did not want to partner with Japan.

In Europe, the signs were increasingly ominous. After taking over an unresisting Austria (the *Anschluss*)—many Austrians being sympathetic to Nazi ideology—and occupying Czechoslovakia, Hitler turned eastward. To the astonishment of communists throughout the world who saw the Soviet Union as the preeminent antifascist state, he persuaded Stalin to agree to a nonaggression pact that allowed Germany and the Soviet Union to divide Poland. Britain and France, although unprepared for war, were committed to defend Poland—and so, in September 1939, World War II began in Europe.

Roosevelt knew war was coming and tried to prepare the nation for it. In October 1937 he delivered his famous "Quarantine Speech," in which he suggested acting to "quarantine" aggressors. The public response was surprisingly favorable, but unsure how to proceed, he chose to be cautious, afraid to lead where his people might not follow him. He began a massive military buildup—which had the added value of providing jobs for needy Americans. He struggled unsuccessfully to revise or repeal the neutrality laws until November 1939, after the war began. Although the cash-and-carry provision was retained, the arms embargo was not. The United States was poised to become the arsenal of democracy.

The fall and winter of 1939–1940 were relatively quiet in Europe, a period eliciting the label "the phony war." Americans relaxed. And then, in the spring, came the "Blitzkrieg," as German forces swept across Western Europe, conquering everything before them. Denmark, Norway, Belgium, and the Netherlands fell quickly. Flying over and racing around France's impenetrable Maginot Line, the Wehrmacht reached the English Channel in May, less than two months after the attack began. Hitler personally accepted the French surrender in June 1940. Only Great Britain remained of his targets in the West.

The fall of France erased any complacency about the security of the United States. Most Americans understood their nation was in danger. Roosevelt encouraged men and women eager to aid the victims of aggression to organize and attempt to influence the media and Congress. The most important of such organizations was the Committee to Defend America by Aiding the Allies formed in May 1940, led by men and women who advocated collective security, many of whom had favored membership in the League. Their task was to mobilize support for aid to Britain, the only remaining obstacle to an attack on the United States.

Britain's immediate need was to defend itself and its supply lifelines from German submarine warfare—the U-boats dominated the eastern Atlantic. The new British prime minister, Winston Churchill, pleaded for help, but Congress opposed the transfer of any arms that might be needed to defend the United States. Roosevelt, who never hesitated to be devious in pursuit of his goals, devised what became known as the destroyer-bases deal. Bypassing Congress, he sent fifty aged destroyers to Britain in exchange for long-term leases for American bases on British territories in the western Atlantic. Obviously, the United States could hardly claim to be a neutral.

There were many Americans whose ultimate concern was to keep the United States out of war. They organized to oppose provocation of Hitler, most prominently in the America First Committee. A few of them may have been Axis sympathizers, some were pacifists, but the overwhelming majority were neither. They simply did not believe that the United States had a stake in what they perceived as a European struggle for power and were persuaded that Roosevelt was leading the country into war. They were surely wrong about the significance of the war for the United States— but not about Roosevelt's direction.

German planes bombed Britain mercilessly in late 1940, but their victims refused to surrender, in what Churchill called his country's "finest hour." Horrified, public support for aid to Britain increased significantly, even as those polled indicated their understanding that the United States would be risking war. When the British ran out of cash to pay for supplies from their friend across the Atlantic, Roosevelt came up with another clever scheme, called "lend-lease." Deeming the defense of Great Britain as vital to the security of the United States, he persuaded Congress to pass legislation that would allow him to sell, lend, or lease to Britain any war materials it needed. He and those who favored his approach, including Wendell Willkie, the Republican candidate opposing him in the election of 1940, argued the law was the country's best hope for staying out of the war. The opposition rightly contended in vain that the law would inevitably lead to war.

Reelected for an unprecedented third term, Roosevelt continued to do what he thought prudent to help Great Britain. Aware that the British navy was overextended and unable to cope with the ravages of German submarine warfare, in spring 1941 he gradually extended American naval patrols far out into the Atlantic, well beyond any previously imagined defensive perimeter of the United States. In April, unwilling to risk a German takeover of the island, he declared the United States the protector of Danish Greenland. In July, as the U.S. Navy patrols reached further across the Atlantic, he announced that Iceland would also be protected as potentially vital to the defense of the United States.

The British gained a moment of respite when Hitler turned on the Soviet Union, ignoring the nonaggression pact the two countries had signed in 1939. A cross-channel invasion was suddenly more remote as German troops marched toward Leningrad and Stalingrad. Roosevelt immediately understood that if the Soviets could stop the Wehrmacht, Germany could be defeated. However grudgingly, given the poor relations between the Soviet Union and the United States and the distaste for Stalin and his brutal regime, Roosevelt perceived value in aiding it.

In August Churchill and Roosevelt met secretly in Newfoundland and planned additional steps to work together. It was at this summit that they announced the Atlantic Charter outlining the principles for which they would fight. Roosevelt's aides also took advantage of British desperation to impose an agreement to open trade within the empire to Americans after the war.

The Germans had a difficult choice. There was no doubt that the United States was not neutral and that it served as the key obstacle to their defeat of Great Britain. On the other hand, it was not in their interest to have the Americans as full participants in the war. U-boat commanders were ordered to do everything possible to avoid confrontation with U.S. ships. That proved extraordinarily difficult as U.S. naval vessels began tracking German submarines and calling in British planes to attack them. Doing precisely that, the USS *Greer* came under attack in September 1941. Roosevelt, expressing shock at what he called an unprovoked attack, commenced an undeclared naval war with Germany. In October an American destroyer was torpedoed and another, the *Reuben James*, sunk. Still, Roosevelt hoped to avoid full-fledged war, and Hitler, still focused on the Soviets, also held back. How much longer the belligerents could fight without declaring war will never be known, because it was Japan that brought the United States into the war openly.

Concerned primarily with the situation in Europe, perceived as more threatening than the Sino-Japanese War, eager to retain flexibility in relations with Tokyo, Roosevelt opposed sanctions against Japan. A massive lobbying effort in Washington in 1939 by men and women demanding sanctions failed in the absence of support from the administration. Nonetheless, to respond to pressure from China's friends, the American government suddenly notified Japan of its wish to terminate the treaty of commerce that existed between the two countries—but there were no plans for sanctions to follow. Not until the summer of 1940, when Japan threatened British and French possessions in Southeast Asia and flirted with Nazi Germany, did the United States take significant action to retard the Japanese war effort. Even then, sales of petroleum products to Japan *increased* dramatically.

The most alert of China's friends, aware of Roosevelt's determination to sustain Great Britain, tried unsuccessfully to tie China to the British war effort. But most foreign policy analysts, in and out of government, viewed the war in Asia as a relatively unimportant war being fought by relatively unimportant people over relatively unimportant issues. The Japanese changed this when, in September 1940, they signed the Tripartite Pact with Germany and Italy. Nothing anyone could have done could have convinced Americans of their stake in the outcome of the Sino-Japanese War as effectively as Japan's decision to ally with Nazi Germany.

Thereafter Japan had to face stepped up American aid to China. In the six months following the Tripartite Pact, Washington extended nearly $100 million in credits to Chiang Kai-shek's government, and in May 1941 China became eligible for lend-lease. But the flow of oil to Japan continued as Roosevelt followed his own estimate of the steps appropriate to encourage China, check Japan, *and* keep the United States out of war in the Pacific.

In July the Japanese appeared in Camranh Bay, on the coast of Indochina. Criticism of Roosevelt's appeasement of Japan mounted among the friends of China and the advocates of collective security. Within the administration there was pressure to freeze Japanese assets and for a complete embargo on oil, but State Department and military leaders, anxious to avoid a showdown with Japan, succeeded in getting Roosevelt to authorize *some* oil sales. The pressure on Japan was severe, approved overwhelmingly by the American people, but it was not complete. High-level Japanese-American talks in Washington worried the Chinese and their supporters in the United States.

At a time when American military leaders were urging the president to seek a modus vivendi with Japan to play for the time they desperately needed to build up American defenses, to concentrate their energies on the vital concerns across the Atlantic, Chiang begged Roosevelt not to appease Japan any longer and implied China might have to surrender. And then Churchill cabled Roosevelt, expressing concern about the situation in China, fearing the collapse of Chiang's regime, endangering British and American interests in East Asia. That same day, Cordell Hull, the American secretary of state, gave the Japanese a reply that he knew would be unacceptable to a proposal he knew would be their last.

Appeasement of Japan had been tolerable until the Japanese added to Britain's distress by their maneuvers in Southeast Asia and then joined the Axis. Afterward, even when the Tripartite Pact might have been expendable to Japan, commitment to the British cause and China's status as an ally prevented a modus vivendi between the Washington and Tokyo. It would be construed as betrayal of a nation so recently labeled a democracy and one of the allies in the war against aggressors. Moreover, Churchill was not alone in fearing that the Chinese might surrender, with ominous consequences. Among these was concern that freed from the morass of China, the Japanese would attack Russia—already reeling from the German invasion—and allow the full force of German military might to be directed against Great Britain.

Now completely denied access to American oil, Japanese leaders watched their oil reserves diminish and knew they would have to strike soon at the Dutch East Indies as the most obvious alternative source. They understood that would mean war with the United States and prepared for it. The attack they planned against the American fleet at Pearl Harbor would have to be carried out before winter, before the seas of the North Pacific became impassable. They gave their negotiators in Washington until late November to gain a lifting of the oil embargo. Failing that, the fleet sailed and the war came. Few in Tokyo imagined they could win a war against the United States, but they hoped destruction of the American fleet would allow them time to consolidate their position in the western Pacific, to dig in so firmly that the Americans would not want to pay the price necessary to drive them out. Clearly they underestimated American resolve, but they had run out of other options for putting in place their vision of a Japanese-dominated new order in East Asia.

The Japanese attack on Pearl Harbor was planned and executed brilliantly. Apart from a few carriers that happened to be out at sea that Sunday morning of December 7, 1941, the notorious "day of infamy," the U.S. Pacific Fleet was destroyed and thousands of Americans killed.

The public demanded immediate revenge for the "sneak attack" on Pearl Harbor, but Roosevelt and his advisers perceived Germany to be the greater threat to American security and were committed to a Europe First strategy. As the country went to war there was an obvious problem: Japan had attacked and declared war; Germany had not. For reasons that will never be known with certainty, Hitler resolved the problem by declaring war on the United States, allowing the Americans to proceed with their plans to join the British and the Soviets in confronting the Third Reich.

As his country reeled under the German attack, Stalin demanded that his allies launch a cross-channel invasion of Europe in 1942 to force Hitler to withdraw troops from his eastern front. Churchill, remembering the high cost of premature assaults in the First World War, was adamantly opposed. He insisted that the American and British forces needed at least a year of preparation for so major an operation. Roosevelt's military advisers agreed that their men were not ready, but they soon became impatient with Churchill's hesitation, with his penchant for proposing smaller actions that they considered peripheral. If he wouldn't fight, they were eager to go into action against Japan. Stalin suspected his new friends in London and Washington of being perfectly willing to allow his people to fight the Germans alone. Indeed, Harry S Truman, a U.S. senator, only months before had proposed allowing the Nazis and the Soviets to destroy each other—a sentiment widely shared among other Americans. Roosevelt managed to keep the alliance functioning.

The U.S. Navy, less encumbered by the need for cooperative efforts among allies, unhesitatingly went on the offensive in the Pacific, led by the carriers that had been at sea on December 7, 1941. In June 1942 naval intelligence discovered the position of a major Japanese task force headed for Hawaii. Carrier-based aircraft attacked and smashed it in the Battle of Midway. The Imperial Japanese Navy was never again able to launch an offensive operation. Slowly, ground forces, primarily American, pushed back across the Pacific, island by island, bloody battle by bloody battle, starting with the assault on Guadalcanal in the Solomon Islands in August 1942. U.S. naval forces thwarted Japanese efforts to support their outnumbered troops, and Japan's retreat had begun.

Determined to send American troops into action against the Germans despite British resistance to the invasion of France, Roosevelt approved plans to attack North Africa in November 1942—to the dismay of his military advisers. Stalin was not impressed. Soviet forces, suffering massive casualties, still engaged approximately 80 percent of Hitler's military. The Americans acquitted themselves well. Their minor victory was a morale booster for them and their British allies—and complicated life for the great German general, Erwin Rommel. Meeting with Churchill in Casablanca in January 1943, Roosevelt again acceded to British plans for peripheral operations, attacks on Sicily and the Italian mainland. Again, Stalin, who was unable to attend the conference, was angered by what he recognized as another delay in the cross-channel invasion necessary to force the Germans to ease pressure on the Soviet Union. Knocking Italy out of the war would not provide his defenders with much relief. On the other hand, the Wehrmacht had been stopped at Stalingrad in December, greatly improving Soviet prospects for survival.

Toward the end of November 1943, Stalin met for the first time with Roosevelt and Churchill, in Tehran. Several months before, at Kursk, the Red Army had won the greatest tank battle in world history, crushing the last German offensive on the eastern front. By the time the three leaders met, Hitler's troops had been driven out of most of the Soviet Union and Stalin was planning offensive operations with Berlin as his target. He and Roosevelt quickly agreed to an Anglo-American invasion of France in the spring of 1944, overcoming Churchill's reluctance. To facilitate the invasion, Stalin promised to launch an offensive at the same time. The demise of the Third Reich was readily imagined. D-Day came on June 6 with the storming of Normandy beaches by Allied forces.

A month later the representatives of forty-four nations assembled at Bretton Woods, New Hampshire, where they agreed to the outlines of a postwar monetary system. Roosevelt and Henry Morgenthau, his secretary of the treasury, perceived the conference and the agreements they sought as the economic basis for the postwar operation of the Grand Alliance. Economic interdependence, a shared stake in a postwar economic order, would bind Great Britain, the Soviet Union, and the United States in peace, as fear of Hitler had brought them together in war. The conference participants created the International Monetary Fund (IMF) and a bank for reconstruction and development that came to be known as the World Bank. The United States, as the wealthiest nation in the world, would provide much of the funding required by these institutions and maintain a proportionate degree of control over their activities.

There was never any doubt, in Washington or abroad, that the Bretton Woods system was designed to serve the long-term interests of the United States. In general, the leaders of other nations accepted the idea that the system that was good for America would be good for the world—that the world would benefit from the responsible and generous position to which the United States had committed itself. There would be a new liberal international economic order with emphasis on increasing trade, increasing productivity, and a larger share for everyone. When the deadline for ratification was reached, the Soviet Union held back, but its trading role was minor—its absence was regretted, but not enough to spoil the party.

The three leaders met for the final time at Yalta in February 1945. Roosevelt, in the last weeks of his life, was pleased by the discussions. He achieved most of his goals at minimal cost to the United States. His primary objective was to obtain Soviet participation in the war against Japan. Stalin agreed to abrogate the nonaggression pact he had negotiated with Tokyo and to attack the vaunted Kwantung Army in Manchuria three months after the German surrender. The Chinese had demonstrated neither the will nor the ability to do the job, and Roosevelt did not scruple to purchase Stalin's cooperation with a diminishment of China's sovereignty: it was understood the Soviet Union would be allowed to retain a sphere of influence in Manchuria.

In addition, Roosevelt sought assurances that the Soviet Union would join the United Nations without a vote for each of the Soviet republics. Stalin settled for three votes instead of the sixteen he had demanded. Finally, Roosevelt asked Stalin to set aside the puppet "Lublin" government he had established for Poland, to respect the principle of self-determination. On this issue, Stalin proved less amenable, agreeing only to prettify a Communist-controlled regime with more posts for non-Communists. He also offered vague assurances of democracy and free elections throughout Eastern Europe. Roosevelt accepted and Churchill went home to praise Stalin's cooperation effusively before Parliament. And Stalin proved worthy of Churchill's praise by launching his spring offensive in February, rescuing British and American soldiers savaged by Hitler's Ardennes offensive.

Unfortunately, Roosevelt lived long enough to see his vision of Soviet cooperation in the postwar new order begin to unravel. Stalin doubtless had every intention of dominating Eastern Europe, "liberated" by the Red Army as it raced toward Berlin. Roosevelt, however, made two decisions that intensified the Soviet dictator's anxieties. One was to withhold information about work on the atomic bomb, of which Stalin had learned from his spies. The other was to authorize American intelligence operatives to meet secretly with senior German officers to discuss the German surrender in Italy, leading Stalin to suspect a deal between the Germans and his Anglo-American allies—a deal that would allow the Germans to concentrate their resistance against the advance of Soviet troops. When Roosevelt joined Churchill in protesting against the ruthless suppression of opponents of the Communist regime Moscow had imposed on Poland, Stalin was unresponsive. At Yalta he had been assured of a friendly government in Poland—all but impossible if the people were permitted to choose one. And then, in April 1945, only weeks before the German surrender, Roosevelt died and it was left to Harry Truman, his successor, to find a path to cooperation with the Soviet Union.

The war against Japan had continued to be a brutal, island-by-island advance by American troops, joined by their allies from the British Empire. Once within reach of the Japanese home islands, the Americans bombed Japanese cities mercilessly, including the firebombing of Tokyo that killed an estimated hundred thousand civilians. On the mainland, however, China's performance failed to meet expectations. Chiang never received as much aid as he wanted, and his armies never engaged the Japanese to the extent his allies wanted. He demanded more aid before he would fight, and the Americans demanded that he fight before they gave him more aid. Both were fighting two wars, but they were not the same two wars. The United States, at war with Germany as well as Japan, gave priority to the campaign in Europe, hoping the Chinese would take the offensive against Japanese troops on the continent. Chiang was at war with the Chinese Communists as well as Japan and saw the Communists as the greater danger to his regime. He husbanded his resources to contain the forces of Mao Zedong, hoping the Americans would intensify their operations against the Japanese, the enemy they shared. General Joseph Stilwell, sent by the United States to advise Chiang and oversee aid, quickly despaired of working with the Chinese leader. The two men became hostile to each other. When Roosevelt asked Chiang to put Stilwell in charge of China's military effort, an enraged Chiang demanded Stilwell's recall. Roosevelt acquiesced in October 1944, but at that point he surrendered hope of the Chinese driving the Japanese off the mainland. At Yalta, he asked Stalin to do what Chiang would not.

Roosevelt had neglected to keep his vice president informed about his policy decisions, military or political. Truman was ill-prepared to succeed him as the Third Reich crumbled and American forces in the Pacific positioned themselves to strike the fatal blow at the Japanese homeland. Nonetheless, he would have to make the decisions necessary to gather the fruits of victory and to preserve the peace that followed. Germany surrendered without much need for presidential direction. Planning for the defeat of Japan required more of his attention, including consideration of the options to minimize American casualties.

According to the advisers he inherited from Roosevelt, his most immediate problem was to manage the tensions that were developing in Soviet-American relations. Despite his distaste for communism and the lack of sympathy he expressed for the Soviet Union when it was attacked by the Germans in 1941, in 1945 Truman indicated no hostility toward the Soviets. He considered them loyal allies and accepted Roosevelt's conviction that Soviet-American cooperation was essential to a peaceful postwar world. Like most Americans, however, he was inclined to measure Soviet cooperativeness by the degree of deference Moscow accorded the United States. The policy decision to be made in the spring of 1945 was how best to achieve cooperation without sacrificing American ideals or interests. Several of his inherited advisers argued that difficulties had arisen because Roosevelt had been too generous with the Soviets. They called for tougher bargaining. Truman accepted the advice to be less gentle with the Soviets and gave Soviet foreign minister Vyacheslav Molotov an undiplomatic dressing down in their first meeting.

Molotov had little difficulty understanding the message: American policy had changed. He and Stalin assumed that Roosevelt's death had resulted in a seizure of power by anti-Soviet forces in the United States. Truman's language had shown little respect for Molotov or the country he represented. He probably raised more questions in the minds of Soviet leaders than he intended. They would be increasingly wary in the months ahead.

In July 1945 Truman went to Potsdam where, amid the ruins of Nazi Germany, he met with Stalin and the British leaders, first Churchill and then his successor Clement Atlee. Initially uneasy given the importance of the issues to be resolved and the experience of Stalin and Churchill, his confidence was greatly bolstered by word that America's secret weapon, the atomic bomb, had been tested successfully and would soon be available for use against Japan. Now the United States had the power to finish the war alone if necessary—and to maintain the peace alone, should that prove necessary.

Truman responded favorably to what he saw of Stalin at Potsdam and was persuaded that they could work together. He knew that Stalin was capable of great brutality, but he did not equate him with Hitler. The ideological differences between the United States and the Soviet Union seemed irrelevant, and there were no fundamental security issues between the two nations. Disagreement over Poland persisted, but Truman understood that Poland was a vital Soviet interest and at most a secondary concern of the United States. Needing American financing for reconstruction, the Soviets would grant the minor adjustments Washington required. Truman and his advisers were confident that he and Stalin could work things out. Truman set sail for home, ordered atom bombs dropped on Hiroshima and Nagasaki, and World War II was over.

10

ORIGINS OF THE COLD WAR

ALONE AMONG THE powers, the United States emerged from the war wealthier and more powerful than ever. Relatively few Americans had died in the fighting. American industry was intact, prosperous on war contracts. American agriculture was ready to feed the world's starving masses. In contrast, the Soviet Union had lost between twenty and forty million of its citizens to the Nazi onslaught. Its industrial infrastructure, along with those of France, Belgium, the Netherlands, Denmark, Norway, and Great Britain, had been severely damaged. In China, civil war loomed, and there was little chance of regaining even the marginal living standards of the prewar period. In the colonial world, millions stood poised to end the age of imperialism, violently if necessary. And Germans and Japanese, devastated in defeat, were dependent for their survival on the whims of the victors—many of whom had suffered terribly at the hands of the Axis powers.

The prewar international system had been shattered. The Eurocentric world was a thing of the past. Only two nations stood in position to extend their power and influence—the United States, most obviously, and the Soviet Union, which had survived at enormous cost and now, in the absence of German, French, and British power, could imagine itself dominating the European continent. For most Americans, the redistribution of world power was not a concern. They had won the war, destroyed their enemies, and this time, unlike after the First World War, had joined the international organization, the United Nations, to which they delegated responsibility for coping with the world's problems. At last they could focus again on domestic affairs, on the creation of a sound peacetime economy.

Those responsible for American foreign policy remained vigilant against potential threats. They developed contingency plans for the next war and sought to secure bases and assets that would make the United States invincible. The military establishment, newly empowered, wanted funds to preserve the massive forces the country had assembled in the course of the war, forces that could now be used to deter aggression. It was clear to the civilians working toward implementation of the new liberal international economic order that reconstruction aid for friends and former enemies was not going to be sufficient. But at war's end, requests for money for the military or for erstwhile allies—let alone those nations that had started the war—were not welcome. The message from the American people was clear enough, and in 1945 the foreign affairs specialists, the nascent national security bureaucracy, had to step aside. They could not ignore the public and congressional demand for demobilization, to release millions of young men from military service. Quickly a mighty fighting force became a shambles.

The handful of Americans still focusing on world affairs noted a number of trouble spots in the Soviet-American relationship during the months immediately following the end of the war. The Soviets needed reconstruction funds that they were not likely to get from the United States. They saw no reason not to squeeze what they needed out of Germany, but there were disagreements over the amount and disposition of German reparations. The Soviets and other American allies were displeased by U.S. monopolization of the occupation of Japan. American journalists and diplomats reported comparably arbitrary behavior by Soviet authorities in Eastern Europe, especially their brutal actions in Poland. In the United States, long-standing hostility to communism resurfaced. Increasingly, Americans equated Stalin with Hitler. The two countries had lost their common enemy, and, in the absence of shared values, a basis for cooperation in peacetime was not readily available.

In China, the Truman administration hoped to prevent a civil war, but its efforts to bring Chiang Kai-shek's Nationalists and Mao Zedong's

Communists together in a coalition government failed. There was no basis for mutual trust. The Soviet Union and the United States were both guilty of unneutral behavior. As Soviet troops withdrew from Manchuria, they left behind arms and facilitated the movement of Communist forces into the areas they had wrenched from Japan's Kwantung Army. The United States attempted to have all Japanese troops in China surrender only to the Nationalists—and U.S. Marines held key coastal cities until Nationalist forces could reach them from the interior. When Patrick Hurley, the volatile American ambassador to China, resigned, Truman dragged George Marshall, the architect of victory in the war, out of retirement to replace him. Marshall's mission was to prevent civil war and to determine Soviet intentions in North China. He failed to prevent the war but was less concerned when he recognized that the Soviets had no intention of pushing into North China. The possibility that the Chinese Communists would prevail over Chiang's forces was troubling but deemed unlikely to have a major impact on American interests in East Asia.

In Washington and Moscow, men with little comprehension of other people's history and culture tried to make decisions for the world. The Soviet experience provided its leaders with no basis for trust in its wartime allies, who, before the threat of Hitler and the Japanese militarists, had tried to isolate and destroy the regime. Americans, repelled by the terror Stalin inflicted on his own people and the totalitarian dictatorship he had consolidated at home, which gave evidence of extending into Eastern Europe, began to lose hope of future cooperation. Nonetheless, each side attempted to ease the apprehension of the other, to overcome the legacy of mistrust, and to create a peace that would endure. They kept at it with decreasing hope to the end of 1945 and on into 1946. Stalin was too prudent to confront the overwhelming power of the United States. Truman hung on to the belief that he and Stalin could work together. By the end of 1945, however, Truman was growing "tired of babying the Soviets."

In 1946 attitudes in Washington shifted significantly. Soviet actions throughout 1946 forced Truman and his advisers to become apprehensive about Stalin's intentions. Some of these actions and American perceptions of them were classic demonstrations of what political scientists call the "security dilemma," where an increase in one state's security will decrease that of another. Aware of historic Western hostility and fearful of superior American power, Moscow took a series of actions designed to enhance Soviet security. But American leaders viewed each of these steps as detracting from the security of the United States. Eventually, the United States responded with policies to enhance its security—which the Soviets saw as imperiling their own. Each side defined its own policies as defensive but viewed the other's as threatening.

In February 1946 Stalin delivered an address in which he called for ideological purity and new sacrifices in a world in which capitalists threatened the survival of communism. Those Americans most fearful of communism perceived the speech as a declaration of war. That same month George Kennan, a Foreign Service officer who had emerged as the leading specialist on the Soviet Union, sent a long, reflective cable from Moscow. He warned that the Soviets were driven by the imperatives of their political system and insecurities to expand their influence and power as far as other nations would permit. Soviet leaders would respond only to clear signs that their actions would not be tolerated. The United States had to draw the line and stand firm until the Soviet system collapsed of its own weight. His "long telegram" struck a chord with a number of American analysts who had reached similar conclusions. They persuaded Truman to delay completion of demobilization of the American military—and to extend the draft. And in March Winston Churchill, with Truman at his side, spoke of an "Iron Curtain" the Soviets had drawn across Europe.

Efforts to arrange for the international control of atomic energy also undermined the ability of the two nations to cooperate. There was no doubt in Washington that the Soviet Union would eventually develop nuclear power. Proposals for UN control of weapons and oversight over the use of nuclear power without jeopardizing American security emerged in the administration, most notably one supported by Dean Acheson of the Department of State and David Lilienthal, chairman of the Tennessee Valley Authority. Their plan provided for the destruction of existing nuclear weapons once UN control had been established. That control and the inspection it entailed would preclude research on weapons development, conceivably leaving the United States as the only nation with that capability. But before the United Nations considered the plan, Bernard Baruch, an adviser to Truman, modified it to include sanctions not subject to the veto, leaving Soviet security at the mercy of a United Nations dominated by the United States and its friends. Not surprisingly, the Soviets rejected the plan when it was introduced in June 1946.

The Soviet-American relationship did not fare well in 1946, but Truman did not want it to become adversarial. Mostly, he wanted the Soviets to behave civilly, defer to American plans for a peaceful and prosperous world, and leave him alone to cope with pressing domestic concerns—not least the resurgence of the Republican Party. And the election of 1946 brought the Republicans back into control of Congress for the first time since 1930.

The Republicans returned to Washington determined to savage Roosevelt's New Deal programs, especially "cryptocommunist" ideas about government responsibility for the welfare of the people. They intended to prevent the administration from wasting money supporting the British Empire. Hating "creeping socialism" at home, they would force Truman to stand up to the Soviet Communists, to reverse Roosevelt's "treason" at Yalta. Truman was overwhelmed by the onslaught, but his foreign affairs advisers forced him to confront a plethora of grave and immediate concerns. First, Western Europe was finding recovery from the war extraordinarily difficult to manage. Second was the collapse of European and especially British power around the world, and the importance of the United States acting promptly to fill the vacuum. In addition, the Communists seemed on the verge of winning control of the governments of France and Italy through democratic elections. And there was fear that the Germans might choose to align with the Soviet Union.

None of Truman's advisers imagined a Soviet attack on the United States or Western Europe, but all recognized the importance of Western Europe to the United States. It was the heart of the civilization with which Americans identified. Its participation was critical to the liberal economic order Americans believed essential to the world's peace and prosperity. Students of geopolitics had long been taught that control of the Eurasian landmass by one state would give that state the power to dominate the world. Conceivably, the Soviet Union could achieve that control, not with bayonets but by the collapse of existing societies unable to recover unaided from war damage and subverted by local Communists.

The activities required of the United States were beyond anything it had ever attempted in peacetime—and the cost would be astronomical. Moreover, Truman faced a hostile Congress determined to cut his budget. Few members of Congress were amenable to appropriating large sums for aid to countries that would become competitors when they recovered. The American people, promised that joining the United Nations would spare them concern about world affairs, would not be persuaded easily of the sacrifices necessary for the United States to exercise leadership in parts of the world that most could not locate on a map.

The most immediate concern was the threat of the expansion of Soviet power and influence in the Middle East, especially in the eastern Mediterranean. The principal architects of the American response were George Marshall, who returned from China to become secretary of state in January 1947; Dean Acheson, his first undersecretary; and George Kennan, whom Marshall appointed head of his newly created policy planning staff. They were troubled particularly by Soviet pressures on Turkey but also uneasy about the situations in Greece and Iran. As early as January 1946 the United States had denounced the postwar presence of Soviet troops in Iran and blunted a Soviet threat to Tehran. In August Truman had ordered the USS *Franklin D. Roosevelt*, the world's mightiest warship, to the eastern Mediterranean to stiffen Turkish resistance to Stalin's demand to share control of the Dardanelles.

Marshall, Acheson, and Kennan accepted the notion that the United States had to assume Britain's historic role of containing Russian expansion in the region. A crisis in Greece provided the opportunity for them to apply and explain what came to be known as the "containment" policy. They knew the Greek government they intended to support was corrupt, repressive, and inept. They also knew there was little evidence of direct Soviet involvement in the Greek civil war, but they were determined to assert American power in the Middle East, to deny the region and its oil reserves to the Soviet Union. They were warning Moscow that the United States had succeeded to Britain's role as the dominant power in the region.

Stalin had told Churchill that he was willing to concede control over Greece to the West. He was much more interested in Turkey and Iran. It was Josip Broz Tito, the independent Yugoslav Communist leader, often indifferent to Moscow's concerns, who was supporting the Greek Communists. Stalin was caught between his fear of provoking the United States and his unwillingness to alienate Tito. Only after the Americans acted did a cautious Stalin persuade Tito to reduce his role in Greece.

In February 1947 the British officially informed Washington they could no longer support the Greek government. Truman called congressional leaders to the White House where Marshall explained the situation and asked for funds necessary for the United States to take over. The leaders of the Eightieth Congress, however, made it clear to the president that they were unwilling to spend taxpayers' money to feed hungry Greeks or solve London's problems. At this point Acheson played to the lawmakers' opposition to communism and the Soviet Union. He warned that the Soviets were on the march; that they were engaged in a bold maneuver to gain access to three continents. If Greece fell to them, Turkey and Iran would follow. Nothing would prevent the Russians from moving into Africa and penetrating Europe through Italy and France. The danger was imminent, and only the United States could stop the Soviets. The congressional leaders told Truman that if he addressed Congress as Acheson had, the administration would get the funds it sought.

Truman's message to Congress in March 1947 requesting aid for Greece and Turkey included the statement that became known as the Truman Doctrine:

> We shall not achieve our objectives unless we are willing to help free peoples to maintain their free institutions and their national integrity against aggressive movements that seek to impose upon them totalitarian regimes. . . . I believe that it must be the policy of the United States to support free peoples who are resisting attempted subjugation by armed minorities or by outside pressures.

Congress appropriated the funds.

The overblown rhetoric Acheson used for the benefit of congressional leaders and Kennan included in his famous "X" article in *Foreign Affairs* (July 1947) was designed to shock Congress and the American public into recognition of an external threat worthy of their attention and their money.

If misleading Congress and the people about the nature and immediacy of the Soviet threat to American interests was necessary to gain the support needed, it was a price the administration was willing to pay. Short of exaggerating the threat, there may have been no alternative means of obtaining the necessary funds.

Truman's words, much like Stalin's in February 1946, were designed primarily for domestic consumption, but the words and actions contemplated could be viewed in Moscow as a threat. Moreover, he implied that the United States was prepared to aid any country threatened by Communist subversion without calculation of the American interests—or lack thereof—involved. He also implied, as several critics noted, a universal crusade, certainly not his intention. When Chiang's friends asked for aid to China, where the Chinese Communists threatened to overthrow his regime, Acheson tried unsuccessfully to persuade them that China was different.

The more critical problem was Western Europe, where the economic situation was desperate. Accounts of terrible suffering filled the press and cables to the Department of State. These evoked humanitarian concerns, but the decision to act was driven by self-interest, by fear of chaos and subversion. It was essential to keep Western Europe out of Stalin's orbit. The area was enormously important to America's trade and defense. It was essential to keep Western Europe free for Americans to feel free, to have any sense of security. European leaders played on American anxieties, exaggerating the Communist threat in hope of obtaining urgently needed aid.

The administration devised a brilliant approach for providing economic assistance to Europe. Washington would invite European governments to develop an integrated plan for the recovery of Europe. American leaders had recognized the importance of the German economy to the economic well-being of Europe and were groping for a politically acceptable way to rebuild Germany. The integration of western Germany into a revitalized European economy might be less threatening to France and tolerable to the American people. Of greatest importance was the central idea of allowing Europeans to design their recovery program rather than imposing one made in Washington. Of course, the Americans who worked on what Truman called the "Marshall Plan" knew what they wanted to emerge. They were intent on creating the liberal international economic order envisaged at Bretton Woods, stressing free trade and currency convertibility and exporting the social ideals of Roosevelt's New Deal—more for everyone rather than class conflict. The Marshall Plan would provide the necessary funds.

The plan had obvious political implications as well. It was intended to shore up Western European economies so that the region would not be susceptible to Moscow-directed subversion. Truman and Marshall chose not to present the program as anti-Soviet. Moscow and Warsaw sent representatives to the first planning meeting. The Soviets, however quickly withdrew, dragging after them reluctant Poles and Czechs. Stalin had no interest in participating in an American-dominated economic order. As Kennan anticipated, the Soviets took on the onus of dividing Europe into those who accepted Marshall Plan aid and those who did not.

Congress, however, was reluctant to appropriate the necessary funds until February 1948 when Stalin gave the administration a little help. Throughout the fall of 1947 and into 1948, the Communist Parties of Western Europe, under orders from Moscow, fought to block implementation of the Marshall Plan. General strikes shook economies and governments in the region. The Cominform was created to coordinate Communist activities around the world, an attempt to give substance to the myth of a monolithic international communist movement. Soviet control over Eastern Europe tightened. Clearly the Marshall Plan, especially indications of American intent to rebuild Germany and integrate it into an anti-Soviet bloc, alarmed Stalin. It was a classic illustration of the security dilemma at work. The Americans and their Western European friends were preparing what they perceived as a defensive action against a potential threat from the Soviet Union—diminishing what little sense of security Moscow enjoyed. As the United States and the Soviet Union moved along the spectrum from allies to adversaries, each lessened the security of the other by attempting to enhance its own.

On February 25, 1948, the Czech Communists, already dominant, staged a coup, assuring the Soviets total control over the country. In Washington, American leaders wondered if war might be imminent. The recently formed Central Intelligence Agency would only assure the president that war would not come in the next sixty days. The American military deliberately heightened anxieties in an effort to extort an increase in congressional appropriations. Shrewdly, Truman used the war scare to ask Congress to fund the Marshall Plan. At the same time, he asked for and obtained restoration of the military draft and additional defense funding. Stalin's "defensive" actions had facilitated passage of the program he dreaded.

Tensions increased significantly in June 1948. The Soviets, fearing the potential creation of a strong German state, attempted to stop the process. They began by harassing traffic between the western occupation zones and Berlin, part of which, although in the Soviet zone, was nonetheless under American, British, and French jurisdiction. And then, on June 24, they stopped all traffic to West Berlin. The general heading the American mission in Germany called for an armed convoy to challenge the blockade. War seemed possible.

Truman and his advisers, including the Joint Chiefs of Staff, did not want to risk starting a war. On the other hand, they could not allow the Soviets to deny access to Berlin, to cut off millions of Berliners from the West. It was essential to demonstrate American resolve to the Soviets and the people of Western Europe. Moreover, 1948 was an election year, and the president could not appear weak. Eventually, the United States responded with an airlift, carrying supplies in extraordinary quantities to the people of Berlin. The operation was a tremendous success. Soviet planes harassed but never threatened the transports. And in May 1949 Stalin, no more ready for war than Truman, lifted the blockade.

The confrontation over Berlin changed the nature of the Soviet-American relationship. Stalin had been annoyed by American reproaches over East European affairs, but he generally brushed them aside, yielding nothing of substance. Obviously, Truman's complaints about Greece were troubling, but Stalin had long since conceded control over Greece to the West. Unfriendly American gestures toward Soviet interests in Turkey and Iran were more troubling, but as Soviet power grew, there would be opportunity to bring about satisfactory results. But the rebuilding of Germany and its integration in an American-led coalition against the Soviet Union was frightening. With the Americans behind them, vengeful Germans could erase all of Stalin's gains since 1945 and again bring misery to the Soviet people. American actions were perceived as hostile, and the Soviets used all means short of war in an unsuccessful effort to persuade the Americans to back off. Unable to contest the power of the United States, Stalin was forced to accept the division of Germany and Europe on American terms.

The perception from Washington was quite different. The United States had demonstrated its recognition of Soviet security concerns and had accepted Soviet spheres of influence in Eastern Europe and Manchuria. It had offered Moscow a role in the international economic order planned at Bretton Woods. But the Soviets had behaved brutally in Eastern Europe, rejected the Bretton Woods agreements, and threatened Iran, Turkey, and Greece. They were directing local Communists to disrupt reconstruction efforts in Western Europe. They had undermined the independence of once democratic Czechoslovakia and now challenged Western rights in Berlin. Truman's advisers suspected Stalin of seeking to dominate the Eurasian landmass. Unless he was stopped, the Soviets would soon threaten the security of the United States.

It was evident that by the end of 1948, the United States and the Soviet Union were no longer allies or friends—adversaries certainly, but perhaps not yet enemies. The term that emerged, "Cold War," seemed apt. Both countries had ended their postwar demobilization and had begun military preparedness programs. But both sides had managed the Berlin crisis cautiously. They left each other room to retreat. The division of Germany—considered essential by Moscow and Washington—had been achieved. There were no remaining issues. The world reflected an uneasy balance, superficially bipolar, in which preponderant American power, including sole possession of nuclear weapons, assured the security of the United States and its friends. With Europe divided tolerably, with no vital interests in conflict, the two greatest powers might have focused their energies on their considerable internal problems. They did not.

European anxieties led to the next step, creation of the North Atlantic Treaty Organization (NATO). The recipients of Marshall Plan aid feared that economic assistance would not be enough to deter the threat they perceived from the Soviet Union. Thousands of miles and an ocean away from the nearest Soviet tank, Americans might feel secure; Europeans did not. In March 1948 Great Britain, France, Belgium, the Netherlands, and Luxembourg joined forces in the Brussels Pact, aimed at protecting themselves from the Soviets—and, if necessary, from a resurgent Germany. Unable to provide for their own security, they were determined to draw the United States into their alliance.

There was no great enthusiasm in Washington for an unprecedented peacetime alliance. The coup in Czechoslovakia, fear of a similar coup in Italy, and Norwegian complaints of Soviet pressures enabled those Americans who favored a mutual security agreement to prevail. The U.S. military, fearful of overcommitment, unwilling to share supplies and secrets with Europeans, grudgingly went along. The Berlin crisis provided another needed stimulus. Washington insisted on reshaping the ultimate organization, demanding, for example, membership for Denmark, Italy, Norway, and Portugal, and the treaty establishing NATO was signed in April 1949.

The diminished sense of urgency in Washington in the closing months of 1948 and early 1949 was striking. The largely covert campaign to prevent a Communist victory in the April 1948 elections in Italy had succeeded. The airlift to Berlin was working. Tito had split with Stalin. If there had been a Soviet threat to Western Europe, it appeared to have subsided. Stalin had launched a peace offensive. Conceivably, confronted by American resolve, satisfied with what they had already gained in East and Central Europe, the Soviets were ready to accept the status quo and exist in peaceful competition with the West.

In 1949, as in 1946, the structure of the international system dictated Soviet-American competition. But by 1949 Moscow and Washington had gained four years of experience coping with each other and had managed their differences without bloodshed. Stalin clearly recognized the superiority of American power and apprehended the circumstances in which it was likely to be used. Truman and his aides had drawn the line and forced Stalin to toe it. But continued Soviet efforts to compete, even peacefully, to strive for equality with the United States, troubled American leaders. The decline of America's relative power proved unacceptable to them.

Harry Truman's surprise reelection in 1948 outraged rank-and-file Republican politicians, deprived of the power and patronage for which American political parties exist. They pressed their leaders for radical changes in strategy, for an end to bipartisanship in foreign policy. They launched a savage attack on the policies of the Truman administration. The charge of "soft on communism" was difficult to substantiate in face of the Truman Doctrine, the Marshall Plan, the Berlin airlift, and the NATO alliance, but the collapse of Chiang's regime in China provided an opportunity.

Despite Marshall's mediation efforts, civil war resumed in China in 1946. Chiang had enormous advantages in manpower and firepower at the outset but was on the verge of defeat by the Communists as Acheson relieved Marshall as secretary of state in January 1949. Chiang and his American friends called for the United States to rescue him. Had they been able to conceive of a way to prevent a Communist victory in China, Marshall and Acheson would have done so, but their advisers insisted the cost in lives and treasure would be more than the United States could bear. Moreover, American strategists had a low regard for China's importance relative to Europe, the Middle East, or Japan. If it fell to the Communists, it would be unfortunate but not catastrophic. In due course the Chinese Communists, like the Yugoslav Communists, would assert their independence from Moscow. But neither Marshall nor Acheson anticipated the domestic political uses to which Chiang's defeat would be put.

The Democratic administrations of Roosevelt and Truman were accused of betraying their loyal Chinese ally to the Soviets. Government officials critical of Chiang's corrupt, repressive, and inefficient regime were accused of being Communist agents. The Democrats were charged with responsibility for the "loss" of China. Contemptuous of their critics, convinced they were on the right course, Acheson and Truman held steady. China would be abandoned, but to be responsive to some of their more reasonable critics, they refrained from recognizing the Communist regime Mao proclaimed on October 1, 1949. They maintained their ties to Chiang's regime, the remnants of which had fled to Taiwan. In a year or two, American intelligence estimated, the Communists would overrun the island and apply the coup de grace—and then the United States would do what was necessary to prevent the Chinese Communists from becoming an adjunct to Soviet power.

Unlike Chiang, West European leaders succeeded in their efforts to protect their societies against the threat of communism. Jean Monet, a French economist, was the principal architect of a structure, the European Coal and Steel Community, designed to alleviate fear of a resurrected

Germany and integrate that country into the Western alliance. The primary supporting role was played by Konrad Adenauer, elected first chancellor of the Federal Republic of Germany in 1949. The plan was to draw Germany into a European framework in which its economic power would accelerate the reconstruction of the rest of Europe. It would place vital German resources, especially those of the Ruhr Valley, under the shared control of participating states, eliminating the threat to France. Adenauer saw the plan as an opportunity to gain recognition of West Germany as an equal state bound to the West. He was not troubled by indications that his prospective allies were determined to prevent Germany from becoming a military threat to them. He was committed to the integration of Europe and alliance with the United States. Confidence in Adenauer eventually won the Federal German Republic restoration of full sovereignty and membership in NATO.

In 1949 the Truman administration also had to make important decisions about defense spending and the military posture the United States would take in its confrontation with the Soviet Union. Truman was satisfied that economic assistance to friends and a substantially increased nuclear arsenal would suffice to protect the security and interests of his country. He opposed the major budget increases demanded by the military. Acheson was more troubled by the size of Soviet conventional forces and arguments that the Red Army could march through Western Europe at will. No one could determine the *intent* of the secretive Stalinist state. Acheson stressed the need to respond to the *capabilities* of the Soviet military. The United States had to prepare for the worst, to be able to overwhelm the Soviets at every point. But Acheson had little support for an extensive program of military preparedness in the White House, Congress, or among the American people.

Before the end of the year, circumstances changed. In August, the Soviets exploded a nuclear advice, creating great anxiety in the United States. Now the American nuclear arsenal might not suffice to deter Stalin from war. The United States had to build a bigger and better bomb. It had to reconsider the size and deployment of its conventional forces. In January 1950 Truman approved development of the hydrogen bomb and authorized a reappraisal of American security policy.

The Communist conquest of China, evidence of significant Soviet spying in the United States, and the Soviet nuclear explosion led to a widespread demand for more aggressive anti-Soviet policies. In fact, the Soviet Union had contributed little to Mao's victory in China—a fact of which the Chinese would remind Moscow often. Spying was a nasty business, in which the United States was also engaged in 1949. And American leaders had known for years that the Soviets were developing a bomb and could not be expected to allow an American nuclear monopoly forever.

Truman and Acheson took steps designed to maintain American military superiority, but they rejected demands from prominent Republican leaders that they intervene in the Chinese civil war. In an important speech in January 1950, Acheson declared that the Asian mainland and the island of Taiwan lay outside the defensive perimeter of the United States.

In March NSC-68, the new study of security policy, was ready. It was intended to justify a major expansion of American military forces, sufficient to ensure the ability of the United States to meet any threat with overwhelming force. It called for a tripling of the military budget. Again, the security dilemma was obvious. The Soviets had no choice but to acquire nuclear weapons. They might reasonably perceive the Marshall Plan and NATO as threats and arm against the latter. But any increase in Soviet power, any effort by Moscow to enhance its security, was perceived in Washington as a threat to the security of the United States. Acheson was preparing to stimulate the next cycle, projecting a major "defensive" buildup by the United States. Truman, however, was not willing to commit the required resources. The program languished, the Cold War stabilized, and Stalin called for peace—and, in the early months of 1950, there seemed a chance he might get it.

Only the United States and the Soviet Union emerged after World War II in position to expand their influence. Predictably, they found themselves competing for dominance over some of the areas between them. Soviet determination to control Eastern Europe had been apparent throughout the war. The reemergence of traditional Russian goals in Northeast Asia, Iran, and Turkey should not have been surprising. That the United States, long content to dominate much of the Western Hemisphere, should assert itself not only in East Asia but in the Middle East and Western and Central

Europe as well might have surprised Roosevelt as much as it did Stalin. In the ensuing struggle for influence, wealth, and power, the economic and technological strength of the United States provided it with a huge advantage.

The nature of the competition that occurred—the hostility, the Cold War—derived from the fact that one of the competing states was a brutal dictatorship that brought intolerable misery to the peoples who came under its control, a totalitarian state whose methods engendered fear everywhere, a closed society whose lack of transparency allowed no means for verifying agreements. The attributes of the American political system exacerbated the problem. The leaders of the world's most powerful nation were constantly constrained by domestic interest groups and the reins given to Congress by the Constitution. Truman and his advisers concluded that overcoming public and congressional lassitude required magnification of the Soviet threat and the Soviet role in undesirable outcomes. This exaggerated description of the Soviet threat worked to the advantage of anticommunist ideologues who dominated American political discourse after 1950.

The leaders of the United States were angered by Soviet unwillingness to accept a subordinate role in the Pax Americana. They were appalled by the political culture of the Soviet Union. Having learned from Hitler of the unspeakable atrocities of which totalitarian dictators were capable, they expected comparable horrors from Stalin. They equated the two men and the systems by which they ruled. But, arguably, the most important point was that despite Stalin's malevolence, despite American arrogance, despite the systemic rivalry, the United States and the Soviet Union had not gone to war. Neither side had incentive to fight. Perhaps in time they would learn how to talk to each other.

11

THE KOREAN WAR AS
TURNING POINT

E UROPE WAS THE principal focus of Soviet-American interests. The
Soviets considered control of Eastern Europe as vital to their security.
The Americans considered a noncommunist Western Europe vital
to theirs. Each feared a united Germany that might ally with the other.
The first serious crisis of the postwar era had come when the United States,
France, and Great Britain indicated their intention to create a strong
Germany out of their occupation zones and to integrate it with the West.
Stalin had responded with the blockade of Berlin.

For both the United States and the Soviet Union, Asia was less important than Europe. Nonetheless, it was a war in East Asia that changed the
nature of the Soviet-American confrontation, changing it from a systemic
political competition into an ideologically driven, militarized conflict.
Local actors played an enormous role in shaping that conflict in Asia and
elsewhere in what came to be known as the Third World. The Soviet
Union, especially after Stalin's death, attempted to assist all movements
hostile to imperialism, most obviously those with "socialist orientation."
American leaders abandoned their determination to be viewed as the
greatest opponent of imperialism and concluded that all leftist movements
were either instruments of Moscow or likely to become adjuncts of Soviet
power and had to be crushed. Too cautious to risk direct confrontation,
the superpowers shed the blood of their surrogates, but over 100,000

American servicemen and women lost their lives fighting communism in East Asia.

Perhaps the most important series of events in Asia in the last half of the twentieth century involved decolonization as the imperial powers, weakened by the war, lost control of their colonies. The Japanese had driven the Westerners out of East Asia, and they were not welcomed back after the defeat of Japan. The peoples of the region were determined to win their freedom and independence. Over the next decade or so they all did, some with terribly destructive wars. The efforts of local leaders to draw in the superpowers intensified the dangers, with another world war a conceivable outcome.

Japan was shielded from most of the unrest that swept Asia. Devastated by the war, by merciless American bombing, the Japanese were relatively docile. They accepted the benign rule of General Douglas MacArthur, the American proconsul, manipulating him as best they could. The American occupation forces demilitarized and democratized the country with considerable success, largely the result of Japanese receptivity. Great concentrations of industrial power, the *zaibatsu*, were broken up, organized labor empowered, women's rights established. Visions of a New Deal for Japan emanated from American civilian planners in Tokyo.

In Washington, however, American leaders, increasingly more fearful of the Soviet Union than of a resurgent Japan, "reversed course," choosing to rebuild Japanese economic power and integrate Japan with the emerging anti-Soviet bloc, much as they were doing with Germany. Led by Yoshida Shigeru, the traditional Japanese elite was anti-Soviet and maneuvered skillfully between the reforms imposed by the occupiers and their own determination to serve Japan's national interests. And, as with the reconstruction of Germany, the reconstruction of Japan was as frightening to America's friends in East Asia as it was to its rivals.

At the end of the war, Franklin Roosevelt's interest in eliminating French rule over Indochina was forgotten, liberation of the territory left to the British and Chinese. The British facilitated the French return. Vietnamese nationalists, the Communist-led Viet Minh, were unable to attain independence peacefully and, by 1946, were engaged in a revolutionary war—in which the United States showed little interest despite Vietnamese appeals to the memory of Thomas Jefferson and Abraham Lincoln. Washington grew unfriendly as American suspicion of Communists anywhere grew. On the other hand, the United States supported the Indonesian fight for independence against the Dutch, largely because of fear that a noncommunist movement would be taken over by the Communists if the struggle continued.

The pattern could be seen in situational variations in two countries in which the United States was more deeply involved: the Philippines and China. In 1946 the United States demonstrated its anti-imperialism by granting independence to the Filipinos. It did not, however, surrender its major bases in the islands and continued to manipulate local politics to assure control by the traditional elites, many of whom had collaborated with the Japanese as they had with Americans before the war. Washington was indifferent to the subsequent collapse of the Philippine economy—until a leftist-led peasant revolution, the Hukbalahap, gathered force. Thereafter the United States provided the assistance necessary to suppress it.

China was more complicated and more important. Washington was unsympathetic to Chiang Kai-shek, who had proved to be a difficult ally. But wartime camaraderie with Mao Zedong's Communist rebels quickly gave way to concern for their connection to Moscow. Visions of bringing together moderates of the left and right, of creating a New Deal for China, could not be fulfilled when dealing with obstreperous patriots such as Chiang and Mao. When George Marshall failed to prevent civil war, American leaders gave up hope for a China that might serve their ends in East Asia. They preferred a victory for Chiang's forces and provided some aid—more than they thought he was worth. Marshall, Acheson, and Kennan perceived Chiang's collapse in 1948 and the subsequent establishment of the People's Republic of China as contrary to American interests but not a catastrophe. Mao would certainly be more responsive to Moscow than to Washington, but they knew he was intensely nationalistic. They assumed that Communist China could be prevented from becoming an "adjunct of Soviet power."

In the course of 1949 Acheson determined to abandon Chiang, who had fled to Taiwan, and to seek accommodation with the People's Republic. Chiang's friends in Congress hampered his efforts, and hostility voiced in

Beijing was unhelpful. Acheson assumed time was on his side: in due course the Communists would eliminate Chiang, and Americans would learn to live with a Communist China. Mao's trip to Moscow in December 1949 and the resultant Sino-Soviet alliance were a setback, but Acheson remained convinced that China and the Soviet Union were not natural allies. Chinese nationalism would prevent Soviet control of China, and the day would come when issues between the two countries would divide them. In January 1950 he spoke publicly of an American defensive perimeter that excluded Taiwan and the Asian mainland. He hinted that the United States would recognize Mao's Beijing government when the dust of civil war had settled. And then, as summer came to Washington, war broke out in Korea.

That a civil war in Korea would provide the critical turning point in the postwar Soviet-American relationship and raise the possibility of world war seems bizarre. In the tense days of 1949 and 1950, American analysts waiting for the Soviets to strike looked toward Europe, and Yugoslavia in particular. The Soviet Army did not move, however, even to punish a deviant Communist leader who had challenged Stalin's authority. But on June 25 troops and tanks of the Soviet-trained and equipped forces of the Democratic People's Republic of Korea launched a major offensive across the 38th parallel, against the American-trained and equipped forces of the Republic of Korea to the south.

American missionaries, businessmen, and naval officers had established contacts with Korea in the nineteenth century, but the United States had little contact with that country after the Russo-Japanese War, when the Japanese established their hegemony there. In the closing days of World War II, the United States and its Soviet allies agreed to liberate Korea jointly, dividing their responsibilities at the 38th parallel. Soviet forces reached Korea first, drove past the 38th parallel, but did not hesitate to move north of it when American forces arrived. Korea was liberated, and the Koreans demanded their independence. Unsure of what to do, the Americans and Soviets came up with the idea of establishing a trusteeship until unspecified conditions for independence were met, outraging the Koreans. As they set about administering their respective sectors, the Soviets turned to local Communists and to Koreans who had fought alongside Soviet forces against the Japanese. The Americans were attracted to those Koreans familiar with the vocabulary of liberal democracy—many of whom had collaborated with the Japanese. As Soviet-American tensions developed, the 38th parallel hardened into something akin to an international border in the eyes of Russians and Americans, if not Koreans.

Although separate governments were established in 1948, Koreans on both sides refused to accept the division of their country. They fought constant skirmishes on the border and did what they could to infiltrate territory controlled by the other. Politics in the American sector were dominated by Syngman Rhee, a ruthless Princeton-educated autocrat, anticommunist but unamenable to American advice. The American military wanted to go home, and in 1949 the National Security Council ordered the withdrawal of American troops from Korea. The Department of State was opposed, fearful that without an American military presence, superior Communist forces would overrun southern Korea. In 1949 both Truman and his secretary of defense were more interested in limiting the defense budget than in Korean affairs. In Washington, Korea was low on nearly everyone's list of priorities. The Asian mainland had been determined to lie beyond the nation's defensive perimeter, and troops stationed in Korea would be useless in the event of war with the Soviet Union.

Stalin, aware of American strategic superiority, did not want war with the United States. He and his agents emphasized the need for peace, spoke of their belief that communists and capitalists could coexist. Stalin's peace offensive was doubtless tactical, designed to buy time until the Soviets could match or surpass American power. He was not ready in 1950: a united Communist Korea was not worth the risk. His Korean protégés, however, like Rhee's regime in the South, were determined to fight, to unite Korea by force.

Stalin's policy in Korea had mirrored American policy. He attempted to keep Korean Communist forces on a tight leash, supplied primarily with defensive weapons. When American troops left the Korean peninsula, however, Stalin and his advisers might reasonably have concluded that the United States was indifferent to the outcome of the Korean civil war and unlikely to intervene. In the spring of 1950 he yielded to the importuning of Kim Il-sung, the North Korean Communist leader, and provided him with the weaponry needed to carry out an offensive that Kim assured him would result in rapid victory. Stalin's one condition was that Kim gain Mao's acquiescence. He wanted to be certain that if the operation went amiss, the Chinese would share responsibility and prevent catastrophe. However grudgingly, Mao—who was focused on attacking Taiwan and destroying the remnants of Chiang's forces—agreed to the plan. Korean troops who had fought alongside the Chinese Communists during the civil war returned to Korea to strengthen Kim's army, and Stalin sent military advisers to direct the invasion.

Arming the North Koreans and supporting their invasion of the South proved to be Stalin's most disastrous Cold War gamble. It postponed détente for twenty years. It intensified a confrontation that continued for forty years at enormous cost to the major antagonists and to much of the rest of the world. The war shifted the balance of forces within the United States to the advantage of the most militant opponents of social justice, to opportunists such as Joe McCarthy and Richard Nixon, and to powerful bureaucrats such as J. Edgar Hoover, allowing them to divert the attention of the American people from needed reform to the hunt for Communists at home and abroad. It enabled the creation of a military-industrial complex that consumed the productive power of the American economy and fueled conflict all over the world. Opposition to reform, the seeds of the military-industrial complex, and men such as McCarthy, Nixon, and Hoover existed in American society independently of any Soviet threat. They might have succeeded in conjuring up a threat from Mars. But it was Stalin's opportunism in Korea that opened the door for them.

The initial response in Washington to the outbreak of war in Korea was relief that Rhee had not started it. The Communists had invaded the South, and Truman had to decide whether to respond. If Korea was outside the defensive perimeter of the United States and deemed relatively unimportant by the National Security Council, why bother? Surprisingly, Truman's advisers all reversed themselves and argued that the invasion had to be repelled, that an act of aggression could not be allowed to go unchallenged. They perceived events in Korea as a test of America's will to resist Soviet attempts to expand their system and their influence. If Stalin were allowed to succeed in Korea, he would probe somewhere else. Now was the time to stop him. The credibility of the United States and the United Nations was at stake.

Another concern was for the political future of Harry Truman. His administration had been accused of betraying China, of allowing the Soviet Union to expand its influence in Asia. Acheson's indifference to Asia was notorious and troubled many of his most loyal aides. Failure to respond in Korea could be politically catastrophic. Successful action could silence the administration's critics.

The combination of reasons for acting—stopping an act of aggression; containing Soviet expansion; demonstrating resolve to Stalin, to America's European allies, to nervous Asians; preserving the credibility of the UN; protecting Truman at home—was overwhelming. To Stalin's dismay, the United States intervened in the Korean civil war. Mobilizing the United Nations, assisted by units as disparate as British, Turkish, and Ethiopian, the United States sent its military forces to fight alongside those of Syngman Rhee. He was an unworthy ally, but the United States could not risk the consequences of inaction.

Initially, UN forces under the command of General MacArthur fared poorly. Rhee's troops were not well equipped, and the American troops included few with combat experience. American airpower functioned ineffectively. Driven back, MacArthur's troops were able to hold a line outside the southeastern port city of Pusan. From there they counterattacked simultaneously with a brilliantly conceived and extraordinarily risky landing the general ordered at Inchon on the northwest coast of southern Korea. By late September they had trapped the North Korean troops in a classic pincer movement and routed them. In less than three months, UN forces under American leadership had defeated the aggressor, were on the verge of liberating the South, and had demonstrated both the viability of the United Nations and the resolve of the United States.

Regrettably, in its moment of triumph, the Truman administration succumbed to the temptation to expand its war aims. Concluding that Stalin would not come to the aid of his Korean surrogates, Truman and his advisers believed they could send UN forces across the 38th parallel, purge the North of Communists, and unite all of Korea, presumably under a government more democratic than that of Rhee. There was a risk that the

Chinese would intervene—as they threatened to do if UN troops crossed the 38th parallel, but Acheson and MacArthur were contemptuous of the Chinese, inclined to believe they were bluffing.

There were voices in Washington favoring a halt to military operations once the South was liberated. Kennan thought there was an opportunity to drive Mao and Stalin apart based on their different responses to an Indian proposal to seat Beijing in the United Nations. Paul Nitze, architect of NSC-68, the plan for a massive military buildup to confront the Soviet threat, argued the United States was not ready for an expanded war that might become World War III. Military leaders were disinclined to commit their forces to what they considered a peripheral area. And there were some who thought the Chinese might well intervene, forcing a larger war.

The opportunity to roll back communism in Korea, the idea of creating a united Korea as a showcase for democracy and an answer to critics who claimed Truman was soft on communism, proved irresistible. MacArthur was authorized to proceed and sent his men racing up the coastal plains on both sides of the peninsula. Uneasy about the Chinese, Truman flew to Wake Island, where MacArthur assured him of a quick victory even if the Chinese were so foolish as to intervene.

In Beijing, Mao and his advisers were apprehensive about American intentions. Ever the realist, Acheson was still looking toward eventual recognition of the People's Republic of China but was in no hurry to reward the ally of his enemy. Mao, on the other hand, was convinced that sooner or later the Americans would attack and try to reverse his victory. American actions following the outbreak of war in Korea intensified his anxiety. Truman ordered warships to the Taiwan Strait to prevent Mao's forces from invading Taiwan and mopping up the remnants of Chiang's army. MacArthur flew to Taipei and indicated his support for Chiang. Once again, the Americans were interfering in China's civil war.

Mao was deeply troubled by the dispatch of American troops to Korea and then by their success at Inchon. Relying on the *New York Times* for their information, his advisers reported growing sentiment in the United States in favor of uniting Korea and then continuing on into China. China was weak and needed time and all its resources to reconstruct and modernize the country. It could hardly expect to win a war against the most powerful country the world had ever known. Chinese leaders did not want to fight, but Mao was convinced the Americans would leave him no choice—better to fight in Korea than on Chinese soil. And Stalin was urging him to intervene.

Even after Stalin reneged on a promise of air support and the Chinese Politburo voted against intervention, Mao was undeterred. As UN forces marched toward the Yalu River, the border between Korea and China, Mao ordered Chinese troops into Korea. Repeatedly, the Chinese warned they would attack if UN forces continued to march north. Arrogantly, the Americans and their allies charged on, confident of a quick victory.

Acheson tried to assure the Chinese that the United States did not intend to attack China, but American assurances lacked credibility in Beijing. The Americans had declared Korea outside their defensive perimeter but had sent their troops anyway. They said they wanted to repel aggression and drive the North Koreans back across the 38th parallel—and now they were headed for the Yalu. American lawmakers were calling for the restoration of Chiang's government, MacArthur and Chiang were conspiring, and American planes were bombing Chinese airfields. Given the absence of trust, given the ambiguous American signals, prudence required China to intervene in Korea.

In mid-October 1950 Chinese forces struck at American troops, bloodied them, and withdrew to observe the American response. MacArthur ordered his men to push on. Two weeks later they were attacked by 200,000 "volunteers" from the Chinese People's Liberation Army. The Chinese shattered discipline among the UN troops who fled south in disarray, suffering severe casualties. By the end of November the American military was preparing to flee Korea, to accept defeat.

In Washington, George Marshall returned to take over the Department of Defense, and he, Kennan, and Dean Rusk, Acheson's assistant secretary for Far Eastern affairs, rallied the U.S. government. They rejected MacArthur's defeatism, vowing to go down fighting. UN forces held again, north of the Pusan perimeter. Fearful of provoking Soviet intervention, Truman rejected MacArthur's demand for permission to attack China. The United States was not ready for World War III. Fierce aerial assaults against overextended Chinese lines took an enormous toll, and gradually the Chinese retreated back across the 38th parallel. Efforts to end the war largely on the basis of prewar conditions began in the spring of 1951.

Instead of the popular victory Truman might have claimed in September 1950, his administration continued the fighting to the point where the war was intensely unpopular with the American people and enormously costly in blood and treasure. It had brought on the United States a war it could not win without risking a world war for which the American military was not ready. It took two more years to end the war, and by then Truman and his aides had returned to private life.

The war prompted the scale of military spending envisioned in NSC-68. American military power, especially nuclear power, increased dramatically. An arms race, in which the Soviet Union could not easily compete, was under way. American military leaders thought they were ready to take on the Soviets. Stalin had permitted the war because he assumed the United States would not fight. He had encouraged the Chinese to be aggressive in their tactics, euphoric over their initial successes. But the Soviets stood back while their Korean and Chinese surrogates were being slaughtered, suggesting to the men in the Pentagon that Stalin perceived the balance of power to favor the Americans. Now the United States could act aggressively in support of its interests.

The Soviet Union supported its Korean and Chinese allies diplomatically and a few Soviet pilots flew missions in the North, but at no time did the Soviet Union threaten military action. It provided the Chinese with military equipment but at a charge the Chinese found outrageous. At no time did it threaten to open a "second front" in Europe. It cheered its allies for confronting American power but took no risks itself. Caution was again the watchword in the Kremlin.

The Korean War ended in 1953, shortly after the death of Stalin. In Moscow the great succession crisis was being played out and Soviet leaders were preoccupied with the power struggle at home. The Chinese had suffered huge casualties, but they had contained the American imperialists and won great prestige for their nation. And they had preserved the North Korean Communist regime as a buffer between their border and unfriendly forces to the south. It was time to return to building socialism at home.

The mood in the United States was ugly. The country had been rent by wartime hysteria, stimulated by demagogues, some seeking personal power, some partisan advantage, some a return to the time when oppression of the poor, the blacks, the Jews, and anyone else outside the mainstream of middle-American culture was condoned. There had long been a streak of nativism in American society that became explosive when combined with fear of radicalism. In the years immediately following World War II, as conservatives attempted to roll back the New Deal, they appealed to fear of radicalism, labeled everything they disliked communism, everyone who opposed them a Communist, and blurred the lines between democratic socialism and communism, even between liberalism and communism. Their cause was strengthened tremendously by the tensions that emerged between the United States and the Soviet Union.

One reason the Red Scare had evaporated so quickly in 1920 was the absurdity of suggesting that Soviet Russia posed a threat to the United States. In the late 1940s that notion was no longer absurd. To gain acceptance of America's new hegemonic role and its costs, the Truman administration had exaggerated the Soviet threat. Stalin unquestionably used Communists and Communist sympathizers all over the world to serve Soviet policy. Though few in number, Communists serving as Soviet agents unquestionably existed in the United States. In the 1930s and 1940s they were more aggressive, more widespread than most Americans realized: there was a danger. As early as 1947 Truman had created a loyalty board to purify the bureaucracy and had indulged in Red-baiting to get himself elected in 1948.

In February 1950 Joseph R. McCarthy, an obscure Republican senator from Wisconsin, bid for recognition with a speech claiming he had a list of 205 card-carrying members of the Communist Party employed by the Department of State. The technique came to be known as the "big lie." McCarthy had a handful of names of men who had been accused previously, generally of being friendly to the Chinese Communists. Several proved guilty of indiscretion. None was a Communist; none was guilty of espionage; most were no longer in the government. But if a U.S. senator claimed there were 205 Communists in the State Department, surely there some— maybe only 200, 100, 50—but *some*. McCarthy had no evidence of any. His charges were investigated and rejected by a bipartisan committee headed by a conservative, anti–New Deal Democrat who Roosevelt had attempted to purge. McCarthy was undaunted and encouraged by other Republican senators, eager to portray Democrats as the "party of treason."

In coping with what he called the "attack of the primitives," Acheson's arrogance initially shielded him and American foreign policy. Disdainfully of public opinion generally, and of Congress in particular, Acheson ignored the charges of McCarthy and others like him. On occasion he yielded to political expediency as directed by Truman, but only on matters he considered tactical. McCarthy and his colleagues were being fed information by friends of Chiang, and Acheson was willing to delay recognition of Mao's government until Chiang was eliminated. He would not reverse his policy of seeking accommodation with Mao—until the anticommunist hysteria generated by the Korean War left him no choice.

Once Americans were dying at the hands of Communists in Korea, the anxieties generated by knowledge that the Soviets had the atom bomb and by awareness that there were Communist agents operating in the United States were channeled into an anticommunist frenzy. Anyone who had ever been associated with a leftist organization, anyone committed to social justice for all Americans, anyone associated with unpopular views—such as support for labor or civil rights in the South—anyone critical of Chiang or thought to be apologizing for Soviet behavior, anyone who had ever angered a neighbor, might be accused of being a Communist. The accusation, the investigation, often sufficed to destroy careers. Blacklists were created in the entertainment industry to prevent suspect actors from getting parts, to prevent suspect writers from having their work produced for the public. A great composer such as Aaron Copeland could be harassed and spared only because a key member of McCarthy's journalistic claque was especially fond of his music. Many officials, teachers, civil rights workers, and labor organizers were less fortunate, losing their jobs and sometimes the opportunity to find comparable work.

If the Korean War created a climate in which McCarthyism could flourish, McCarthyism created a climate in which reducing Soviet-American tensions became extraordinarily difficult. Red-baiting at home was unquestionably disagreeable. As the basis of foreign policy, it resulted in the wasting of millions of lives and countless billions of dollars. The intersection of McCarthyism and the Korean War, of American paranoia and Soviet opportunism, brought recurring misery for the next four decades.

The first major victim of McCarthy and Korea was Acheson's policy toward China. Mao's Red hordes had killed thousands of Americans. Gone were the images of a weak, docile China, hungering for Christianity and democracy. Now hundreds of millions of Chinese were perceived as instruments of the international Communist conspiracy. Mao's China became America's most feared enemy, the return of the "yellow peril." Recognition of Mao's regime was impossible, as was acquiescence in seating it in the United Nations.

Direct confrontation led to intense hostility between the United States and China, but American leaders did not forget that their principal adversary was the Soviet Union. If, as the chairman of the Joints Chiefs argued in response to calls to attack China, it would be the wrong war in the wrong place at the wrong time, the right war would be against the Soviet Union when the American military buildup was complete. By the end of 1952 the American military was ready, eager to launch a preventive strike against the Soviets.

To meet the Soviet threat, European leaders wanted a stronger NATO. Fearful the Americans would be distracted on the Asian periphery, they sought a larger, permanent U.S. military force on the continent. The American government shared some European apprehensions but wanted Europeans to contribute more to their own defense. Increasingly, Truman's advisers thought in terms of a rearmed Germany, of a German Army that would provide the critical manpower for NATO forces in Central Europe. There was considerable hesitation along the way, but in December 1950, at the same time that Dwight D. Eisenhower was named supreme commander of allied forces in Europe, formal discussions of German remilitarization began.

Perhaps the greatest beneficiaries of the Korean War were the Japanese. When the U.S. Navy had trouble clearing mines in Korean harbors, remnants of the Imperial Japanese Navy were activated to do the job. Most of the goods and services required by American forces were procured in Japan, providing the economy with a $4 billion stimulus. In May 1951 forty-eight nations, led by the United States, signed a peace treaty with Japan, leading to an end of the occupation in May 1952. On the same day the treaty was signed, Japan and the United States signed a mutual security treaty to provide for the protection of a demilitarized Japan. Retaining bases in Japan, the Americans had simultaneously restored Japanese sovereignty and integrated the country into the anticommunist alliance.

The Korean War was a momentous turning point in the Cold War. An almost inevitable civil war among a people, Communist and non-Communist, determined to unite their country became an international war and the catalyst for a terrifying arms race. Whatever Stalin's expectations, the results could hardly have been more disastrous for the Soviet Union or unfortunate for the rest of the world. His peace offensive was compromised, and American wealth rapidly extended American military superiority. The process of rearming Germany began. American aid to the French in Indochina was increased. What little reluctance to replace British power in the Middle East remained in Washington was overcome. For the people of the Soviet Union, the Korean War produced a nightmare, mitigated only by the coincidence of Stalin's death before it was over. In addition to Japan, the winners were Rhee, Chiang, and all the other merciless dictators who, professing anticommunism, could count on American support. In the United States the winners were the advocates of rolling back Communists abroad and programs of social justice at home.

12

NEW LEADERS AND NEW ARENAS

J OSEPH STALIN DIED and the world was a better place, but not necessarily less dangerous. His principal successor in the 1950s, Nikita Khrushchev, was not nearly as vicious, to the benefit of the people of the Soviet Union, but he was a less prudent man who nearly started a nuclear war. His confidence that communism would prevail in the competition with capitalism, with the United States, led him to involve his nation in the affairs of countries in Africa, the Middle East, and Asia that Stalin had deemed unworthy of Soviet support.

The new Soviet leadership inherited a world in which the dominant power, the United States, had just undertaken a rapid military buildup and demonstrated its ability to project power thousands of miles from its shores. And a new administration had arrived in Washington, led by men who called for a more aggressive anti-Soviet policy, including the liberation of Eastern Europe. In addition, Stalin's death had prompted the Chinese government to become more independent, ultimately to challenge the Soviet Union for leadership of the Communist world. A revolt in East Germany and unrest in Poland and Hungary all threatened the stability of the new Soviet empire and its gains from the World War.

The legacy of Stalinism handicapped the new leadership in Moscow. Few had any experience with foreign affairs or knew more of Soviet policies than Stalin had chosen to tell them. The study of international relations, of the social sciences generally, hardly existed in the years of Stalin's rule.

Similarly, Stalin's unhappy experience with Chiang Kai-shek's "bourgeois nationalist" revolution in the 1920s had convinced him that supporting noncommunist nationalist leaders, such as Jawaharwal Nehru of India, Sukarno of Indonesia, or Gamal Abdel Nasser of Egypt, would be another mistake. He was contemptuous of the newly independent states, and they found few defenders in Moscow during his lifetime.

After Stalin's death, the study of international relations was revived, and analysts warned that neither war nor depression was imminent among capitalist countries. They reported the rapid recovery of European economies as a result of the Marshall Plan. They reevaluated the role of newly independent states and saw some as potential allies. When representatives of African and Asian governments met in Bandung, Indonesia, in April 1955, they expressed the determination not to be drawn into the Cold War, but their rhetoric indicated hostility toward European imperialism, positions not far from those taken in Moscow and Beijing—to the chagrin of American leaders.

In February 1956, at the Twentieth Party Congress, Khrushchev denounced Stalin and his crimes against his people. Stalin was gone and the apparatus of terror was being dismantled, but the Soviet Union remained a Communist state. It continued to hold against their will most of the peoples of Eastern Europe. It had five million men and women under arms, and in August 1953 it had exploded a thermonuclear (hydrogen) bomb. The Soviets would continue to be dangerous rivals in the competition for power and influence. Nonetheless, the post-Stalinist Soviet Union was a different country, led by relatively reasonable men with whom an agreement on peaceful competition might be attainable. Khrushchev was a bold and innovative leader, eager for good relations with the United States but unwilling to surrender the vision of an ultimately Communist world.

In Dwight Eisenhower and his secretary of state, John Foster Dulles, the Republican Party and the American people had selected two men extraordinarily well qualified to manage world affairs. Dulles had been active in international politics since the Paris Peace Conference of 1919. He had been a prominent spokesman on foreign policy issues throughout the Roosevelt and Truman presidencies. He was intelligent, knowledgeable, and highly respected at home and abroad. Eisenhower had been the commander of the allied assault on Europe that led to the defeat of Hitler's legions. He had served as supreme allied commander, Europe, after the creation of a NATO military force. He had had extensive contact with European leaders and with the Soviets. He was a highly popular, avuncular figure, sought after as a candidate by both major parties. He seemed the ideal man to calm the anxieties of the American people and unite the country for the grave domestic and international tasks it confronted.

Both Eisenhower and Dulles, however, were viewed with suspicion by the right wing of their party. Throughout the campaign of 1952, they tailored their activities to appease the Right. Eisenhower accepted Richard M. Nixon, a young senator with a reputation for Red-baiting, as his running mate. He allowed Joe McCarthy to campaign for him and stood by silently as McCarthy impugned the loyalty of George Marshall, to whom Eisenhower's career owed so much. Dulles condemned the containment policy of Truman and Acheson as immoral and promised the "liberation of captive nations," the rollback of Soviet influence. For Eisenhower and Dulles, the dogmatism of the Right created shoals only marginally easier to navigate than the Stalinist dogma Khrushchev had to maneuver through.

The massive military buildup the United States carried out between 1951 and 1953 eased fears in the American military and intelligence community of a Soviet attack in the mid-1950s. But the enormous increase in military spending worried Eisenhower. An experienced planner, he considered the military budgets excessive. As an economic thinker, Eisenhower, like Truman, was pre-Keynesian, determined to balance the budget. He feared that deficits caused by the arms race would weaken the United States and result in an economic collapse that would leave it vulnerable.

To cut military expenses, Eisenhower revised American strategy. Whereas the Truman administration was attempting to expand both conventional and nuclear forces to meet any Soviet action with overwhelming force of the same kind, Eisenhower's "New Look" policy stressed air and nuclear power. His strategy implied the possibility of a nuclear response even if the offending Soviet action had been carried out by conventional means.

Dulles labeled the approach "massive retaliation." Others, aware of the president's fiscal conservatism, referred to the New Look as "more bang for the buck."

Eisenhower and Dulles were aware of the changes occurring in the Soviet Union but responded cautiously. They were constrained by the intensity of anticommunism in the United States and aware that the Soviet Union was still a dangerous adversary. Nonetheless, they were confident the Soviets would not challenge NATO. And they had no intention of launching a military challenge to the Soviet sphere of influence in Eastern Europe. By the mid-1950s, with West Germany in NATO and Austria free, and with impressive economic growth in those countries receiving Marshall Plan aid, Eisenhower and Dulles perceived little reason for fear in Europe. The superpowers had achieved a stalemate in the central arena of their competition, and the United States enjoyed an enormous advantage in ability to project power overseas.

Despite frequent suggestions that he viewed nuclear weapons like any others and the implications of his New Look emphasis on such weapons, Eisenhower was eager to find a way both to reduce the danger of nuclear war and to respond favorably to the overtures of the new Soviet leaders. Neither his "Atoms for Peace" nor his "Open Skies" proposals won support from the Soviets, however. The best Eisenhower and Khrushchev could accomplish was a moratorium on nuclear testing, gingerly reached and unenforceable—but an indication that both men recognized the dangers of radioactive fallout and that the two nations, slowly and ineptly, were learning to work together.

In July 1955, responding to pressures from European allies and to the markedly less threatening Soviet posture, Eisenhower attended a summit meeting with Soviet leaders in Geneva, where he met Khrushchev for the first time. Little of substance came out of the meeting, but the symbolic import was enormous. Soviet and American leaders were meeting for the first time since Potsdam in 1945 and attempting to persuade rather than bludgeon each other. The "spirit of Geneva," the reemergence of the idea that problems might be solved by diplomacy, was a source of hope everywhere. It was evident that the existing division of Europe was acceptable to both sides. War was unnecessary as well as unthinkable.

The year after the summit, there were further indications that the Cold War might be winding down. Khrushchev's speech of February 1956 denouncing Stalin and endorsing peaceful coexistence was followed by dissolution of the Cominform, relinquishing Moscow's claim to control of all foreign Communist Parties. In May the Soviets announced major troop reductions. Stalinist Russia was slowly being dismantled, and the Soviets were changing both their approach to foreign affairs and the nature of the regime.

Events in Eastern Europe soon tested the limits of Soviet tolerance. In Poland and in Hungary, demands for an end to Soviet domination erupted in riots in the summer of 1956. The Poles won the right to a Communist leader of their own choosing, but the Hungarians, encouraged by Voice of America and Radio Free Europe broadcasts, pushed harder, tried to withdraw from the Warsaw Pact—Moscow's response to NATO—and were crushed by Soviet tanks. Much of the world was appalled by the brutality with which the Soviets put down the Hungarian rebels, but no one came to their rescue. For all the prattle about liberating captive nations, the Eisenhower administration would not risk World War III by intervening in the Soviet sphere of influence—where Soviet interests were vital and the Soviets were certain to fight.

Soviet actions in Hungary, like Stalin's in Berlin and Korea, were a boon to those determined to maintain a high level of readiness to fight the Soviet Union. And when the Soviets took the lead in the space race, sending *Sputnik*, the first space capsule, into orbit in 1957, Eisenhower found himself under attack for disregarding the security of the United States, for putting a price limit on America's defense.

The Eisenhower-Dulles campaign promise to be more assertive in East Asia had pleased the American Right, especially the friends of Chiang Kai-shek. Visions of rolling back the Communists and restoring Chiang to power on the Chinese mainland danced in their minds. But Eisenhower was eager to disengage American forces from the Asian mainland, to end the war in Korea and contain Communism in the region from bases offshore. Neither he nor Dulles trusted Chiang, and both were apprehensive of his efforts to involve the United States in a war with the People's Republic. Had the domestic political climate been less inhibiting,

Eisenhower would have sought accommodation with Mao's government. He argued publicly against the trade embargo, and his administration secretly permitted American firms to trade with China through their Canadian affiliates.

Both Eisenhower and Dulles considered East Asia less important than Europe. They were unwilling, however, to acquiesce in the expansion of communism that they equated with Soviet influence. They were prepared to use American power and influence to halt the Red tide. The principal threat they perceived came from Beijing. They knew China was not a Soviet puppet and were interested in fomenting friction between the Communist giants. After Chinese intervention in Korea, the intensity of public hostility to the Chinese Communists prevented the administration from attempting to woo the Chinese away from the Soviets by friendly gestures. When the Chinese, eager to lessen their dependence on the Soviets, reached out to the United States, Dulles was unwilling to respond.

The first post-Korean crisis in the region came in Indochina, where the Vietnamese were fighting to be freed from the French empire. American anticommunism proved stronger than American anti-imperialism. Eager for French support for the rearming of Germany and European integration, the United States had become, by 1953, an active supporter of France against the Communist-led Vietnamese revolutionaries. But American money and equipment did not suffice. By March 1953 the French faced certain defeat—unless American military forces came to their rescue.

As the French made their last stand at Dienbienphu, Eisenhower and Dulles considered intervention. Their air force chief of staff was persuaded that a few small nuclear bombs dropped on Vietnamese forces in the hills overlooking the French camp would turn the tide of battle. The chairman of the Joint Chiefs, a naval aviator, thought a carrier task force would be right for the assignment. General Matthew Ridgeway, army chief of staff, the man who had cleaned up after MacArthur in Korea, argued that airpower would not suffice, that a half million American troops would probably be necessary, and that it would be a mistake to put them on the Asian mainland. Eisenhower did not want to send troops, but he was unwilling to see the Communists overrun Indochina. Conceding that Indochina was of little importance to the United States, he outlined his "domino theory":

if Indochina fell, the remaining states of Southeast Asia would fall, one after another, like a row of dominoes. He sought congressional approval, British participation, and a French commitment to grant independence to Vietnam. Failing on all three counts, he chose not to intervene and the French were defeated in May, on the eve of great power talks on Indochina at Geneva.

Ho Chi Minh's forces had won a great victory in their long battle against French imperialism, but the accords reached at the Geneva Conference did not reflect the triumph adequately. A truce was arranged between Vietnamese and French forces, and Vietnam was partitioned *temporarily* to allow the combatants to disengage. The temporary partition, to be followed by a nationwide election in 1956, was forced on Ho by his Soviet and Chinese supporters to protect their own interests. But Ho could count on an easy victory in the election and accepted the delay in the creation of a united independent Vietnam.

The United States had participated in the conference but did not sign the accords, promising only that it would not upset them by force. Immediately, however, the American government subverted the agreement, substituting American influence for French and attempting to convert the truce line into a permanent boundary. It attempted to create a separate Vietnamese state in the South, to be part of the anticommunist bloc. There would be no election in 1956. In addition to southern Vietnam, Cambodia and Laos would become American protectorates. None of these nations individually was important to the United States, but the domino theory suggested that the fall of any one of them would result in the "loss" of all of Southeast Asia. Eisenhower had invested each tiny state with the importance of the entire region. He was directing the United States toward disaster.

In September 1954, at a meeting in Manila, Dulles forged the Southeast Asia Treaty Organization (SEATO). The United States joined Great Britain, France, Australia, New Zealand, Thailand, the Philippines, and Pakistan in an attempt to deter the further expansion of Communist influence in the area. India and Indonesia, the most important states of South and Southeast Asia, rejected membership, as did Burma. SEATO was but a shadow analog of NATO, but Washington now claimed a legal basis for intervention. Ho and Mao were forewarned.

One issue that plagued Eisenhower and Dulles was the shape of the security relationship with the Republic of China, Chiang's rump regime on Taiwan. Chiang's friends urged including Taiwan in some kind of mutual defense pact. Most of the SEATO participants opposed such a provocation to Beijing. A bilateral pact seemed to be the only option, but as the historian Nancy Bernkopf Tucker demonstrated, Dulles was convinced Chiang was trying to entangle the United States in a war with the Chinese Communists to facilitate his return to the mainland. But a miscalculation by Mao forced Dulles into Chiang's embrace.

Uneasy about SEATO and fearful of an alliance between Chiang's government and the United States, Mao precipitated a crisis in the Taiwan Strait, bombarding islands held by Chiang's forces a few miles from the mainland. Chinese leaders perceived an American plot to separate Taiwan from the mainland permanently. They thought they could forestall the alliance by demonstrating its potential danger to the Americans: the danger of becoming embroiled in a war over tiny islands within range of mainland batteries. Eisenhower and Dulles understood but refused to be intimidated. Chiang got his treaty. Mao's display of power proved counterproductive.

Mao had failed to prevent the treaty, but he succeeded in alarming many of the allies of the United States, especially Europeans unwilling to be drawn into a world war precipitated by confrontation over the islands. Having gained Washington's attention, the Chinese offered to negotiate existing differences, including the release of Americans held in China and Chinese stranded in the United States when the two countries became enemies in 1950. Agreement was reached on ambassadorial-level talks in the summer of 1955 and the crisis passed.

After a quick agreement on the exchange of each other's nationals, the talks concluded with a stalemate on the Taiwan issue. The Americans demanded that China renounce the use of force against the island and the Chinese refused, insisting the Taiwan issue was a domestic issue, unfinished business in their civil war. They stressed the likelihood of peaceful liberation of the island but would not give the explicit assurances the United States required. Dulles was inflexible, and in the summer of 1957, despite Chinese efforts to continue the dialogue, the Americans broke off talks.

Mao concluded that a more aggressive approach was necessary. Buoyed by Soviet success in the space race, he argued that the time had come for a Communist offensive. He found Khrushchev unresponsive. Mao decided to challenge the Americans alone, initiating a campaign in August 1958 to seize the offshore islands of Jinmen and Mazu—a second crisis in the Taiwan Strait.

In the years between crises, Chiang had reinforced his garrisons on the islands, hoping to compel the United States to defend them. Eisenhower, failing to get Chiang to withdraw his troops, threatened to use nuclear weapons against China. He sent a large battle fleet, including seven carriers, to the Strait. Khrushchev warned the Soviets would retaliate if the United States launched a nuclear strike. Fortunately Chiang's air force maintained supremacy over the islands, staving off the attack without an American offensive—to the relief of Khrushchev as well as Eisenhower.

Mao had gained the attention of the Americans again, and they agreed to resume ambassadorial-level discussions. Responding to public outrage at home and abroad over the administration's willingness to risk world war over Jinmen and Mazu, Dulles openly criticized Chiang and began to explore the possibility of recognizing the Beijing government. Nothing substantive came of the conversations, but the regularly scheduled talks provided a mechanism for venting rage, providing and obtaining explanations, exploring and even inching toward resolution of differences.

Mao's tactics in the Strait crises troubled Khrushchev. Like Eisenhower, Khrushchev worried about his nation's credibility. He could not stand by idly while the United States pummeled his principal ally—not without sending the wrong message to uncommitted nations the Soviets were wooing. No Third World leader could be expected to cast his or her country's lot with the Soviet Union if the Soviets could not be relied on for protection. On the other hand, if the Soviet Union was to risk a nuclear confrontation with the United States, Khrushchev wanted to be sure that war would come over an issue *he* deemed worthy of fighting and dying for, at a time and place of *his* choosing. But Mao, jealous of his prerogatives as leader of a great nation, was not amenable to Soviet advice.

The ties that bound the Communist giants began to fray. Soviet advice designed to moderate Chinese policy irritated Mao. He was not satisfied with the terms of Soviet economic and technical assistance. He was contemptuous of Soviet foreign policy and horrified by criticism of Stalin, by de-Stalinization. Khrushchev's suggestion that Beijing accept the two Chinas policy toward which the United States had moved struck at the core of Mao's nationalism and confirmed Mao's sense of Soviet indifference to China's interests. Angry exchanges led to Khrushchev's recall of Soviet technicians in 1959 and an effort to undermine China's atomic bomb project.

The Eisenhower administration could not devise a policy to capitalize on the Sino-Soviet split. Containment of communism did not provide a useful framework for exploiting a situation in which the two major Communist powers were at each other's throat. Only a growing involvement in Indochina and awareness of a falling domino in Laos marked Eisenhower's last days in office.

If Mao's assertiveness roiled the Kremlin, some American allies did what they could to prevent complacency in Washington. Foremost of these was the imperious Charles de Gaulle, who objected strenuously to what he perceived as Anglo-American control of NATO and the relegation of France to an inferior role. He raised a question fundamental to the alliance: would the United States risk a nuclear attack on its own cities by responding to a Soviet attack on Western Europe? Unpersuaded by American assurances, he developed an independent nuclear force for France. Dissatisfied by American unwillingness to share responsibility for directing the alliance, he began to withdraw French forces from NATO control. France remained a loyal ally but on de Gaulle's terms.

Less dramatically, the Japanese, too, became more assertive in the 1950s. Freed of the occupation in 1952, its security assured by alliance with the United States, Japan concentrated on economic growth. Eisenhower considered Japan's economic stability as essential to American security interests. He argued frequently against protectionism at home and against posing obstacles to Japan's trade with Beijing. The Japanese were also eager to regain territories lost to the Soviets at the close of World War II and were responsive to Soviet initiatives that led to reestablishment of diplomatic relations with Moscow. Japanese assertiveness worried American analysts, who warned that Japan might dissociate itself from the West. The Japanese public was intensely angered by American nuclear testing in the Pacific, especially after the crew of a Japanese fishing boat was irradiated by a thermonuclear test on Bikini atoll. In 1960 anti-American riots in Japan in opposition to renewal of the Japanese-American security treaty, reflecting pacifist and neutralist tendencies, gave cause for alarm in Washington.

Much of the world went about its business with minimal regard for the antics of the United States and the Soviet Union. The ethnic and religious strife, the class struggles that have always been the stuff of human existence persisted, quite apart from the Cold War. But as the United States and the Soviet Union acquired the ability to project their power all over the world and as they achieved an uneasy balance in Europe, the area of vital concern, they began to intervene in local struggles. Some of their activity could be justified strategically and some of it involved vital economic interests, such as American concern for oil in the Middle East. Some of it was merely mechanical: the power to intervene existed; use it.

Eisenhower was relatively relaxed about the struggle for control of the Third World, doubting that his nation's future rested on the outcome. But there were those dominoes and the need to contain communism. Some Third World countries were sources of important raw materials or potential trading partners for the United States, Japan, or Western Europe. Brandishing nuclear weapons might protect American interests when the Soviets or Chinese were involved, and demonstrations of power might suffice in other situations. Eisenhower, however, was intrigued by covert operations.

One of the administration's first major Third World interventions occurred in Guatemala. Latin America was the lowest priority for American leaders, who assumed Soviet intervention in the region was highly unlikely. And there was no evidence of Soviet involvement in Guatemala. There was, however, a nationalist, reformist government that came to power by constitutional means and dared to expropriate holdings of the United Fruit Company, an American-based firm that was a major force in Guatemalan politics as well as in the economy. The Guatemalan president rejected demands for compensation deemed adequate by United Fruit. Prodded by United Fruit executives, the American government determined that Guatemalan recalcitrance was Communist-inspired. The cancer of communism had appeared in the American sphere. The Central Intelligence Agency (CIA) developed plans to remedy the situation.

Learning that the Americans were preparing an exile invasion of Guatemala, its president searched desperately for arms, ultimately turning to the Soviets—who were delighted by the opportunity to worry the United States. The discovery that Czech arms were en route to Guatemala proved to be a public relations coup for those who blamed reform on international communism. A CIA-organized raid (150 attackers and a handful of planes) sufficed to trigger the collapse of the Guatemalan government. An American-supported regime seized power and quickly made the country one of the world's most repressive. From Washington's perspective, however, it had won an important victory in the Cold War, at minimal cost and almost without showing its hand—impressive evidence of the value of covert operations.

Judaism, Christianity, and Islam all had their roots in the Middle East. For centuries Christians and Muslims fought for control of the Holy Land. For centuries Jews in the diaspora called for a return to Jerusalem as part of their Passover tradition. Secular Jewish nationalism, Zionism, emerged in Europe late in the nineteenth century, and a few thousand Jews trickled into Palestine in the years that followed. The British, who took control of Palestine during World War I (and were subsequently awarded a Mandate to govern the region by the League of Nations), made conflicting promises to the Arabs who lived there and to European Jews who sought a homeland. After the Holocaust, the murder of six millions Jews during World War II, American and British leaders saw Palestine as a convenient refuge for the Jewish survivors of Nazi death camps.

Palestinian Arabs and the Arabs of neighboring states forcibly opposed the UN decision to partition Palestine in order to create a Jewish homeland there. In April 1948 the Jews declared the existence of the state of Israel on that part of Palestine allotted to them by the United Nations. A major war followed in which the Jews, thanks in part to arms provided by Soviet-dominated Czechoslovakia, prevailed over vastly larger armies and created a state even larger than the United Nations had intended. Israel had won the first round in an Arab-Israeli conflict that was to plague the region for decades to come.

Some American leaders, including Harry Truman, seem to have been genuinely sympathetic to the survivors of Auschwitz, Buchenwald, and other camps. They also knew that in the aftermath of the Holocaust, there was enormous support among American Christians as well as Jews for the creation of a Jewish homeland. Politicians were not unaware that there were votes to be gained from supporting creation of the state of Israel. Truman moved quickly to recognize Israel, undermining efforts by the American UN delegation to find a peaceful solution to the partition question.

Other American leaders had argued that the national interest required the United States to align itself with the Arabs. The Middle East contained an enormous percentage of the world's oil reserves. The area was almost entirely Muslim, largely Arab, and broadly hostile to the encroachment of Europeans. Support for a handful of Jews would alienate many millions of Muslims who controlled the strategic crossroads connecting three continents—and vast quantities of oil, on which the United States, increasingly, and its European and Japanese friends were dependent. Moreover, with part of it constituting the rimland of the Soviet Union, it was a critical area for the Soviet-American confrontation.

The Truman Doctrine had demonstrated the intent of the United States to succeed to the British role in the region. Stalin's attempts to appropriate Iranian and Turkish territory had been relatively easy to counter. His meddling in the Arab-Israel War of 1948, intended to aggravate Britain's problems as regional hegemon, were more worrisome. It was Soviet economic and military support for Middle Eastern states that posed the threat to American interests after Stalin's death. American leaders were unwilling to oppose British and French imperialism to facilitate Soviet imperialism. Support for Israel was an irritating complication, driven by humanitarian and domestic political concerns—and a prayer that somehow it could be reconciled with concrete interests. But the Arab-Israeli conflict could not be isolated from the Soviet-American rivalry. Nor could a historic commitment to anti-imperialism inoculate Americans against the virus of imperialism when the opportunity appeared. Once again, it would act as a nation like all others.

Policy toward Iran in the early 1950s illustrates the corrupting influence of imperial responsibilities. The Soviet threat had been countered successfully in 1946. The British had withdrawn their forces, but their interest in Iranian oil remained intense. When tensions arose between an Iranian nationalist regime determined to command its own resources and the British, the Truman administration attempted unsuccessfully to broker an Anglo-Iranian compromise. By the time Eisenhower became president, Washington had come to fear that Communist influence was growing in Tehran, that Mohammed Mossadegh, the democratically elected Iranian prime minister, might allow his country to slip under Soviet control. Like any nineteenth-century imperial power exercising suzerainty over a client state, the United States decided to replace the Iranian leadership. With the assistance of British operatives, the CIA facilitated a military coup, resulting in the arrest of Mossadegh and a shift of power to the shah, the reigning monarch. For many years afterward, the shah responded to American needs with appropriate gratitude, including increased access to Iranian oil. His own people fared less well.

As Eisenhower and Dulles surveyed the world, they noted that the Middle East constituted a gap in the network of alliances with which they were determined to encircle the communist bloc. Between Turkey and Pakistan sat the Arab states, Iran, and two-thirds of the oil reserves accessible to the West—all vulnerable to a Soviet thrust. The Truman administration had tried but failed to create a Middle Eastern command. Eisenhower would try again. Turkey, Iraq, and Pakistan were interested, each for its own purposes. Washington and London hovered in the background, groping for a formula that would not enrage the Israelis or the Egyptians. The Turks seized the initiative, forging the Baghdad Pact with Iraq in February 1956—to which the British, Pakistanis, and Iranians adhered. Unable to pacify the Israelis or Egyptians, both resentful of Iraqi access to Western military aid, the United States never joined what became the Middle East Treaty Organization (METO), although it was the principal source of its support.

The Soviet bloc was ringed by hostile nations, all receiving military assistance from or protected by the Americans. But for most denizens of the Middle East, the Soviet threat was imperceptible. Western domination had blighted their lives for generations, and they preferred to assert themselves against Western imperialism and Zionism, which they perceived as its most recent manifestation. There was little popular support for the containment of the Soviet Union. There was, however, a vast quantity of combustible material waiting to be ignited by a leader who would strike out against Israel and reverse decades of humiliation by the West.

The man most likely to lead the Arab world to renewed glory and respect was Gamal Abdul Nasser of Egypt. He emerged as master of Egypt after a group of young officers overthrew a decadent king in 1952. Nasser and his colleagues demanded elimination of European restrictions on Egyptian sovereignty, and the British had neither the will nor the resources to resist. Nasser impressed American leaders favorably and, eager to win his friendship, they favored the British retreat. But he disappointed them: he was unwilling to enlist in the containment of the Soviet Union, nor was he willing to moderate the anti-Israel, anti-imperialist rhetoric so popular in the Arab world. Indeed he was outraged by the Baghdad Pact. Iraq was undermining his vision of rejecting Western hegemony and uniting the Arab peoples under his leadership. He understood that the Soviets were equally unhappy with the pact and increasingly supportive of the Arabs against both Israel and the West. When Israel launched a humiliating raid into Egyptian-controlled territory in February 1956, retaliating for commando raids originating there, Nasser turned to the Soviets for help.

Khrushchev was interested in competing with the United States for influence among the Arabs. He accepted the challenge of the Baghdad Pact and the opportunity Nasser provided. The Soviets were prepared to provide economic and military assistance to nonaligned leaders who sought an alternative to dependence on the West or a more radical model for rapid development. In September 1955 they shipped Czech arms to Egypt. By inducing Iraq to join in the effort to contain the Soviet Union, the Americans had facilitated Soviet penetration of the region.

As Nasser's relations with the communist bloc warmed, the United States continued to court him. He and other African and Asian leaders who mastered the art manipulated the competing superpowers that contributed generously to their treasuries, their technology, and their weapons. With Czech arms on the way, Nasser found the Americans eager to build a dam that would allow him to irrigate and electrify the Nile Valley. He wanted the aid, but with Soviet assistance available, he saw no need to trim his sails to comfort Washington. The arms deal, a slap at the West, had enhanced his stature among the Arab masses. He promised to do something unpleasant to Israel. To demonstrate further his independence from the United States, he ignored American pleas and recognized the People's Republic of China in May 1956.

Giving foreign aid to countries that demonstrated no gratitude, that performed in a manner contrary to American wishes, was not popular with a Congress that never liked giving money to foreigners—and Nasser had blatantly antagonized politicians sympathetic to Israel or Chiang. Eisenhower and Dulles, skeptical of Soviet willingness to commit the necessary funds, decided to back away from Nasser's dam project.

Enraged, Nasser nationalized the Suez Canal, owned by a British-controlled corporation, hoping to finance the dam with the canal's revenues. Eisenhower and Dulles responded cautiously; British prime minister Anthony Eden did not. To the Americans, the question of who controlled the canal was less important than keeping the Arabs friendly, keeping oil flowing to the West, and keeping Soviet influence out of the region. To Eden, the canal was a critical artery linking West European industry to Persian Gulf oil. As he had opposed the appeasement of Hitler in the 1930s, he was determined not to appease Nasser, who had committed a wanton act of aggression. He was convinced that Nasser, like Hitler, could be stopped only with force.

London found willing accomplices in Paris and Tel Aviv. The French shared British concerns about the canal and were angered by Nasser's support for Algerian efforts to gain independence from France. The Israelis were troubled by the shipment of Soviet arms to Egypt and the refusal of the United States to provide additional arms or assurances. Israeli leaders perceived Eisenhower to have abandoned the Jews as the Arabs prepared to destroy them. They would not watch passively. After the Holocaust, never again!

On October 29, 1956, while much of the world focused on the Soviet response to the Hungarian Revolution, Israeli tanks raced across the Sinai and quickly destroyed much of the Egyptian Army. The following day, in a move coordinated with Israel, Britain and France warned Israeli and Egyptian forces to stay away from the canal and, in a move to "protect" the canal, attacked nearby Egyptian forces. America's allies had resorted to a classic nineteenth-century means of coping with unruly natives.

Eisenhower was in an extraordinarily difficult position. To support the British, French, and Israelis would alienate the Arab world and much of the rest of the Third World. It would mean abandoning traditional opposition to imperialism and allow the Soviets to claim the high ground in the region as the sole supporters of the Arabs against Western and Zionist imperialism. It would give Khrushchev, who was threatening the British and French with nuclear weapons, an enormous propaganda victory at a time when the world should have been railing against Soviet brutality in Hungary. Instead, the United States chose to lead the attack on the British and French in the United Nations. For once the United States and the Soviet Union were on the same side, denouncing imperialism as they vied for influence in the Arab world. The British, the French, and ultimately the Israelis withdrew under American pressure. Relations with its NATO allies might never be the same, but the United States had preserved its influence in the Middle East. Unfortunately, from Washington's perspective, so had the Soviets, who seemed poised to improve their position in the region.

In the aftermath of the Suez crisis, Eisenhower asked for and received from Congress a resolution declaring the Middle East a vital national interest. It gave the president discretion to send American troops to aid any country in the region that asked for help to repel "overt armed aggression from any nation controlled by international communism." The "Eisenhower Doctrine," designed to check Nasser's influence, was applicable to no known situation. It was used in 1957 when the king of Jordan, threatened by pro-Nasser forces within his country, appealed for help, claiming that the danger came from "international communism." The U.S. Sixth Fleet showed the flag in the eastern Mediterranean and the king received $10 million in aid.

A more dangerous situation shook Washington in the summer of 1958. The Christian president of Lebanon had been appealing for help against pro-Nasser forces. There was no evidence that international communism was involved, but Egypt and Syria, with links to the Soviets, were. Eisenhower was unresponsive until a coup in Iraq substituted a pro-Nasser, pro-Soviet regime for the one that had signed the Baghdad Pact. Confronted by a situation in which Nasser seemed to have united the Arab world, eliminated the West's principal ally, and enhanced Soviet influence in the area, the United States sent marines to Lebanon. Khrushchev, fearing American intervention in Iraq, threatened war. Quickly, the United States determined that the Soviets were not involved in the coup and that the new Iraqi leaders had no interest in becoming a Soviet satellite. Recognition of the Baghdad regime by Washington defused the crisis. Nasser, fearing a permanent American military presence in the region, used his influence to calm his friends in Lebanon and Syria, facilitating the withdrawal of the marines.

The American position in the Middle East, as it developed in the 1950s, was that of a traditional great power. The principal interest of the United States was in an uninterrupted flow of oil at a reasonable price. To that end, it desired order and stability—exotic commodities in the Middle East, as in most of the developing world. The problems for American policymakers would have been similar even if the Soviet Union had not existed. Intra-Arab rivalries, especially those involving Egypt, Syria, and Iraq, states seeking to lead pan-Arab movements, but also between secular and religious nations, would have created turbulence. These issues bubbled in a cauldron in which the addition of Israel's presence guaranteed an explosive mixture.

The Soviets played the classic role of the competing but weaker great power. It was unable to dislodge the United States from the region, but it could and did facilitate local resistance to American visions, raising the cost of the Pax Americana. To Arabs dissatisfied with their relations with the United States, the Soviet Union provided an alternative.

Two other examples, Indonesia and the Congo (Zaire), illustrate Khrushchev's confidence that the Soviets could compete on the periphery. Moscow had no historic concerns or vital interests in either, but to establish footholds in Southeast Asia and Africa, to demonstrate that the Soviet Union was a world power, Khrushchev committed Soviet resources at critical moments in the development of both countries.

Sukarno of Indonesia had hosted the Bandung Conference of non-aligned states in 1955 and perceived himself to be a world leader. Dissatisfied with the extent and conditions of American aid, he flew off to Moscow, where Khrushchev offered a $100 million credit. Sukarno then attempted to use the Soviet offer to encourage greater generosity in Washington.

American leaders were troubled by Sukarno's flirtation with the Soviets, his support from Indonesian Communists, and his claims to Dutch-held territory in New Guinea. The United States increased its aid in 1957 but was unwilling to provide the Indonesians with weapons they might use against the Dutch. Khrushchev was delighted to provide the desired arms and became principal supplier to the Indonesian military.

Eisenhower and Dulles preferred several smaller states to a unified Indonesia aligned with international communism. In 1958 the CIA, Eisenhower's weapon of choice, was instructed to support Sumatran secession. Sumatran rebels were armed and trained, and CIA-operated planes flew bombing missions in their support. The effort failed and was exposed when one of the bombers was shot down, the pilot captured, and Washington's efforts to deny culpability failed. Khrushchev was delighted—although the Soviets gained little from wooing Sukarno.

Khrushchev was less successful in the Congo, where the Soviets were outmatched by the CIA. Belgium granted the Republic of the Congo independence in June 1960. Its first premier was Patrice Lumumba, a man American Africanists perceived as the only national leader in a country threatened seriously by tribalism. No one in the Eisenhower administration thought American economic interests in the Congo were endangered—or perceived of strategic interests in Central Africa.

Shortly after the Congo became independent, Lumumba realized the Belgians were not willing to surrender their holdings. They reinforced their troops, engineered the secession of Katanga province, the center of European investment, and prevented Lumumba from going there. He appealed successively to the United States, the United Nations, and the Soviet Union.

Initially, the Americans and Soviets both deferred to the United Nations—which proved ineffective. Lumumba appealed again to the Soviet Union, and Khrushchev could resist no longer. He sent large quantities of equipment and technicians. The American perception of Lumumba and of the strategic import of the Congo changed immediately. Despite the fact that Lumumba had appealed to Washington first, the Eisenhower administration decided he was a dangerous radical likely to facilitate Communist inroads into Central Africa, and the Congo became the keystone of sub-Saharan Africa. Once again, the value of a peripheral area was enhanced by imbuing it with the weight of a dozen or more countries in its vicinity. Its loss might mean loss of the region, of the continent. The world balance of power was at stake. The Soviets had to be stopped.

Eisenhower hoped the United Nations could manage with the assistance of a CIA plan to assassinate Lumumba. The president of the Congo was persuaded to dismiss Lumumba, who tried unsuccessfully to seize power. UN forces closed the airports, preventing Soviet planes from moving pro-Lumumba forces. Lumumba was placed under house arrest and eventually murdered at the direction of Joseph Mobutu (later Mobutu Sese Seke), the CIA-selected strong man. The Soviets had been outmatched. They could not match American ability to project power into the region.

Khrushchev craved respect for his country and worked to plant the Hammer and Sickle around the world. The desire to make the Soviet Union a power at least equal to the United States drove him to invest Soviet resources in remote regions of dubious importance. He would not concede the periphery to the Americans. Soviet activity in the Third World raised the stakes for the United States. The American national security apparatus was eager to counter it. Because Soviet capabilities were limited in the 1950s, the American response was usually a CIA operation. Some were arguably successful, as in Iran, Guatemala, and the Congo; others, as in Indonesia, were not.

In the 1950s in Europe, the central arena for both the United States and the Soviet Union, the great power contest was stalemated. Both countries looked to the Third World for opportunities to gain an edge, to test the allure of their ideas and the skill of their operatives. If one superpower became involved, a peripheral concern became an important one. The other had to demonstrate its resolve, lest its image as a would-be hegemon would be questioned, its ability to lead its bloc suspect, as indeed occurred when Mao challenged Soviet leadership and de Gaulle refused to defer to the Americans.

13

ON THE BRINK OF NUCLEAR WAR

THE TENSEST YEARS of the Cold War were probably 1958 to 1962, when issues over Berlin and Cuba led the United States and the Soviet Union to the brink of nuclear war. Situations arose in which a rash action by an aggressive officer might have led to the incineration of much of the world. Nikita Khrushchev provoked each of these crises. He delighted in calling Berlin the "testicles" of the West: "Every time I give them a yank they holler." Cuba provided a convenient platform for placing nuclear missiles that would teach Americans what it felt like to live under the shadow of the bomb.

Although provoked by the Soviets, these crises are best understood by recognizing the interactive quality of Soviet actions, the extent to which they were responses to American policies. Khrushchev and his colleagues feared a resurgent Germany, especially the likelihood that West Germans would gain access to the nuclear weapons the United States was stockpiling on German soil. They were anxious to negotiate a settlement of European issues that would recognize the status quo, including a divided Germany. Soviet overtures were unwelcome in Washington. Provoking a crisis was a crude and dangerous way of winning Eisenhower's attention, but Khrushchev was not known for finesse.

Similarly, widespread evidence of American efforts to overthrow the regime of Fidel Castro in Cuba led Soviet and Cuban leaders to anticipate an American attack in 1962. CIA and U.S.-backed émigré operations against Cuba were frequent, the development of contingency plans for an invasion of Cuba by American forces was known to Soviet and Cuban intelligence, and plans for major U.S. military exercises in the Caribbean in the fall were no secret. Among Khrushchev's reasons for installing nuclear missiles on the island was the desire to protect his newfound Cuban friend.

Each step the Soviets and Americans took was based on an assessment of the other's intentions. Soviet activity in Berlin and Cuba was prompted by Soviet perceptions of German and American aggressiveness. Perceiving themselves as defenders of the status quo in Europe and Cuba, Soviet leaders sought to forestall change in both while simultaneously using missiles in Cuba to redress the strategic balance. American officials who sent missiles to Germany out of fear of superior Soviet conventional capabilities could not conceive of Khrushchev's pressures on Berlin as defensive. When they determined to destroy Castro, they were defending vital American interests in the Western Hemisphere. As always, each saw the other's actions as threatening, its own as defensive.

Late in 1958 Khrushchev announced that the Western powers had six months in which to negotiate the status of West Berlin with East German authorities. After the deadline, Moscow would sign a separate treaty with the East Germans, leaving them responsible for Western access to Berlin. Dulles warned that the West would use force if necessary to ensure access to Berlin. Khrushchev replied that the West would be starting World War III. Eisenhower defused the potential crisis by inviting Khrushchev to visit the United States, where he spent a weekend at Camp David and toured Hollywood. Security precautions cheated him out of an opportunity to visit Disneyland, but he lifted the deadline on Berlin nonetheless. The issue, however, did not go away. Hopes of resolving it at a summit planned for May 1960 were dashed when Khrushchev walked out of the meeting, ostensibly angered over the downing of an American spy plane, a U-2, over Soviet territory on the eve of the conference.

Closer to home, the Eisenhower administration became intensely irritated with Castro, the Cuban leader once viewed as a Robin Hood–like figure who, in January 1959, had liberated his people from an evil Fulgencio Batista. Castro's government was passionately nationalistic and moderately leftist. In Latin America, that meant suspicion of the United States, long-time regional hegemon—and especially American economic power. But initially the regime was non-Communist, including many proponents of democratic capitalism. Quickly, however, moderates gave way to radicals, the pace of reform accelerated, and the prospects for liberal democracy dimmed. The Cuban Communist Party was legalized and began to play a minor role in implementing Castro's programs, but the CIA found no evidence of a Soviet role, no evidence that Castro was a Communist, easing Eisenhower's concerns.

In February 1960, however, responding to Castro's overtures, Khrushchev sent his deputy premier to Cuba. A Cuban-Soviet trade agreement followed—enough to galvanize Eisenhower. An alternative to Castro, a government of the kind of democratic reformers who had helped overthrow Batista, was necessary. Eisenhower would not send in the marines, as Teddy Roosevelt and Woodrow Wilson might have, but he had the CIA.

Eisenhower preferred minimizing overt American involvement when reining in unruly Third World leaders. As with Iran and Guatemala, he wanted the CIA to orchestrate a coup by local forces more receptive to American political and economic values. Soon the CIA was training Cuban exiles for the invasion of their homeland. Eisenhower would not send them ashore until they had formed a government-in-exile. In the interim, Washington initiated a series of economic pressures, beginning with reduction of the quota of Cuban sugar the United States was committed to buy. Ultimately, the CIA developed a series of bizarre plots to assassinate Castro, including subcontracting the assignment to the Mafia.

American hostility served Castro well, rallying the Cuban people behind him and gaining the support of a wary Khrushchev. In May 1960 Cuba and the Soviet Union established diplomatic relations and Khrushchev warned Washington not to attack Cuba. Soviet leaders were still skeptical about Castro but enjoyed the opportunity to twit the United States in its sphere of interest. A pattern that men such as Nasser and Sukarno had exploited developed quickly. As Washington intensified its pressures on Castro, he turned more and more to the Soviet bloc. Unlike Nasser and Sukarno, in late 1960 or early 1961 Castro decided to become a Marxist-Leninist.

In December 1960 Havana declared its support for Soviet foreign policy, and in January 1961 Castro ordered a drastic reduction of American Embassy personnel. Eisenhower angrily withdrew American recognition of the Castro regime, and plans for CIA-sponsored exile invasion gained momentum. As he prepared to leave office, he was warned that the operation might soon become irreversible—but in a few days, Castro became John F. Kennedy's problem.

The key player in the interaction between Cuba, the United States, and the Soviet Union was Castro. He dominated the Cuban revolution and decided correctly that the United States would be an obstacle and the Soviet Union might prove a useful counterweight. He needled the Americans and reeled in Khrushchev. He played the great powers with consummate skill and by declaring himself a Communist made it difficult for Moscow to abandon him.

American policy might have been wiser, but American political culture precluded support for the radical revolution Castro wanted. Friendly relations were not readily imaginable between Cuban revolutionaries weaned on tales of American imperialism and American leaders convinced of the benign role their country had played since liberating Cuba in 1898. A less hostile policy might have lessened Castro's need for Soviet assistance and left Khrushchev less of an opportunity for mischief. The odds were poor: Soviet-American competition was simply too easy for a clever leader like Castro to exploit, and American responses to a whiff of communism too reflexive.

Immediately after the election, Khrushchev reached out to President-elect Kennedy. The Soviets were eager to signal their desire to work with the new administration, to give and gain assurances on the status quo in Europe, to establish mutually acceptable guidelines for peaceful competition in the Third World. They hoped the Kennedy administration would be more respectful of Soviet interests, more accepting of the Soviet right to compete for influence around the world.

Soviet hopes for accommodation were matched in Washington but not on Khrushchev's terms. No less than its predecessors, the Kennedy administration was committed to containing communism, preventing the expansion of Soviet influence and maintaining American strategic superiority.

Kennedy and his advisers were profoundly troubled by Khrushchev's threats regarding Berlin and Soviet activities in the Congo, Laos, and Cuba. They found Khrushchev's signals confusing, a mixture of appeals for peaceful co-existence and attempts to intimidate. However peaceful his intentions may have been, American analysts perceived him as a volatile and dangerous adversary.

In his first days in office, Kennedy found crises in Laos, the Congo, and Cuba, all tilting toward the Soviet Union. CIA efforts in Laos had been counterproductive, destabilizing a neutralist government and stimulating Soviet and Vietnamese efforts to support the Laotian Left. The Agency was faring better in the Congo, where efforts to eliminate Lumumba were on track. Implementation of the planned exile invasion of Cuba required the new president's immediate attention. If the exiles were not sent in, there would be a "disposal problem"—one could not simply send hundreds of armed Cubans back to Miami.

Kennedy and his advisers considered themselves supportive of social revolution in the developing world but not if Communists were involved. Castro had brought known Communists into his government and opened the door to Soviet influence in the Caribbean. He had betrayed the dream of freedom that drove the Cuban people when they rose against Batista. His regime had to be destroyed.

In meetings among Kennedy's advisers, the CIA and the Department of Defense pressed for orders to proceed with the exile invasion. Dean Rusk, secretary of state, suspecting that American involvement would be exposed, preferred economic sanctions. But Kennedy feared that if he rejected the plan after criticizing Eisenhower for "losing" Cuba, he would be perceived as weak. To meet Rusk's concerns, the operation was whittled back, the invaders denied air cover the CIA deemed essential. On April 17, 1961, the Cuban exiles were sent ashore at the Bay of Pigs.

Air raids by CIA-operated bombers two days earlier had failed to eliminate the tiny Cuban Air Force but had prompted a Cuban military alert and protest to the United Nations. A raid scheduled for the morning of the invasion was canceled to avoid further implicating the United States. The exiles landed on inhospitable terrain without air cover and communication equipment, lost in the landing. The Cuban Air Force pinned down the invaders, and the Cuban Army mopped them up. The predicted uprising of the Cuban people, essential to the success of the operation, never occurred. The CIA scheme was poorly conceived, and implementation was undermined by administration modifications. Only a major assault by American forces could have succeeded—and Kennedy was not ready for that.

The Bay of Pigs invasion was a humiliating defeat for the United States. Having castigated its British and French allies for resorting to atavistic imperialism at Suez, American leaders violated their much beloved principle of nonintervention. Adlai Stevenson, American ambassador to the United Nations, having denied vehemently that his government would ever commit such an act, was greatly embarrassed to discover that his president had deceived him. There was little room for moral imagination in the White House during the Cold War.

Castro's popularity with his people increased, as did his appeal to Khrushchev. In July 1961 a Soviet-Cuban alliance was announced. With Washington's assistance, Castro transformed revolutionary Cuba from an irritant into a powder keg.

After accepting responsibility for the Cuban debacle, Kennedy agreed to a June summit meeting with Khrushchev in Vienna. Whatever good intentions either may have had evaporated in an atmosphere of confrontation. Khrushchev, insisting that socialism was on the rise, accused Kennedy of trying to deny the Soviet Union the fruits of impending victory. Kennedy denied the Soviets a right to support any new radical movements that might emerge. Surprisingly in that context, they were able to agree to neutralize Laos.

The most troublesome issue at Vienna was Berlin. Khrushchev was convinced that Kennedy could be pushed around, that he was inexperienced and less intelligent than Eisenhower. He presented him with an ultimatum, threatening to sign a peace treaty with the East Germans that would terminate Western access to Berlin. Kennedy replied that the United States would stand by its commitment. Each man warned that war would follow if the other did not back down. Each went home to take steps to increase the credibility of his threat.

Kennedy's advisers had been preparing for a crisis over Berlin. Dean Acheson, Truman's secretary of state, had been consulted, and he insisted the Western position on Germany and West Berlin was nonnegotiable; American forces should be mobilized to demonstrate a willingness to fight. Kennedy thought Acheson rigid, that agreement to negotiate was superior to brinksmanship. He was not willing to surrender anything of substance, but before the Vienna summit he had thought negotiations would ease tensions. Khrushchev's attempts to intimidate him in Vienna provoked a more Achesonian, macho response.

On July 25, 1961, Kennedy spoke on national television, explaining the importance of Berlin and declaring the American military position there and access to Berlin as nonnegotiable. He then announced a large increase in American conventional forces, expanding the draft and ordering a partial mobilization of the reserves. He warned the Soviets against miscalculating the determination of the United States to preserve its position in Germany. Khrushchev had created the crisis, and the decision for war or peace would have to be made in Moscow.

Khrushchev retreated immediately. He sent assurances that he did not want war and called for an easing of tensions. He promised to take no military action and softened his position on Berlin: the Soviets would not "infringe upon any lawful interests of the Western powers. Any barring of access to West Berlin, any blockade of West Berlin is entirely out of the question."

Even as Khrushchev spoke, the crisis took a new direction. West Berlin had long been the principal escape route for East Germans fleeing to the West. In July, fearful that the West would surrender to Khrushchev's threats, thirty thousand East Germans slipped into West Berlin. On August 12 four thousand crossed into West Berlin. The East German regime, faced with collapse, begged Khrushchev for permission to staunch the flow.

Soviet analysts examining Kennedy's speech of July 25 noted he had said nothing of guaranteeing access between East and West Berlin. They decided to gamble. They would block access between the Western and Soviet sectors of Berlin, preventing escape from the East—and hope the American response would not be violent. On August 13 barriers started going up, and the United States did not respond. No vital American interest was threatened. The Soviet gambit worked, and barbed wire obstacles became the Berlin Wall. The crisis subsided. The United States would not attack the barriers, would not take the offensive when the stakes were very high for Khrushchev. He achieved his minimum goal, an end to the bleeding of the East German regime.

American strategic superiority left Khrushchev little room to maneuver, but the Soviets increased the pressure again in February 1962, harassing Western flights into Berlin. This time talks between Rusk and the Soviet foreign minister, Andrei Gromyko, eased the tension. The issue did not disappear, but Rusk suggested that Moscow might have postponed attempting to resolve it until they had achieved strategic parity. Kennedy and Gromyko were scheduled to meet on October 18, 1962, and the president's advisers wanted him to leave no doubt in Soviet minds that the West was united and would fight if necessary over Berlin. What they did not know was that the United States and the Soviet Union were on the verge of nuclear war over Cuba.

On October 14 a U-2 flight obtained unmistakable evidence that the Soviets were building missile sites in Cuba. For Kennedy, Berlin became a secondary issue. His administration had not been inactive toward Cuba since the Bay of Pigs fiasco. It had worked with modest success to isolate Cuba diplomatically and economically and did little to suppress piratical acts by exiles against Cuban vessels. It was also experimenting with a variety of covert operations designed to humiliate Castro—even murder him. Perhaps most threatening were the contingency plans for American forces to invade the island, of which Soviet and Cuban intelligence services were aware. The Cuban government had reason to be anxious, to allow the Soviets to build missile sites directed against the United States.

Although eager to have Soviet protection against the threat to his regime, Castro preferred to perceive his acceptance of the missiles as a contribution to the international Communist movement, a means to gain a strategic advantage for it. He was doing Khrushchev a favor. Khrushchev and his advisers always insisted, however, that they acted to defend the Cubans—that the missiles, planes, and Soviet combat troops they sent to Cuba were intended to deter an American invasion.

Khrushchev apparently conceived of placing Soviet intermediate range missiles (IRBMs) off the coast of the United States after learning that American IRBMs near the Turkish-Soviet border had become operational.

Something had to be done to minimize the world's perception of American strategic primacy. The fact that Cuba would simultaneously be protected was a collateral virtue. The Soviets did not anticipate a crisis. They expected to install the missiles secretly and confront the United States with a fait accompli, to which Washington would have to acquiesce, however grudgingly.

In late August 1962 the director of the CIA informed Kennedy and his senior advisers that he suspected the Soviets of placing offensive missiles in Cuba. A review of the evidence led Rusk and the others to reject the idea. There was no doubt that the Soviets were providing the Cubans with military equipment, but they had been warned that offensive weapons would not be tolerated, and there was no inclination to believe they would take the risk.

As the midterm election of 1962 approached, the Republican opposition was increasingly critical of the administration's failure to eliminate the Communist regime in Cuba. Kennedy's aides argued that Cuba was not a threat and dismissed allegations of Soviet missiles. They discounted mounting evidence of Khrushchev's gamble. On October 14 Kennedy's national security adviser assured a television audience that there was no evidence the Soviets were preparing an offensive capability in Cuba. That day the U-2 returned with photos of a missile site under construction. The United States, and especially the Kennedy administration, faced catastrophe.

Kennedy and his senior advisers met to try to determine what the Soviets were doing and how the United States might respond. Contingency plans called for an invasion or an air strike, and the military commenced preparations for both. There was considerable support for an air strike, but the opposition prevailed. Secretary of Defense Robert McNamara argued that Soviet missiles in Cuba meant little more than Soviet missiles in Russia. Should the Soviets launch an attack, the United States would destroy the Soviet Union no matter where the attack originated. Unmoved by the contention that missiles in Cuba might undermine the U.S. strategic advantage, he insisted strategic parity was inevitable.

After two days of discussion, even McNamara was persuaded that a strong response was necessary. For domestic political reasons as well as his image abroad, the president had to demonstrate that the United States could not be deceived and challenged with impunity. The choice of options narrowed to an air strike against the missile sites or a blockade, to be followed by an air strike or invasion if the Soviets did not respond adequately. Dean Acheson, supported by the military leadership, called for military action. Ultimately, not convinced that an air strike would suffice, fearful of an irrational response by Khrushchev if Soviet troops were killed by it, and hoping to avoid an invasion, Kennedy opted to begin with a blockade. American forces began to move into position, and on October 22 the Soviets, the American people, and the rest of the world were informed.

To knowledgeable people everywhere there came an awareness that they hovered on the edge of extinction. The danger of nuclear incineration hung over Rusk's briefing of the ambassadors of nonaligned nations. With a sense that they might never see each other again, each ambassador shook Rusk's hand on the way out, murmuring a word of hope. The initiative had returned to Khrushchev. His choice was war or surrender.

The Soviet leader and his advisers were taken by surprise and badly shaken by Kennedy's address. Soviet intelligence had failed to pick up any indication that the United States had discovered the missiles. Firing the missiles and provoking certain retaliation against the Soviet Union was inconceivable. The central question was what could be salvaged. Was some sort of face-saving deal possible? Would the Americans use the opportunity to invade Cuba, and, if so, how would the Soviet Union respond?

Initially, Moscow denied the charges, condemned the blockade as piracy, sent submarines to probe the blockade and ordered Soviet forces in Cuba readied for combat. They were 42,000 strong, far in excess of American intelligence estimates, and armed with tactical nuclear weapons, to be used at the discretion of the local commander. Castro mobilized his reserves, tripling his forces under arms to 270,000. Construction at the missile sites accelerated. World War III was rapidly approaching.

The U.S. Navy used low-explosive depth charges to force Soviet submarines to the surface. The Strategic Air Command (SAC) was put on full alert, with the order given "in the clear." Khrushchev could have no illusions as to the seriousness of American intent. He chose not to challenge the blockade. On October 25 the last Soviet ships heading for Cuba turned back.

Kennedy and his advisers were greatly relieved by reports of Soviet ship movements, but they were also aware that Soviet forces in Cuba were working around the clock to get their missiles operational. The United States would have to attack before any of them were ready, an eventuality estimated to be only two or three days away. The Soviets were informed of American intent. Castro, urging Khrushchev to stand firm, took refuge in a bomb shelter in the Soviet Embassy.

On October 26 the senior KGB officer in Washington suddenly contacted John Scali, ABC's State Department reporter, to ask if his friends in the State Department would be willing to offer a public pledge not to invade Cuba if the Soviets removed the missiles and allowed UN verification. After receiving the message, Rusk thought a breakthrough was possible and sent a favorable response. Later that day, Khrushchev sent a cable indicating his awareness of the danger of the situation and his willingness to negotiate. He implied that if the United States agreed not to invade Cuba, the missiles could be removed. That night Robert Kennedy, the president's brother, met with the Soviet ambassador, who indicated that removal of the American missiles in Turkey might help resolve the matter. The president authorized his brother to tell the Soviets he had considered removing the missiles and expected to do so shortly after the crisis ended.

On the morning of October 27 a second cable from Khrushchev demanded that the missiles in Turkey be removed as a condition for removal of the missiles in Cuba. Shortly afterward, Kennedy's advisers were informed that a U-2 had been shot down over Cuba. Later that morning, for the first time, low-level reconnaissance flights were fired on. The advisers concluded that the Soviet position was stiffening and military action might still be necessary. Acheson and American military leaders suspected the Soviets were stalling until some of the missiles were operational. They still favored air strikes and an invasion.

That afternoon, the president's advisers agreed to a proposal offered by Robert Kennedy. Khrushchev's second cable would be ignored, and the president would agree to the terms implied in the first cable. Robert Kennedy informed the Soviet ambassador that his brother was prepared to give the required assurances that the United States would not invade Cuba, but he could not remove the missiles from Turkey unilaterally. Nonetheless the president was confident that NATO would withdraw them shortly. If, on the other hand, the Soviets did not agree promptly to remove their missiles from Cuba, the United States would remove them. Although Khrushchev was not told, plans for an air strike on October 29 or 30 had been developed. Again, the decision for war or peace rested with the Soviet leader—unless one of his officers or an American naval or SAC commander acted precipitously.

On Sunday morning, October 28, it was all over. Khrushchev announced he ordered the missiles to be dismantled and returned to the Soviet Union. The joy in Washington was not matched in Cuba, where Soviet officers wept at the news and Castro was enraged. He never permitted UN supervision or verification of the removal of the missiles. The United States never gave assurances that it would not invade Cuba and remained hostile to the Cuban regime for a quarter of a century after the Cold War had ended. Nonetheless, the gravest crisis of the Cold War had ended with a victory for the forces of peace.

In 1962 Khrushchev brought the world close to nuclear war. He gambled impulsively, risking the lives of hundreds of millions of people. He acted deceitfully, putting missiles in Cuba while sending Kennedy assurances he would do nothing of the sort. He hoped to score a diplomatic and military coup against the United States. Kennedy's response brought the world a step closer to disaster, perhaps unnecessarily. McNamara was probably right—that strategic parity between the United States and the Soviet Union was inevitable and that the gap was merely being closed sooner rather than later; that Soviet missiles in Cuba were strategically tolerable. It might be argued that the only grave threat posed by discovery of the missiles was to the political future of the Kennedy administration; that the Republican opposition would use the missiles, the existence of which the administration had consistently denied, to ride the Cuban issue to victory in the congressional elections in 1962 and in the presidential election of 1964.

Once the administration decided on a strong response, its plans were conceived carefully and executed with an appropriate balance of courage and flexibility. Interestingly, Kennedy kept his flexibility secret from the American people. It was six years before they learned he had agreed American missiles would come out of Turkey, and more than a quarter of a century before Americans, including most of his advisers, learned that his brother had discussed the trade with the Soviet ambassador before Khrushchev offered it. Obsessed with a need to present a public image of toughness, Kennedy preferred to have the American people believe he had won in a man-to-man showdown with the Soviet premier.

The missile crisis came to be seen as a watershed in Soviet-American relations. Both American and Soviet leaders thereafter acted with greater prudence. A Moscow-Washington "hot line" was set up to permit direct and immediate communication between the leaders. Agreement was reached on a treaty banning atmospheric nuclear testing by the superpowers. These may not have been major steps, but they reversed the direction of the previous two years, suggesting that the future might well be one of peaceful coexistence. Further improvement of relations would depend on the performance of each country, on the respect and confidence that might develop between its leaders. Unanticipated in 1963 was the rapid disappearance of both Kennedy and Khrushchev, the one murdered and the other forcibly retired by his colleagues.

There were fleeting moments of crisis in the years that followed, but the United States and the Soviet Union deterred each other by spending enormous sums on nuclear warheads and delivery systems sufficient to destroy each other several times over. Out of this emerged the strategic doctrine of Mutual Assured Destruction (MAD), based on the fact that each side would be vulnerable to destruction by the other side, no matter which one started a war. Given such incentive to avoid direct confrontation, they indulged in costly games on the periphery, largely in areas where neither had a vital interest. There, in countries such as Vietnam, Afghanistan, and Ethiopia, they brought misery to the local peoples, squandered the lives of their own young, and expended resources desperately needed for the shoring up of their own societies.

14

VIETNAM AND THE LESSONS OF GREAT POWER ARROGANCE

MERICA'S WAR IN Vietnam was an example of great power arrogance. Neither American leaders nor American scholars knew or cared much about the people of Vietnam, their history, their culture, or their aspirations. Vietnam was of no intrinsic importance to the United States. In the years when France controlled Indochina, it allowed little foreign involvement in the region's economy. American business acquired no stake there. The area was potentially rich in natural resources, but there was nothing there that could not be obtained elsewhere or that the locals could afford to deny to the world market. Similarly, the region was of minimal strategic importance. A case could be made for keeping Cambodia, Laos, and Vietnam—or any place else on earth—from being controlled by an adversary, whether Japan in 1941 or China or the Soviet Union in the Cold War. French control was desirable, but if all of Indochina were hostile to the United States, the shift in the world balance of power would be imperceptible. No vital American interest would be threatened. Nonetheless, more than fifty thousand Americans gave their lives in a war in Indochina, as did millions of Cambodians, Laotians, and Vietnamese.

Once a nation develops the ability to project its power to distant regions of the globe, to intervene in the affairs of other peoples, the temptation to do so seems nearly irresistible—at least until its leaders are sobered by disaster. American power in the first two decades after World War II, relative and absolute, was extraordinary. No place in the world was beyond the reach of the United States. And for American policymakers the lessons of the past demonstrated that their nation had a responsibility to use its power to stop aggressors and to thwart those who would extend totalitarian systems.

American leaders discovered Indochina early in World War II, when the Japanese intruded on the French empire. Japanese pressures on Southeast Asia worried Franklin Roosevelt, who feared their maneuvers would distract the British from the task of containing Germany in Europe, North Africa, and the Middle East. Toward the end of the war, when the retreat of Japanese forces was imminent, Roosevelt suggested that the people of Indochina be put under a UN trusteeship rather than be subjected again to French imperialism. The few Americans who reached the area before the end of the war discovered a well-organized resistance movement that had harassed the Japanese and had no intention of submitting to the French. In Vietnam in particular, the will to independence was strong and deemed worthy of American support. Indeed, the leader of the Vietnamese resistance, Ho Chi Minh, worked with American intelligence operatives on the eve of Japan's surrender.

When the war ended, the French returned, determined to reassert their control. French leaders warned Washington that opposition to French suppression of the Vietnamese independence movement would alienate the French people, strengthen the French Communists, and, conceivably, drive France into the arms of the Soviets. Ho invoked Thomas Jefferson and the Declaration of Independence, to no avail. He was, after all, a Communist, and Vietnam was distant and unimportant. American leaders intended France to be a major partner in the new world order they envisaged in the late 1940s. French leaders angered by American opposition to their imperial vision could undermine American plans for Europe. The United States chose to facilitate the return of French power to Southeast Asia, subordinating traditional American anti-imperialism to the exigencies of great power politics, abandoning the principles on which America's claim to moral superiority, to exceptionalism, had rested.

When the French failed and were forced to come to terms with Ho's Viet Minh in 1954, the United States decided to do the job itself.

Eisenhower and Dulles imagined that the United States could intervene in Vietnam untainted by colonialism and help those Vietnamese nationalists who wanted independence not only from France but from international communism as well. The president and his secretary of state were prepared to concede Vietnam above the 17th parallel, where the Viet Minh had regrouped, to Ho's Communist regime. They intended to build a separate noncommunist nation to the south where the French and their collaborators had regrouped.

Indochina became important to the Eisenhower administration because it was perceived in 1954 as the site of the next round in the battle with the Sino-Soviet bloc. The Communists were quiet in Europe and lacked a toehold in Africa or the Middle East. They had been stopped in Korea but retained enormous potential for mischief in East Asia. Chinese support for the Viet Minh against the French as well as Chinese and Soviet recognition of Ho's regime in 1950 helped shape Eisenhower's expectations. He and his aides overlooked Soviet and Chinese indifference to Vietnamese goals at Geneva. Domestic political pressures from the Republican Right also shaped their need to act: those who found the Truman administration guilty of losing China did not want to be charged with losing Indochina.

Indochina may have lacked economic or strategic import, but, by applying his domino theory, Eisenhower concluded that if it fell to the Communists, all of Southeast Asia would follow. That would put at risk the gateway to South Asia and the western Pacific. He appears to have developed a rationale for intervention after he had decided to intervene and to have strained to offer something plausible to the American people. In 1956 and 1958 his National Security Council dutifully declared that the security of the United States would be endangered by Communist domination of Southeast Asia; that the loss of any country there would encourage accommodation by the rest, including more distant India and Japan, hurting the U.S. position in East Asia.

The South Vietnamese regime created by the Eisenhower administration proved an imperfect instrument for achieving American ends. Ngo Dinh Diem, the anticommunist prime minister, failed to become the popular leader who would draw his people away from Ho Chi Minh. The elections mandated by the Geneva accords had to be avoided because

American intelligence estimated that Ho would win 80 percent of the votes. The principle of support for free elections lost its attractiveness in Washington when the victor was likely to be a Communist.

Diem had some success in consolidating control of the South, but his methods alienated much of rural Vietnam and antagonized Buddhist activists, intellectuals, and politicians. American-promoted land reform was less attractive to the peasants than the more radical programs instituted by the Viet Minh. Diem's efforts to root out the Viet Minh infrastructure required villagers to leave their homes and burial grounds to take refuge in "strategic hamlets." Buddhists were angered by the preference enjoyed by Diem's Catholic coreligionists, both in government positions and in religious freedom. Intellectuals and much of the rest of the political elite, repressed by his secret police, turned hostile. There was minimal support for Diem outside the Catholic minority in the cities. The American nation-building experiment in Vietnam was in trouble.

John F. Kennedy shared Eisenhower's views: Indochina had to be denied to the Communists; American antiimperialists could succeed where French imperialists had failed. His first test came in Laos, where Eisenhower's attempts to create a pro-Western government had proven counterproductive. In January 1961 the right-wing general Washington was supporting was on the ropes. Kennedy's advisers concluded that pro-Western forces couldn't win: a neutral Laos was the best possible outcome. The president rejected a major military intervention when the Joint Chiefs, unwilling to fight another limited war, demanded freedom to use nuclear weapons and attack China. Instead, Kennedy sent a carrier into the Gulf of Siam and put forces in Okinawa on alert, signaling to the Soviets American willingness to fight rather than allow a Communist takeover. Khrushchev recognized the risk, did not consider control of Laos worth what it might take to overcome an American escalation, and agreed to settle for a neutral Laos.

Kennedy's willingness to compromise over Laos did not extend to Vietnam. There he would make his stand. Initially, his principal concerns were standing up to Khrushchev and avoiding being labeled "soft on communism." He was troubled by Khrushchev's advocacy of wars of national liberation. Success in Vietnam would teach Khrushchev that the indirect aggression constituted by wars of national liberation did not pay, might erase the embarrassment of failure at the Bay of Pigs, and would ensure Kennedy a second term in the White House.

For Kennedy and his advisers, Vietnam became a convenient ground for demonstrating America's will and power. To those who feared that the United States was intimidated by Soviet missiles and nuclear capability, there would be proof that the Americans would still ride to the rescue, even in places as distant and inhospitable as the jungles of Vietnam. To those at home who worried that a Democratic president would not stand up to the Communists, there would be evidence to the contrary. To the men in Moscow and Beijing who thought they could accomplish through subversion the conquest they dared not seek through overt acts of aggression, there would be a warning that this, too, would fail. In Vietnam, Kennedy could test the counterinsurgency techniques to which he had become attracted, and the Pentagon could test a myriad of technological innovations, products of billions spent on weapons development. The brilliant men who served Kennedy, named the "best and the brightest" by the journalist David Halberstam, were confident that they had the ideas necessary for nation building, to succeed in the great-power contest in Vietnam—and all over the globe.

As they confronted the initial crises inherited from Eisenhower, Kennedy and his advisers found time to focus on Vietnam. They found a deteriorating situation, with the Diem government losing influence and the Viet Minh increasingly active in the South and obtaining support from the North. American intelligence concluded that the insurgency in the South was indigenous and that Ho, while hardly disinterested, was husbanding his resources to strengthen that part of Vietnam he controlled. There was no evidence of significant Chinese or Soviet involvement. Kennedy's colleagues concluded that the insurgency could be defeated at minimal cost to the United States; that an increase in military supplies and advisers to Diem's forces would suffice.

The president began by increasing the number of American military "advisers" in Vietnam, including four hundred members of the special forces, in direct violation of the limits impose by the Geneva agreements. He wanted more aggressive tactics and was untroubled when these required Americans to engage in combat, a further violation of the Geneva agreements. He authorized the dropping of napalm and herbicidal defoli-ants, the former a jellied petroleum product that clung to the skin while it burned, the latter chemicals that would denude the forest, destroy the pro-ductivity of the soil, and have unpredictable effects on humans who came in contact with it.

The Joint Chiefs, skeptical of counterinsurgency operations, called for sending regular combat troops to Vietnam. Diem, apprehensive about being perceived as an American puppet, indicated American combat troops were not needed. But the insurgency became increasingly threatening, and a mis-sion Kennedy sent to assess the situation recommended introducing combat forces in the guise of a flood relief team. Kennedy procrastinated. He did not want to send American troops, he did not want to negotiate with the insur-gents, known as the Viet Cong—and he did not want to risk a Communist victory. Finally he decided to send American "support" units that dribbled in, first by the hundreds and then by the thousands. There were 16,000 when Kennedy died in 1963, more than twenty-five times the amount allowed by the Geneva agreements. And these support units quickly engaged in combat operations. Despite Diem's opposition and Kennedy's reluctance, the United States had taken a major step toward Americanization of the war.

If sending a few thousand troops would suffice to turn things around, it seemed a safe, sensible move, less provocative, less dangerous than a major military escalation, politically wiser than withdrawal. Kennedy and his ad-visers deluded themselves into believing that they were still in control, that they retained their freedom of action. A little military action, however, turned out to be like "a little pregnant." The process could not be reversed easily.

Throughout 1962 the president was told by his aides that American pol-icy was working, that the insurgents had lost their momentum. He was irritated by press accounts that the battle was going less well, that the Diem regime was repressive and corrupt, that reports of its strategic suc-cesses were exaggerated. Angrily, he demanded that the *New York Times* recall its correspondent. He failed in that endeavor but more easily intimi-dated the television networks.

By January 1963 Kennedy was receiving indications that all was not well in Vietnam. His friend Senator Mike Mansfield (D-Mont.) went there at the president's request and confirmed the negative reports of the journalists. He warned that the battle was becoming an American war likely to cost the United States far more in lives and dollars than Vietnam was worth. But the American military advisory group in Vietnam remained optimistic, and the president preferred to hear that his policy was working.

In April 1963 the CIA considered the situation in Vietnam to be "fragile." Its analysts doubted that Diem would carry out the reforms necessary to convert any military successes into "lasting political stability." The fragile situation shattered in June 1963, and not even hundreds of thousands of American troops could put the Saigon regime back together again. Diem's government had become increasingly repressive and was facing widespread Buddhist protests. The Americans urged Diem to be conciliatory. His brother, Ngo Dinh Nhu, urged him to crush the Buddhists. On June 11 a Buddhist priest seated himself cross-legged in a major Saigon intersection, other priests poured gasoline over him, and he set himself afire—an incredible scene that horrified Americans and people all over the world who watched it soon afterward on television.

Pressed by the United States, Diem agreed to end both the special privileges of the Catholic Church and the harassment of Buddhists. The protests intensified and Diem seemed immobilized. His brother was not: on August 21 he sent his security forces into the pagodas. Wielding billy clubs and truncheons, they suppressed the Buddhist movement—to the horror of Kennedy and his advisers. They preferred not to associate the United States with a dictatorship that survived by Gestapo methods. They concluded that it was time to consider alternatives to Diem.

A few days later the American ambassador in Saigon received a cable from Washington containing a thinly veiled instruction to encourage a coup against the Diem regime. He was to inform Vietnamese military leaders that the United States could not long support a government that included Nhu or suppressed Buddhists. Should the government collapse, the generals were assured of a continued flow of supplies. With the arrogance in which great powers can indulge, the Kennedy administration had decided to invite a coup against a regime that had been created by the United States. Heaven, now located on Pennsylvania Avenue, had withdrawn its Mandate from the Diem dynasty.

The generals proved timid, and Kennedy's advisers had second thoughts. The president decided to muddle on, gradually increasing pressure on Diem to liberalize his administration, to rein in his brother. But reports that Nhu was dallying with the Viet Cong generated unease in Washington. Kennedy's men feared that Diem and Nhu might respond to pressure by coming to terms with the National Liberation Front (NLF) and Hanoi and demand that the Americans leave. Once more, advocates of a military coup prevailed. On November 1 the generals launched their operation. In the course of coup, Diem and Nhu were murdered. With their liquidation the American-supported cause in Vietnam had been purged of the stigma of repression.

The United States, a nation whose people had long prided themselves on their adherence to the principles of nonintervention and anti-imperialism, had arrogated to itself the privileges of imperial power. Out of the southern portion of Vietnam it attempted to build a nation. "Southern Vietnam" became "South Vietnam." It designated the leaders of that nation, armed their troops, and had them removed when they did not meet American standards of performance. The best interests of the people of Vietnam were determined by men in Washington. By preventing elections scheduled for 1956, the American government deliberately denied the Vietnamese their only chance to express their preferences peacefully. By introducing American military power into Vietnam, the United States attempted to deny the Vietnamese the right to overthrow a government they had come to despise. The result was to bring extraordinary misery to the Vietnamese, to come close to destroying their country in order to save it from communism.

Eisenhower eagerly seized imperial responsibility in 1955 and warned Kennedy against "losing" Southeast Asia. Kennedy's fear of appearing weak and his own intense anticommunism precluded the alternative of leaving the future of Vietnam to be decided by the Vietnamese. It was Kennedy who began the Americanization of the war, who increased the 600 military advisers Eisenhower had sent to more than 16,000—and Kennedy's men in Vietnam were not merely advising. His death, only a few weeks after that of Diem, left a perilous situation in the hand of Lyndon Johnson.

A popular general, Duong Van Minh, headed the junta that replaced Diem's regime. In the closing weeks of 1963, the level of violence in Vietnam declined as the NLF and Hanoi explored the possibility of negotiated peace with Minh. Relative calm in Vietnam suited Lyndon Johnson. He did not want an escalation of the American role; he did not want a wider war. His principal concern in late 1963 and early 1964 was the presidential election scheduled for 1964—and he wanted to concentrate on his domestic programs, his vision of building the Great Society.

Neither the Vietnamese nor the American military accepted Johnson's priorities. American military men in Saigon were disappointed by Minh's lack of aggressiveness and his resistance to greater American control over his forces. Before long his American military advisers were shopping for a new Vietnamese leader. With their assistance, General Nguyen Khanh mounted a successful coup, and he proved eager to receive American political advice and to participate in covert operations against Hanoi. American aid increased rapidly, but to no avail.

Johnson did not want any major initiatives before November 1964 but could hardly accept the loss of Vietnam during the campaign. The major danger to his election came from the Right, from people such as Senator Barry Goldwater (R-Ariz.), demanding more vigorous prosecution of the war and probably aware of the Pentagon's desire to bomb northern Vietnam. Johnson chose to pose as the peace candidate, the man who would keep extremists from widening the war, costing the United States tens of thousands of casualties. But as the collapse of the Saigon regime loomed, the need for American boys to go over and do the job right, to subject the North to American power, became harder to deny.

Pressure to attack the North mounted through early 1964. Some of the president's advisers thought an attack would demonstrate American resolve and bolster Khanh. The Joint Chiefs wanted to provoke Hanoi into acts that would justify systematic bombing. Ambassador Henry Cabot Lodge Jr. thought nuclear weapons might be necessary. In May Johnson's advisers agreed to an *eventual* program of using force against the North. The principal barrier to an immediate attack was the president's perception of his domestic political needs. When that perception changed, no one could restrain the application of America's great power against the Hanoi regime.

On August 2, 1964, an American destroyer was attacked by North Vietnamese torpedo boats while patrolling in the Gulf of Tonkin, off the coast of North Vietnam. American analysts suggested that the assault was the result of an assumption by North Vietnamese leaders that the ship was involved in clandestine operations such as the South Vietnamese had just completed in the area. The ship was ordered to return to the site of the attack, accompanied by a second U.S. warship. On August 4 the North Vietnamese allegedly launched a second attack. The incident came at night and there was uncertainty as to whether it occurred, but naval authorities assured the president it had (they were wrong). Johnson ordered reprisals against what he called aggression on the high seas. It was an opportunity to demonstrate American power and determination and to undercut Goldwater's criticism. The peace candidate left no doubt he would respond fiercely to provocation.

The incident in the Gulf of Tonkin not only gave the Johnson administration the desired excuse to attack North Vietnam but also provided the occasion for the president to ask Congress for the authority to take whatever action he deemed necessary to protect any state in Southeast Asia. His advisers considered a congressional resolution an essential part of carrying the war to Hanoi. In August the House voted 416–0 and the Senate 88–2 to give Johnson a blank check.

Although Hanoi's role in the insurrection was known to have been marginal, the United States was preparing to go to war against Ho Chi Minh's regime. The war in the South was going badly. Johnson's advisers, excepting only George Ball, undersecretary of state, could not accept defeat, would not countenance American withdrawal. They could not tolerate the "loss" of southern Vietnam to the Communists, its domestic consequences, its impact on the credibility of the American imperium. They could not believe that the greatest power the world had ever known lacked the means to crush a peasant rebellion in what Johnson called some "pissant" country. The historian Frederick Logevall has argued persuasively that they had other choices. Opposition to escalation was broad, including from Vice President Hubert Humphrey, Senate Democratic leaders, the mainstream press, and the country's allies. But Johnson and his advisers chose to invest the revolutionary struggle in Vietnam with the potential of tipping the scales in the world balance of power in favor of international communism. They chose to widen the war, to impose an American vision of their future on an unwilling and uncomprehending Vietnamese people.

On November 3, 1964, Americans gave Lyndon Johnson an enormous victory over Barry Goldwater. In much of the world, men and women concerned with issues of world affairs rejoiced at what they perceived as a victory for peace. In Washington, preparations for war were complete. The president resisted an argument for commencing systematic bombing of the North. The dogs of war strained at their leashes.

Suddenly, on February 7, 1965, the insurgents attacked an American installation at Pleiku, killing seven Americans and wounding more than a hundred others. Johnson immediately ordered attacks on barracks and staging areas in North Vietnam. A few days later he authorized implementation of the full-scale bombing plan. In March two battalions of U.S. Marines went ashore at Danang to protect the airfields. Johnson hoped Hanoi and the Viet Cong could be brought to heel without a major combat role for American ground forces. But intelligence reports indicated that the bombing had not affected Hanoi's will and that North Vietnamese regular army troops were beginning to cross into the South. On April 1 the president approved the use of American troops for offensive operations. On Election Day, November 1964, there had been 25,000 American military men and women in Vietnam. In July 1965 there 75,000. In November there were 165,000 and more on the way. American boys were trying to do what candidate Lyndon Johnson had promised Asian boys would be allowed to do for themselves. Gradually Americans realized they were at war.

Unhappiness with the American role in Vietnam manifested itself as early as March 1965 as student activists, religious pacifists, and academics specializing in Southeast Asian affairs began to challenge the administration. The first antiwar demonstration was mounted in Washington in April. In May there was a national teach-in involving over a hundred college campuses. Opposition to the war grew in intensity as the Americanization of the struggle intensified. Attempts by Johnson and his advisers to counter criticism were often disingenuous, increasing doubts.

Johnson's handling of an unrelated crisis in the Dominican Republic in April and May 1965 further undermined his credibility. The deviousness with which he justified sending in the marines cost him the trust of a powerful ally, Senator J. William Fulbright (D-Ark.), chairman of the Committee on Foreign Relations. Fearing Communists might be turning the Dominican Republic into another Cuba, Johnson first sent a small detachment of marines and then more than twenty thousand soldiers to suppress a mutiny by democratically inclined officers against a conservative military junta. He exaggerated both the danger to Americans resident there and of Communist involvement. Skepticism about Johnson's shifting explanations and distaste for his eagerness to assume imperial responsibilities stimulated Fulbright to reexamine policy toward Vietnam.

Between January 18 and February 18, 1966, Fulbright held six televised hearings on the war. Secretary of State Rusk insisted that the war was an act of aggression by the Hanoi regime and that the United States had commitments to repel that aggression. He argued that the credibility of American commitments all over the world, the whole edifice of postwar collective security, was at stake. Others spoke in support of the administration's policy, but of greatest consequence was the appearance of George Kennan, architect of the containment policy, in opposition. He argued that the war was foolish and might lead to a disastrous encounter with China. He insisted that withdrawal—and, by implication, Communist control of the South—would not hurt any major American interest. The hearings, highlighting the doubts of prominent and highly respected observers, assured millions of Americans of the respectability of dissent.

Johnson and his advisers were unmoved by their critics. Every week scores, sometimes hundreds, of Americans and thousands of Vietnamese died. Billions of dollars that might have been spent on Johnson's vision of a Great Society were drained away. Slowly the fabric of American society strained and was ultimately torn apart as the administration concentrated time, energy, and resources on the war. Around the world, contempt for the United States grew. America the liberator, the protector, was gone, replaced by the brutal oppressor of tiny Vietnam.

Johnson's advisers saw the criticism as a public relations issue. The American public and critics all over the world would have to be pacified with evidence that the president was second to none in his desire for peace. The administration agreed to several bombing halts and accepted or sponsored a series of missions—Canadian, Russian, Hungarian, Polish, and British, as well as American—in search of peace. Johnson offered Vietnam a rural electrification program for the Mekong Valley to rival the Tennessee Valley Authority. But it was all a charade: American terms for peace required surrender of Hanoi's dream of unifying Vietnam, of the NLF's demand for a share of the government in the South, of everything for which the opposition had been fighting and had every expectation of winning.

The massive use of American airpower failed. Estimates by the intelligence community indicated that the bombing had not affected North Vietnamese morale significantly. Equipment destroyed by the bombing was being replaced by the Soviets and the Chinese, who vied with each other for Ho's fealty. To all indications that the military effort was ineffective, the Joint Chiefs replied with demands for more men, more bombs, more freedom to select targets. In June 1966 the president authorized a troop buildup of 431,000. Robert McNamara, his secretary of defense, began to question the value of the escalation. But Johnson was determined to win, irritated by doubters, and turned increasingly to those who assured him the war was going well.

In May 1967 the CIA reported that "short of a major invasion or nuclear attack, there is probably no level of air or naval actions against North Vietnam which Hanoi has determined in advance would be so intolerable that the war had to be stopped." The Communist regime was confident of victory, and the Pentagon's own analysts contended that more American troops would do little good and probably great harm, especially to the economy of South Vietnam.

The United States could not win and could not seem to end the war. As American casualties multiplied, demonstrations, draft resistance, and desertions from the military increased. In the field, the phenomenon of "fragging," of the murder of officers by men resisting being led into battle, spread ominously. In July riots exploded in Newark and Detroit, adding to the sense of a society breaking apart. There were demands that funds being used to kill in Vietnam be used for saving lives at home, for a War on Poverty. It was clear that the government lacked the resources for both the Great Society and Vietnam. In August Johnson averted financial disaster by agreeing to a 10 percent surcharge on income taxes. The response in the public opinion polls was immediate. For the first time, a plurality of Americans, most of those with an opinion, thought the war was a mistake. Pressure to end the war intensified. Even the pope called for a suspension of the bombing.

At the outset of 1968 the military braced for a major North Vietnamese attack at Khesanh, perceived as a replay of the Battle of Dienbienphu in 1954. There the Vietnamese would learn the difference between the United States and France. American military leaders were convinced they were on the verge of victory, that the insurgents no longer had any offensive capability.

The president and his aides received a rude shock on the morning of January 30, while most Vietnamese relaxed during the Tet (lunar New Year) holiday. As Americans focused on the base at Khesanh, the Viet Cong penetrated the American Embassy compound in Saigon, besieging it for six hours before they were overcome. Elsewhere in Saigon, the airport, the presidential palace, and the headquarters of the general staff came under attack. Simultaneously, the insurgents attacked four of the other five major cities, capturing the ancient Citadel in Hue and scores of provincial and district capitals. It was a brilliantly conceived attack that demonstrated that they were far from being liquidated.

The Viet Cong and the North Vietnamese took very heavy losses in their Tet offensive. The Viet Cong did most of the fighting, suffered most of the casualties, and never recovered. All the territory they seized was retaken by South Vietnamese and American troops. The people in the cities did not rise to welcome their Communist liberators. The American military command, pleased by the performance of Vietnamese troops it had trained, claimed victory. In terms of kill ratios and territory controlled, the Americans were unquestionably correct.

Hanoi's hope for a South Vietnamese uprising came to naught, but its secondary target was American public opinion—and with that audience they were strikingly effective. The optimism expressed by the president and military leaders seemed absurd. The war would be endless. Every week in February, at least four hundred Americans were killed in Vietnam, with little indication of any accomplishment. Walter Cronkite, the most respected of American television news commentators, declared the war a hopeless stalemate.

Americans in and out of government were shocked by the demonstration of Viet Cong capability and the failure of the intelligence community to anticipate the attacks. The ability of the Saigon regime to recover was widely doubted. Support for the war eroded within the foreign policy establishment, the "in-and-outers" to whom presidents and cabinet officers were most responsive. The Communists won the psychological victory they sought. Johnson could not hold course.

In March it became clear the president was in political trouble. Eugene McCarthy, the quixotic peace candidate for the Democratic nomination, came close to defeating him in the New Hampshire primary. Robert Kennedy declared his candidacy. Antiwar activists organized massive "Dump Johnson" rallies. Johnson needed to end the war.

In addition, the economy was verging on disaster. There were long-standing balance-of-payments difficulties exacerbated by the war. Gold was flowing out of the country at an alarming rate. Unless there was a tax increase, difficult to obtain in an election year, there would be serious inflation in the United States and possibly a collapse of the international monetary system.

On March 25 a group of leading establishment figures, the so-called Wise Men—highly prominent former government officials—assembled in Washington to be briefed on Vietnam and to advise the president. They concluded that the war was absorbing too much of the nation's energy, too much of its resources. They urged a scaling down of American objectives. Two insisted on a bombing halt. A few months earlier, most of these men had supported the war. No one anticipated so radical a change in attitude. The Wise Men were troubled by divisions in American society, the decline of American standing in the world, the gold drain, and most thought it was time to find a way out. Johnson was shaken by their response.

On March 31 the president addressed the American people. He spoke of his past efforts to achieve peace and announced a cessation of attacks on North Vietnam except for staging areas just north of the demilitarized zone—and those attacks would cease if Hanoi showed restraint. Then he made a striking bid for national unity and to demonstrate the serious of his peace initiative by announcing he would not seek another term as president. He contended the stakes were too high to allow the presidency to become involved in election-year partisanship. Three days later Hanoi agreed to negotiate. But peace remained many years away. Indeed the air war in the South intensified. The air force had the planes, the pilots, and the bombs. Deprived of targets in the North, they simply concentrated on the South.

On April 4 Martin Luther King Jr. was murdered in Memphis. Hours later Washington was in flames, and riots followed across the nation. In June Robert Kennedy was murdered in Los Angeles. In August antiwar demonstrators outside the Democratic Convention in Chicago were attacked viciously by the police, in what a subsequent investigation labeled a "police riot." When Governor Abraham Ribicoff of Connecticut protested on the convention floor against police action, Mayor Richard Daley led his claque in chanting "kike, kike." This was not the America God had blessed, liberator of oppressed people. The war had changed all that, and another side of American life surfaced, ugly, brutal, reminding some of the rise of fascism.

In Vietnam, American boys were destroying villages "to save them," committing unspeakable atrocities against an alien people whose savage struggle for independence frightened and confused them. At home, Americans were turning on each other, divided by the war, by race, by class. The tension caused by the war in Vietnam and racism at home had infected almost every aspect of American life. Johnson and his advisers were pitted against the hour hand. Could they find an acceptable peace in Vietnam before the bell tolled for America?

It was May before Washington and Hanoi agreed on a site for the talks, and May 13 before the first formal session was held. That week, 562 Americans were killed in Vietnam, the highest weekly total of the war. It was July before the American negotiators perceived a breakthrough and a chance for peace. By late August Henry Kissinger, a sometime adviser to the Johnson administration, having become a supporter of Richard M. Nixon, Republican presidential candidate, had persuaded the South Vietnamese to reject any peace terms Johnson might be prepared to accept. He and his colleagues assured the Saigon regime they would get better terms after the election, after Richard Nixon became president.

In October Johnson's negotiators convinced him that an agreement was in reach. He authorized them to try, and they succeeded with the help of the Soviet Union. The Soviets pressed the Vietnamese to accept American terms, and on October 31 Johnson ordered the cessation of all attacks on North Vietnam. But the struggle for control of the South continued. The Saigon regime, convinced Nixon would gain more for it, accused Johnson of betrayal and refused to participate in the talks if the NLF was present as a separate delegation. Nixon's victory had the opposite effect on Hanoi. The North Vietnamese were eager to reach a settlement before facing the Nixon administration. Concessions by Hanoi won Saigon's representation at the talks, but nothing came of them. The war went on.

Nixon and Kissinger, his principal foreign policy adviser, had no illusions about the importance of Vietnam to the security of the United States. Both were ruthless practitioners of great power politics, eager to be relieved of the burden of an unpopular war, eager to concentrate on relations with the Soviet Union and China. But the president had to be perceived as strong at home and abroad. His dilemma was to find a way out of Vietnam short of surrender yet quickly enough to stay ahead of antiwar sentiment at home. He chose to approximate Eisenhower's New Look, relying on American airpower and local forces, in this instance called "Vietnamization." Gradually, American troops were pulled back from combat and out of the country. The air war was stepped up and extended to infiltration and staging areas in Cambodia and Laos. The killing went on, but fewer of the corpses were American.

Hopes for a quick end to the American military presence faded as the North Vietnamese held their ground, confident the American people would tire of the war and bring their children home. But the performance of Saigon's forces improved, largely because the Viet Cong had suffered enormous losses during their Tet offensive. By 1970 the balance of forces in the South had shifted in favor of the government. Increasingly, the burden of fighting Saigon and its American supporters fell to North Vietnamese regulars. Supplied with Soviet SAM ground-to-air missiles and the latest Soviet tanks, Ho Chi Minh and his colleagues assumed they could counter any invasion. It was evident to Nixon that the infiltration of North Vietnamese had to be stopped.

The American military had long advocated a strike at Vietnamese sanctuaries in Cambodia. Johnson had refused, but Nixon authorized secret bombings in 1969—secret from the American people, not from the recipients of the bombs. Early in 1970 the Cambodian government fell to a military coup led by officers friendly to the United States. In May American troops invaded neutral Cambodia, determined to destroy North Vietnamese sanctuaries there. The results were disastrous for Cambodians and led to anti-American demonstrations around the world and death on American college campuses.

Caught between the Americans and the Vietnamese, hundreds of thousands of Cambodians died. Their country was devastated and control gradually shifted to a murderous group of Communist insurgents, the Khmer Rouge, who slaughtered as many as two million more of their countrymen and women. The invasion also resurrected the antiwar movement in the United States. Protesters at Jackson State and Kent State were shot and killed by police and the National Guard. The president was besieged in the White House, with troops posted on the premises in case of attack.

The Nixon administration withstood the aftermath of the invasion of Cambodia, but the situation in the field and at home deteriorated. In February 1971 South Vietnamese forces supported by American planes and helicopters struck at North Vietnamese sanctuaries in Laos, resulting in another disaster. Hanoi knew they were coming, met them with new Soviet tanks, and decimated Saigon's troops. At home, Lieutenant William Calley was convicted for his role in the massacre of women and children in the village of My Lai, and other veterans revealed that such atrocities were not isolated incidents. Then in June 1971 the *New York Times* began publishing a secret Defense Department documentary history of American decision making in Vietnam, revealing many of the ways the Kennedy and Johnson administrations had deceived the American people.

Polls taken soon afterward indicated that 71 percent of the American people thought it had been a mistake to intervene in Vietnam—and 58 percent thought the war was immoral. Nixon knew he had to find a way out before he ran for reelection in 1972—and so did his adversaries in Hanoi.

Intensive efforts to reach agreement in 1971 failed, but Nixon and Kissinger succeeded in their efforts to move closer to the Soviet Union and China, gaining the support of Moscow and Beijing for the peace process. They assumed they could isolate North Vietnam and force it to come to terms. The response from Hanoi was a conventional attack across the demilitarized zone that caught the Americans and their Vietnamese protégés by surprise. The United States responded with more massive air attacks on the North and the mining of Haiphong harbor. The North Vietnamese were stopped short of the collapse of the Saigon government.

Renewed military stalemate, additional American concessions, pressure from Hanoi's Soviet and Chinese allies—both eager to improve relations with the United States—and the realization that Nixon was likely to be reelected led the North to accept a diplomatic arrangement short of victory in the fall of 1972. Saigon rejected the agreement, but on the eve of the American election, Kissinger declared: "Peace is at hand." The announcement was designed to help bury George McGovern, the Democrats' peace candidate.

After the election, Nixon proved more responsive to Saigon's cries and demanded changes in the agreement. When the North Vietnamese balked, at Christmas time he ordered the most devastating bombing of the war, a series of raids in which more bombs were dropped in twelve days that had been dropped in the two years between 1969 and 1971. At the same time, massive supplies of military equipment were delivered to the Saigon regime, with Nixon's promise that the United States would return if the North violated the agreement. Finally, in March 1973, the war ended for Americans.

Nixon continued efforts to sustain Saigon after American troops withdrew but was crippled by the Watergate scandal that led to his resignation. Congress reasserted itself and restricted the president's power to reinvolve the United States in Vietnam. American support for the Saigon regime declined and with it one of the regime's principal reasons for existing. The departure of the Americans and the reduction of American aid affected morale adversely, and Saigon's will to fight ebbed palpably by early 1975. Enormous numbers of government troops deserted. When the North Vietnamese struck in March 1975, the South Vietnamese Army panicked and then disintegrated. Calls for help from the United States were not answered. Nixon was gone, and his secret promises could not be honored by President Gerald Ford. A few weeks later the fighting stopped with the Communists in control of the entire country—and Saigon became Ho Chi Minh City. After thirty years of war, the Vietnamese revolution had triumphed over the French, the Americans, and all internal opposition.

Fifty-five thousand Americans and millions of Vietnamese died in the American phase of the Vietnamese revolution. It was a struggle in which the United States should never have intervened. No vital American interest was threatened by events in Indochina. Defeat in Vietnam was of little consequence, without impact on the strategic balance between the United States and its adversaries. Before the war ended, the United States had taken major strides toward reconciliation with the Soviet Union and the People's Republic of China, the very nations the Americans had sought to contain by killing and dying in Vietnam. The dominoes of Southeast Asia did not fall. To be sure, the Khmer Rouge had triumphed in Cambodia and the Pathet Lao seized control of Laos, but the remaining nations of the region remained independent, noncommunist, and friendly to the United States, ultimately creating the Association of Southeast Asian Nations (ASEAN), an important force in world affairs.

Nonetheless, the cost of fighting the war hurt the United States, accelerating its decline as a hegemonic power. The achievement of strategic parity by the Soviet Union and the regaining of their economic edge by Japan and Western Europe were all but inevitable, but the disastrous economic policies of the 1960s and early 1970s, including the means of financing the war in Vietnam, contributed mightily to the timing and depth of the slide.

The dollar had been weak since the late 1950s and balance-of-payments deficits had troubled Kennedy, but the deficit did not get out of control until 1964. After Eisenhower, no president gave adequate consideration to the cost of American security. Kennedy, Johnson, and Nixon proudly refused to put a price tag on the foreign policy goals they pursued. There was a sharp increase in the rate of inflation in the 1960s as the government printed more and more dollars to pay for its imperial activities. Both the Johnson and Nixon administrations tried to export the cost of the war, export inflation, to their trading partners, but the French, British, and Germans rebelled. The world had grown tired of collecting inflated American dollars in return for protection against a Soviet threat they perceived as diminished or to support an American war in Vietnam of which most Europeans disapproved. The political scientist Robert Gilpin suggested that the United States had become "the rogue elephant of the global economy."

15

THE QUEST FOR DÉTENTE

B Y 1969, WHEN Richard Nixon entered the White House, the endless war in Vietnam had eroded public support for overseas military adventures. The United States had to disengage from Vietnam, and, perhaps, it was time to end the Cold War as well. No one was better able to free the country from hysterical anticommunism than the man who had contributed so much to creating it. As one commentator remarked, he would be the first president since the end of World War II who did not have be on guard against Richard Nixon.

Nixon and Kissinger, like their predecessors, sought a stable world order in which American interests would be preserved—and considered containment of Soviet influence central to that end. But Nixon and Kissinger faced a Soviet Union that had achieved strategic parity and was striving for preeminence. They were constrained in their response by congressional weariness with the battle and by an economy weakened by Lyndon Johnson's attempt to provide guns *and* butter.

Central to their approach was the determination to control foreign policy from the White House, to prevent interference from the bureaucracies or Congress. They wanted to be free to act as quickly and as ruthlessly as they imagined the Soviet Politburo did and to that end would finesse constitutional restraints on the president as they deemed necessary. Neither man had great respect for American political culture. At home and abroad they practiced power politics, no holds barred. Moral imagination was not in their genes.

To contain the Soviets when the wealth and power of the United States were in relative decline and public support at low ebb was the task that confronted the new administration. Nixon and Kissinger offered the Soviets recognition of their strategic parity, tolerance of the aberrant political philosophies and human rights abuses of which the Soviets and their satellites were guilty, and access to Western capital and technology. In return they asked Moscow to recognize the mutuality of superpower interest in stability, especially in maintaining order in the Third World. They were telling Soviet leaders that it was in their interest to cooperate with the United States rather than attempt to capitalize on unrest in peripheral areas. They were asking the Soviets to contain themselves when America's will to hold the line was in doubt.

Desperately eager to regain public support for America's role as world leader, they imagined ending the war in Vietnam and easing tensions with the Soviet Union might achieve that goal. In addition there was a tactic the president liked to have called the "Nixon Doctrine," the devolution of American responsibilities in the Third World upon regional powers such as Brazil, Iran, Indonesia, and Zaire. Rather than intervening with American troops, the United States would arm surrogate forces to do the fighting and dying.

Soviet leaders watched the antiwar demonstrations, racial unrest, and chaos in American streets and were confirmed in their contempt for democratic society. Clearly, the United States was in decline and would soon be supplanted by the Soviet Union as the world's hegemonic power. And they did not wait passively for the Americans to self-destruct. They provided large-scale aid to the Hanoi regime, did what they could to undermine the American position in the Middle East, and expanded their own military power significantly. They were prepared to act aggressively to achieve a position of dominance.

Moscow was unresponsive to the Nixon administration's requests for pressure on Hanoi to help extricate the United States from Vietnam. America's war in Vietnam could not have been more advantageous to the Soviets had it been planned in the Kremlin. It drained American resources, exacerbated tensions within American society, alienated NATO allies as well as Third World countries, and increased Vietnamese dependence on the Soviet Union. In blood, in treasure, in the sullying of America's image in the world, the war in Vietnam was enormously costly to the United States—and a great boon to the Soviet Union.

Nikita Khrushchev's successor, Leonid Brezhnev, and his colleagues were no more willing than Khrushchev had been to end efforts to expand Soviet influence in the world. They perceived momentum to be on their side. On the other hand, the Soviet Union did have problems that might be alleviated through better relations with the United States. Like Lyndon Johnson, Brezhnev was trying to provide both guns and butter, trying to project Soviet power abroad while improving the lives of his people—and the economy was beginning to strain. The Soviet Union would benefit from an infusion of capital and technology from the West. A reduction of tension between Washington and Moscow seemed to be a prerequisite.

Once the massive military buildup of 1965–1968 had pacified the Soviet military-industrial complex, Brezhnev was free to pursue his dream of becoming the great peacemaker. His action to crush the "Prague Spring" in the summer of 1968 had assured his more aggressive colleagues that he would act as necessary to protect Soviet interests. The historians Melvyn Leffler and Vladislav Zubock perceive him as a man convinced that nuclear war had to be avoided and that the pursuit of détente was the surest route to peace and security for the Soviet Union—and international acclaim for its leader.

Moreover, Brezhnev's efforts to conciliate the Chinese had been unsuccessful. Announcement of the Brezhnev Doctrine, claiming the right to use force to defend Soviet-style "socialism," coming on the heels of the Red Army's invasion of Czechoslovakia to crush a deviant Communist Party, failed to intimidate Mao Zedong. Incidents along the Sino-Soviet border increased in number and intensity. As Soviet leaders considered their options for punishing the Chinese, it seemed advisable to neutralize the United States. A Chinese-American connection would not be in the interest of the Soviet Union. There might be some value derived from improving relations with the United States—provided the Soviet Union remained free to outmaneuver the Americans throughout the Third World.

In Beijing, the turmoil of the Great Proletarian Cultural Revolution did not blind Chinese leaders to the danger from the Soviet Union. In November 1968 Zhou Enlai called for talks with the newly elected Nixon administration, but more radical leaders forced cancellation of a scheduled meeting. In the months that followed, Sino-Soviet tensions erupted in serious border incidents, provoked by the Chinese and followed by a sharp retaliatory strike by the Soviets. Fearful of a preemptive attack on their nuclear installations, the Chinese backed off. With their hostility toward the Soviets greater than ever, they proved receptive to overtures from the Nixon administration. Ambassadorial talks were renewed early in 1970, but it was the end of the year before Zhou persuaded the aging Mao Zedong that the United States might prove a valuable counter to Soviet pressure.

Nixon and Kissinger were eager to engage China diplomatically, primarily to seek help ending the war in Vietnam, but also to use China as a potential lever against the Soviet Union. Rapprochement with Beijing would facilitate the withdrawal of American forces from East Asia. American troops would no longer need to be prepared to fight major wars in Europe and Asia simultaneously, reducing force requirements. American resources could all be focused on the Soviets in Europe. Détente with China fit magnificently with the Nixon-Kissinger approach to the Soviet Union and with the Nixon Doctrine.

On July 15, 1971, without warning to friend or foe, Nixon announced that Kissinger had met secretly with Zhou and that he, the president of the United States, had accepted an invitation to visit China. By September Beijing had replaced the Kuomintang regime in Taipei at the United Nations. And in 1972 Nixon flew to China, where the old Red-baiter enjoyed a personal audience with Mao. A new era in Chinese-American relations had begun.

The principal obstacle to regular diplomatic relations, to "normalization," was American policy toward Taiwan. The Chinese opposed all variations of the idea of two Chinas and demanded that American forces be withdrawn from Taiwan. The Americans conceded that Chinese on both sides of the Taiwan Strait insisted that Taiwan was a part of China, that there was but one China. Washington would accept the idea of one China with a tacit understanding that the future of Taiwan would be determined later, by the Chinese, peacefully. The Americans agreed to the ultimate withdrawal of their forces and installations from Taiwan, promising to do so progressively as tensions in the region subsided. Fearing a reaction from Chiang's friends in the United States, Nixon and Kissinger concealed the full extent of their concessions. In fact, Kissinger left no doubt of American willingness to abandon Taiwan as soon as feasible.

Soviet leaders watched uneasily, but their worst fears had not been realized. There was no indication of any military understanding between the United States and China. The Kremlin was certain that Sino-American relations would not advance appreciably until the Americans found a way out of their commitment to Taiwan. To the men in Moscow, it was apparent, however, that they would have to include the Sino-American relationship in their calculation, to try to control the strategic triangle that had emerged. The Soviet Union could not appear so indifferent to American overtures for détente as to drive Washington and Beijing closer together.

The Soviets correctly estimated that an arms control agreement would be the most effective instrument for demonstrating their surpassing importance to the United States. Once an agreement was reached, the Americans were unlikely to jeopardize it by entering into a military alliance with China. Moreover, the Soviets were troubled by Nixon's interest in deploying an anti-ballistic missile (ABM) system. This was not only an area in which Soviet technology was inferior; at least as worrisome was the potential cost of an extensive ABM system. Military expenditures already stretched the Soviet budget to the limit. Brezhnev was ready for a deal.

Nixon and Kissinger were not much interested in an arms control agreement for the sake of limiting the development and deployment of weapons. The particulars of an agreement concerned them less than the fact of an accord. They wanted to signal a change in the superpower relationship from one of confrontations to one in which differences were resolved through negotiations. Kissinger and the Soviet ambassador bypassed the official negotiators, spared themselves mastery of the technical details, and came up with a document Nixon and Brezhnev could sign.

The first Strategic Arms Limitation Talks (SALT) agreement, signed in Moscow in May 1972, brought Nixon and Brezhnev the political capital they sought. The Soviet ruling class was pleased by the indication that the United States had conceded strategic parity. Shortly afterward, a Soviet-American trade agreement brought closer the economic gains the Soviets expected. The American people warmed to the prospect of ending the Cold War, and the "new" Nixon glowed with the aura of a man who had achieved rapprochement with his nation's two principal adversaries. Around the world there was a perception of a new and less dangerous era dawning.

One likely glimpse of the future emerged when tensions arose between the United States and Japan over trade issues. Japan's prime minister, Sato Eisaku, failed to respond quickly to Nixon's request for restraints on textile exports. Washington retaliated in 1971 with the "Nixon shocks," designed in part to undermine Sato. First, the president announced his opening to China without consulting the Japanese, who, out of loyalty to Washington, had resisted internal pressures to recognize the Beijing government. Second, Nixon unilaterally declared that dollars could no longer be converted into gold and that a 10 percent surcharge would be levied on all imports—forcing the Japanese to revalue the yen and limit exports to the United States. Economic issues, long subordinated to security concerns, were becoming paramount in Japanese-American affairs.

Both Nixon and Kissinger were uninterested in Latin America—except when it came to Cuba and Castro. When Salvador Allende, a Marxist and friend of Castro, was elected president of Chile in 1970, they feared the emergence of another Communist state in the Americas, for which they would be held accountable. Failing to prevent Allende's election despite spending millions interfering, they were complicit in a military coup that resulted in Allende's death and the seizure of power by General Augusto Pinochet in 1973. Pinochet established a brutal dictatorship that lasted until 1990. He was responsible for the murder of thousands of dissidents, including one assassinated in Washington, D.C.

And then there was the dirty little war in Vietnam in which the United States was still engaged. If it had ever made sense for American resources to be deeply committed to Indochina, Nixon's maneuvers in Beijing and Moscow obviated two imperatives. In 1972 Nixon, who had argued in 1968 that anyone who could not end the war in four years did not deserve to be president, was up for reelection. On the eve of the election, Kissinger announced that peace was at hand. It took a ruthless bombing campaign in December to finalize the agreement with Hanoi, but the last American troops left in February 1973. For Americans the ordeal was over—but not so for the Vietnamese, for whom there were two more years of fighting and dying. For the Cambodians, the worst was yet to come.

Briefly, Nixon basked in the glory of his landslide victory over George McGovern. Americans, with the atrocities of Southeast Asia relegated to the back pages of their newspapers, gone from their television screens, might have imagined a world at peace. But the Watergate scandal that was to destroy Nixon had already surfaced, and trouble was just over the horizon in the Middle East.

The Middle East has long been—and perhaps always will be—an area of exceptional volatility. Communal strife, primarily religious, plagues the region. Shiites and Sunnis seem incapable of resolving centuries-old differences peaceably. The great power decision to grant Jews a homeland in Palestine and the creation in 1948 of the state of Israel overshadowed most prior grievances among Arab Muslims. And Israel survived the first onslaught against it, in 1948, in large part thanks to Stalin's facilitating of Czech arms shipments to the embattled Jews. As the Soviet leader anticipated, the Jewish nation was perpetually at odds with its Arab neighbors, creating difficulties for first the British and then the Americans, the principal Western influences in the area.

Stalin had paid little further attention to the Arab Middle East, but his successors extended Soviet influence to those states confronting Israel, most importantly Egypt and Syria. The historic Russian claim to influence in a region that it bordered was reasserted by Moscow in the 1950s.

In 1967 Soviet agents in Syria spread false allegations of an impending Israeli attack. The Soviets then repeated their allegations to the Egyptians, who regarded the information as independent confirmation of Syrian fears. Attempting to intimidate the Israelis with the threat of a two-front war, Nasser demanded withdrawal of UN peacekeeping forces separating his troops from the Israelis. He sent his forces toward the Gulf of Aqaba, threatening Israel's vital port of Elat. Provoked, the Israelis attacked preemptively, in what came to be known as the Six-Day War. They routed

Egyptian, Syrian, and Jordanian troops, seizing control of the Sinai Peninsula, the west bank of the Jordan River and Jerusalem, and the Golan Heights. When the Israelis seemed likely to continue on to Damascus, the Soviets threatened to intervene. The Soviets quickly resupplied their Syrian and Egyptian friends and sent them thousands of military advisers. In return they obtained naval rights in Arab ports and air bases from which they could counter the operations of the U.S. Sixth Fleet in the future.

In 1969 Nasser began a "war of attrition" against Israel. The Israeli Air Force responded with air attacks that penetrated deeply into the Egyptian heartland, demonstrating that it could fly wherever it pleased. Nasser turned to Moscow and the Soviets sent missiles, planes, and thousands of air-defense personnel, including fighter pilots. Soviet warplanes, flown by Soviet pilots, changed the nature of the war—although in one engagement the Israelis shot down five Soviet interceptors. As the war escalated and the Israelis threatened to invade Egypt to knock out the missile sites, the Soviets agreed to American calls for a cease-fire in August 1970—but they retained 20,000 "advisers" in Egypt.

A month after the cease-fire, Nasser died of a heart attack. His successor, Anwar Sadat, was dissatisfied with Soviet support. He suspected Brezhnev of betraying Egyptian interests to facilitate détente with the United States. Abruptly, in July 1972, he expelled his Soviet advisers. American leaders viewed Sadat's action as evidence of the wisdom of their policy. Their support of Israel had demonstrated that the Arabs could achieve their goals only through the United States. Soviet influence had been checked.

Sadat and his Syrian counterpart were preparing to attack Israel in 1973, intending to force Israel to disgorge the spoils of the Six-Day War. Kissinger had been warned by the State Department's intelligence analysts but underestimated Sadat's determination. The Israelis, too, were surprised by the attack, which caught them as they observed the holiest of the Jewish holidays, Yom Kippur. The Egyptians punched through Israeli defenses in the Sinai and the Syrians scaled the approaches to the Golan Heights. The Soviets, hoping to retain influence, launched a massive airlift to resupply their Arab allies and appealed to other Arab states to join the battle. The United States failed to support the Israelis until Golda Meir, the Israeli premier, threatened to use nuclear weapons to save her country. Then the

American airlift began, followed immediately by an Israeli counteroffensive. Quickly the Israelis drove back the attackers on both fronts and in a few days were in position to annihilate the Egyptian Army. Sadat, who thought his forces were winning, resisted calls for a cease-fire until Soviet satellite photographs demonstrated the precariousness of his position. Brezhnev and Kissinger then worked out the terms for a cease-fire acceptable to all the combatants.

The Israelis, however, took advantage of minor Egyptian provocations to justify further advances. Brezhnev proposed sending Soviet and American troops to stop the Israelis. He warned he would send Soviet forces in alone, if necessary, and mobilized airborne troops to demonstrate that he was serious. Nixon and Kissinger responded by putting American forces on strategic alert and compelling the Israelis to comply with the cease-fire. A confrontation was averted.

The October 1973 war in the Middle East dispelled illusions about the meaning of détente. In Washington, there was disappointment in the Soviet effort to undermine the American position in the Middle East. The Soviets had tried to incite the Arab world against the United States, disseminating lies about the American role in the conflict. In Moscow, the outcome of the war was probably the major source of frustration, but the American strategic alert and the implication that the United States had forced the Soviets to back down rankled Brezhnev and his colleagues. Sadat's decision for rapprochement with the United States was a serious setback. The United States had conceded strategic parity to the Soviet Union, but it clearly had no intention of allowing the Soviets a major role in the Middle East. The rivalry seemed little changed.

The most stunning event of the mid-1970s was the forced resignation of Richard Nixon from the presidency in August 1974. It was the culmination of years of illegal activities directed from the White House to destroy opponents, uncover disloyalty to the president, and preserve the secrecy with which he and Kissinger conducted foreign policy. As the evidence of wrongdoing mounted, the president's power ebbed and Congress reasserted itself in the realm of foreign policy. The once troubling "imperial presidency" faltered, and the system of checks and balances created by the Founding Fathers came back into play.

In 1973 Congress passed the War Powers Act, designed to restrain the president's use of force. It ordered an end to bombing of Cambodia, passed a law preventing American troops from returning to Vietnam, and signaled its intent to hold trade relations with the Soviet Union hostage to Soviet performance on human rights issues, specifically the freedom of Soviet Jews to emigrate. These limits on the ability of Nixon and Kissinger to manage foreign affairs brought about the collapse of the intricate schema they had devised. They could not deliver on promises to allies in Indochina or adversaries in Moscow. The Nixon administration and the administration of Gerald Ford that succeeded it were not strong enough to act as they wished in world affairs. In Nixon's mind, the United States was becoming "a pitiful, helpless giant."

When the North Vietnamese launched their final assault on the Saigon regime, the United States did not ride to the rescue and the war ended. The suffering of the Vietnamese people did not end, as thousands of refugees demonstrated in the years that followed, but peace was a blessing for most of the country. Cambodians, relieved of the terror of American bombers, enjoyed little respite before facing even greater horrors at the hands of their new Communist leaders, the Khmer Rouge. Congressional actions indicated that the economic rewards Brezhnev had anticipated from détente would not be forthcoming and reduced the likelihood of moderating Soviet behavior. The unraveling of détente was probably the inevitable outcome of the deviousness of Nixon and Kissinger, their contempt for democratic practices, and the mistrust they provoked in the bureaucracy, in Congress, and ultimately among the American people.

Chinese-American relations also fell victim to Nixon's disgrace. The Chinese expected the United States to abandon the pretense that Taiwan was China, disengage from Chiang Kai-shek's regime, and establish formal diplomatic relations with the People's Republic. Struggling to stave off impeachment, the president was dependent on the support of conservative lawmakers, many of whom were supporters of Chiang. Unwilling to risk alienating them, Nixon chose not to abrogate the defense treaty with Taiwan. Recognition of Mao's China was not quite equal in importance to the preservation of Richard Nixon's presidency. His successor, Gerald Ford, likewise needed the support of the Republican right wing. Recognition of the People's Republic would have to wait. In China, American delays undermined advocates of rapprochement and a dying Zhou Enlai lost control of policy. Succession crises in both countries precluded decisive action in the mid-1970s.

Perhaps the most serious problem the United States faced in the 1970s was posed by the decline of its economic power, aggravated by the policies of the Johnson and Nixon administrations. The decline was only *relative*; although the United States ceased to dominate the international economic order, it remained an enormously wealthy and powerful country. The American economy was troubled and mismanaged but never in danger of collapse.

The American economy had provided the engine that drove the nations linked to it to extraordinary prosperity in the 1950s and 1960s. The United States had accepted the imperial burden of protecting its friends and allies while they reconstructed or developed their economies. The system that evolved out of Bretton Woods had worked. Real wealth had increased among the countries participating in the American-led liberal order. But by 1960 problems emerged. First, European countries and Japan recovered from the war and became more competitive and more assertive in their trade policies. They were prepared to continue cooperation with an American-led system but demanded a voice in its direction. Second, the American people became increasingly sensitive to the inequities within their society, the persistence of poverty amid plenty. The Kennedy administration devised a series of innovative steps to meet demands for social justice by expanding the economy, but a simultaneous increase in defense and foreign assistance spending precluded success. Keynesian methods of achieving full employment might have succeeded in a quiescent world: added to the expense required to meet the challenge of a Khrushchev-invigorated Soviet Union, they meant excessive federal deficits, inflation, and a balance-of-payments deficit that threatened the stability of the international economic order established at Bretton Woods.

Lyndon Johnson was even more committed to social justice for people in the United States. His reforms rivaled those of Franklin Roosevelt's New Deal for boldness of vision. But Johnson was also committed to winning the war in Vietnam and squandered billions of dollars in that benighted cause. A powerful president who dominated the executive branch and manipulated the legislative branch with ease, he lacked the courage to tax the American people to pay for his Great Society and his war. The budget deficit grew, inflation increased, the rate of economic growth declined, and the domestic and foreign economic policies of the United States were left in disarray for Richard Nixon.

Nixon and Kissinger were confronted with a politically damaging recession in 1969 and concluded that inflationary tactics, including devaluation of the dollar, were essential. The Bretton Woods system had always been costly to the United States, but it had borne the cost to enable its friends to reconstruct and to preserve vital security relations. By 1971 Nixon had decided the price was too high, the system too restrictive. He was confident that he could change the rules and destroy the system at an acceptable cost. The steps he ordered, however disruptive to the international economic order, helped stimulate a boom in the United States in 1972, easing his path to reelection. To increase its freedom of maneuver, the United States wrecked the system it had created.

But in the new era that began in the 1970s, Washington no longer dominated the international financial system. In 1971 the United States recorded its first balance-of-trade deficit of the twentieth century. Increasingly, it required the acquiescence of Germany and Japan, German and Japanese capital, to maintain domestic prosperity and to project its military power across the world. Gradually American leaders discovered they no longer had the freedom of action their predecessors had enjoyed in the quarter of a century following World War II. The United States needed foreign capital, and that capital did not come without strings.

The relative decline of American power had been underscored by the oil crisis of the mid-1970s, induced by the Organization of Petroleum Exporting Countries (OPEC). Until then the United States had controlled the world energy market as well as the monetary system. But as American automobiles and industry consumed more and more of the world's oil each year, American reserves declined. The United States, for the first time, became dependent on foreign suppliers. It could no longer use its vast reserves to keep world prices down and to assure Americans of an endless supply of inexpensive fuel. The Saudis replaced Americans as the arbiter of world oil prices.

The year Nixon resigned the presidency, 1974, was a particularly bad year for the American economy. President Ford was confronted with a stagnant economy and a high rate of inflation, an unusual combination economists called "stagflation." The American people were more concerned about jobs and the cost of living than about competing with the Soviets on the periphery. With the collapse of the Saigon regime in 1975, there was a widespread unwillingness, in Congress and across the country, to throw scarce resources into relatively unimportant, probably hopeless causes abroad.

Kissinger was deeply troubled by the message that American ennui sent to the Soviets. He feared that an indication that the United States was withdrawing from the field would be perceived in Moscow as an opportunity to expand Soviet influence. When, in May 1975, Cambodian Communists seized an American vessel, the Ford administration reacted muscularly, sending in the marines. The operation proved to be unnecessary as the captives had been released before it began. Although more lives were lost among the would-be rescuers than there had been prisoners, Kissinger had demonstrated, to his satisfaction, that the United States was not to be trifled with.

Angola, an African nation in which the United States had little interest, emerged as the major point of contention during the Ford administration. A bewildering array of indigenous groups, each with external sources of support, had been fighting for independence from the Portuguese, who abandoned the field after their own revolution in 1974. Tribal as well as ideological differences separated the Angolan factions.

Heavy fighting in mid-1975 resulted in unexpected successes for the Cuban and Soviet-backed MPLA. The Chinese, Americans, South Africans, and various and sundry other governments backed the other two leading organizations, the FNLA and UNITA. Ultimately the Cubans turned the tide by sending combat troops, some air-lifted by the Soviets, to assist the MPLA. Angola may not have been important to the United States, but Kissinger was unwilling to allow the Cubans and Soviets to act unopposed. The administration turned to Congress for more money for its preferred Angolan revolutionaries. To Kissinger's horror, Congress said no. In January 1976, unwilling to step into another morass on the periphery, it banned further covert aid to Angola.

Freed of the risk of confrontation with the United States, the Soviets and Cubans deepened their involvement. The People's Republic of Angola quickly won recognition from other black African states and by March 1976 had reached agreements to relieve most external pressures. The dominant influence was Cuban. The Cuban-backed Angolan government crushed pro-Soviet competitors. But neither Cuban- nor Soviet-backed members of the Angolan government could be restrained from reaching out to the West, including the United States, for trade and investments.

The Soviets had gained little in Angola, but that was not Kissinger's perception. The victory of the Soviet-backed MPLA reduced his tolerance for Soviet competition in the Third World. Kissinger feared the Soviets would be emboldened to further interventions, feared Americans had lost the will to meet the Soviet challenge.

The Soviets, on the other hand, were confronted by a different challenge: China. Not only did they have to prove to themselves and the rest of the world that their country was a superpower as deserving of deference as was the United States, but they also had to demonstrate to Communists and radicals all over the world that Moscow and not Beijing was their Mecca, that the Soviet Union would do more for them than would China. Chinese-American collusion in Angola touched a raw nerve among Brezhnev's colleagues.

As American willingness to use military power abroad declined, Soviet willingness increased. The Soviets perceived a clear field in Angola. In addition, the Soviet military was eager to test its newly developed air- and sealift capabilities. Despite evidence of how the cost of American interventions in the Third World had eroded the power of the United States, the Soviets were determined to defy the lessons of history. Starting with a far weaker economic base, the Soviets wanted to believe that their great military power, the one area in which they excelled, would enable them to succeed where the Americans had failed, to gain advantage on the periphery.

In the central arena, Europe, détente held. Europeans were less concerned with Soviet-American rivalry in the Third World and eager to avoid becoming battlegrounds for testing Soviet and American tactical nuclear weapons. Willy Brandt, chancellor of West Germany, made enormous strides with his *Ostpolitik*. Trade grew between Eastern and Western European countries. In 1970 West Germany and the Soviet Union signed a nonaggression pact. In 1971 accord was reached on Western access to Berlin, to be guaranteed by Moscow. By 1972 East and West Germany had recognized each other. Uneasy about German initiatives but preoccupied by Vietnam, Nixon and Kissinger could do little but acquiesce.

The Soviets pressed hard for détente with Western Europe. They sought technology not easily obtained from the United States and hoped to drive a wedge between the Americans and their NATO allies. Brezhnev and his colleagues wanted formal acceptance by all European countries of their post-1945 borders and proposed a conference from which they hoped to exclude non-European nations, most obviously the United States. By 1973 they succeeded in bringing about a Conference on Security and Cooperation in Europe but had to accept American participation—and that of Canada and the Vatican.

Two years of negotiations resulted in the Helsinki Agreements of August 1975, giving the Soviets the assurances they wanted on the European status quo. To get those assurances, the Soviets were forced to commit to improving their record on human rights, specifically to allow the free movement of people and ideas. Were they to honor their Helsinki commitments, the political system from which Brezhnev and Soviet bloc leaders derived their power would be destroyed. Perhaps little of substance had been achieved, but like the American Declaration of Independence, the Helsinki Agreements established a standard toward which the signatories might strive and to which they might be held.

The decision of President Ford to sign the Helsinki accords was derided by his opponents as naiveté in foreign affairs. Ford, a popular conservative, fought off the challenge of the right wing of his party, in the person of Ronald Reagan, and won the Republican presidential nomination in 1976 but lost the election to the Democrat Jimmy Carter. It was Carter who would have to determine how the United States would respond to Brezhnev's opportunism in Africa and whether efforts to extend détente would continue.

The American people were wary of the sacrifices demanded of them— the lives of their children spent senselessly in distant wars, the impact of stagflation on their standard of living. Not unreasonably, they blamed their government. Unlike their counterparts in the Soviet Union, China, and many other parts of the world, they had a remedy: they voted out their rulers and started fresh, with a new government headed by a man uncontaminated by previous contact with Washington and unassociated with any of the tired policies of the past.

Unfortunately, the new American president, however well he had once run the state of Georgia, was ill-prepared to manage the foreign policy of the world's greatest power. In the nuclear age, in the volatile world of the late 1970s, it was terrifying to think that the man who had his hand on the levers of American power had no experience in international relations. It was not a job for an amateur; it was not a time for an amateur. But Jimmy Carter was the people's choice.

The result was four years of disarray. A good and decent man, Carter was sufficiently arrogant to think that he could put aside the misguided efforts of his predecessors and start anew. Like Woodrow Wilson, he denounced the selfish realpolitik of the preceding administration and proclaimed America's intention to return to its ideals. Insistence on respect for human rights would be the centerpiece of his foreign policy. He was determined to alleviate tensions with the Soviets but was slow to comprehend that his criticism of their performance on human rights complicated his efforts. His principal advisers on foreign policy, Cyrus Vance, secretary of state, and Zbigniew Brzezinski, national security adviser—pulled him in opposite directions on Soviet issues in particular. The president attempted to fashion a policy out of ideas offered by both and succeeded only in confusing friends and enemies alike.

For Vance, the principal objective of American policy was to revive détente, to work closely with the Soviets to reduce bilateral tensions and to resolve some of the world's less tractable problems. He was persuaded that beneath the geriatric leadership of the Brezhnev Politburo was a generation free of Stalinist dogma, eager to end the Cold War and anxious to modernize their country. Specifically, he wanted a further arms control agreement, a SALT II treaty, to slow the arms race and to reduce American defense expenditures that were straining the economy. He was prepared to accept a Soviet role in the Middle East, convinced that giving them a stake in the peace of the region was the best way to stop malicious Soviet agitation of radical Arab forces.

Vance suspected the Chinese were attempting to manipulate the United States, exacerbating Soviet-American tensions to maximize China's room to maneuver. He insisted the best hope for the future was to encourage modification of Soviet behavior. Change would not come overnight, but if détente were back on track, the next cycle of Soviet leaders might accelerate the process.

Brzezinski never doubted that the Soviet Union was central to American concerns but did not believe that solutions could be found in Moscow. The Soviets had to be defeated, and to do so the United States had to strengthen itself and its allies and maintain relentless pressure on them. SALT II was less important than gaining strategic advantage, revitalizing NATO, enlisting China, promoting dissent within the Soviet empire, and countering Soviet interventions everywhere.

Vance was clearly right about the imminence of change in the Soviet Union. But the "new thinking," the intellectual turmoil that Vance's advisers had noted, was having little impact on Brezhnev and the other party elders. They were not receptive to fresh ideas. Vance's vision was probably not realizable in the 1970s.

Brezhnev perceived a United States weakened by Vietnam and Watergate, led by an irresolute and uninformed president. The moment was opportune for the Soviet Union to press its advantage. Brezhnev was heartened by the Communist seizure of power in Afghanistan in April 1978 and his Vietnamese protégés' victory over the Chinese-backed Khmer Rouge in December. In January 1979 the shah of Iran, the American surrogate in the Middle East and Southwest Asia, fled his country, and the ensuing civil strife undermined the strategic position of the United States in the region. Even on the doorstep of the United States, first in tiny Grenada and then in Nicaragua, forces friendly to Cuba and the Soviet Union seized power.

From the perspective of the Kremlin, Carter had been ineffectual in responding to each of these situations. Soviet power could no longer be checked anywhere. The men of the Politburo saw no need for new approaches and behaved much as Brzezinski had anticipated. Soviet leaders undermined Vance and drove Carter into Brzezinski's arms.

Although ground was lost in the effort to end the Cold War, the Carter administration enjoyed important successes in Latin America, the Middle East, and East Asia. In 1977, despite the opposition of some American conservatives, Carter signed several treaties that ultimately would permit Panama to gain control of the canal. The ratification process, however, cost the administration votes it would need for acceptance of SALT II. Some of the conservative senators who helped the administration with the Panama treaty would have to vote against arms control to renew their conservative credentials.

Perhaps Carter's greatest success was with the Camp David accords, important agreements between Israel and Egypt that he brokered. Sadat had lost faith in the Soviet ability to aid his cause and relied increasingly on American leverage with the Israelis. To help Carter overcome Israeli rigidity, he heroically traveled to Israel to demonstrate to American friends of Israel, as well as Israelis, his willingness to live in peace with his erstwhile enemies. The agreements Carter oversaw allowed Egypt to regain its Sinai territory and won Egyptian recognition of the state of Israel, breaking the back of the Arab coalition against Israel.

Egypt's rapprochement with the United States and Israel deprived the Soviets of their most important friend in the Middle East. The odds on Israel's survival had increased greatly, but without at least a gesture toward Soviet interests in the region there was little chance of enduring peace. And Soviet support of Arab belligerence against Israel intensified anti-Soviet attitudes in the United States, creating a political climate unreceptive to détente.

The normalization of relations between the United States and the People's Republic of China was also one of Carter's accomplishments. Regrettably, the issue of when and how to achieve this goal was caught up in the Vance-Brzezinski rivalry. Vance was convinced that showing favoritism toward the Chinese would aggravate Soviet-American relations, that relations with China were less important than relations with the Soviets. Brzezinski demonstrated less concern for Soviet sensibilities and thought frequent jabs to the head reminded Soviet leaders of the need to conciliate the United States. Brzezinski prevailed.

Chinese ends were not congruent with those of the United States. There was a shared interest in containing Soviet power, but the Chinese were apprehensive about improvement in Soviet-American relations. They were eager to play the Soviets and Americans off against each other. Deng Xiaoping, who emerged as China's leader in the late 1970s, recognized the Vance-Brzezinski rivalry and used it to China's advantage. Whenever possible, Chinese leaders attempted to stir trouble between the Soviet Union and the West. Deng was at least as successful at using the Americans as they were at using China.

Carter's last effort to salvage détente came in 1979 when the Soviets agreed to a summit meeting and the signing of the SALT II agreement. Vance was interested in regaining momentum toward accommodation, and Brzezinski thought Brezhnev's willingness to meet with Carter and sign the treaty was evidence of the success of his efforts to intimidate the Soviets. American analysts thought the agreement very much in the interest of the United States. On the Soviet side, there was an intense need to reduce military expenditures. The economy was disintegrating and the cost of empire more than the people could bear. At the meeting, Carter managed not to berate Brezhnev on human rights violations. Briefly, the possibility of revitalizing détente seemed to exist, but it was not to be.

Soviet actions in the Third World and the Kremlin's suppression of dissidents at home, combined with Carter's inept leadership, allowed anti-Soviet elements in American society to seize the initiative. In late summer of 1979 Frank Church (D-Idaho), a senator friendly to détente, doomed the SALT II treaty by calling attention to a Soviet combat brigade in Cuba and demanding its removal. In fact, the Soviet brigade had been in Cuba for years with the acquiescence of the American government. Carter, responding to the domestic political furor Church had aroused, demanded withdrawal of the Soviet troops. Brezhnev was outraged: the Soviets had done nothing wrong. They had honored their promise not to reinforce their forces in Cuba. They would not retreat from a position they had held since the early 1960s to assist the American president with his domestic political problems.

The issue of the Soviet brigade in Cuba was quickly overshadowed by the hostage crisis in Iran that began in November 1979 and the Soviet invasion of Afghanistan in December. The shah of Iran, reestablished in power by the CIA-directed coup of 1953, fled in January 1979 as forces hostile to his autocratic rule became increasingly threatening. A democratic successor regime was quickly overthrown by Islamic fundamentalists who looked to the Ayatollah Khomeini as their leader. In November Khomeini's followers seized the American Embassy and took those inside hostage, holding them for fourteen months, the remainder of Carter's presidency. The inability of the administration to obtain the freedom of the hostages through negotiations or a bizarre rescue attempt intensified frustration with the president's leadership. Americans wanted their leader to act forcefully to command the respect due the world's greatest power. They could not understand why he could not get the Soviets out of Cuba or the hostages out of Iran.

In December the Soviets gave Carter an opportunity to assume the mantle of greatness Brzezinski held out for him—at the cost of détente. In Afghanistan, the Communist regime that had come to power in April 1978 was disintegrating, partly under attack from Islamic fundamentalists but largely because of ethnic factionalism within the Afghan Communist Party. The Soviets had failed to ameliorate the situation and felt threatened by unrest in a nation on its border, among people ethnically related to restive Soviet peoples in Central Asia. When political pressure failed, the Soviets resorted to force. The mighty Red Army marched into Afghanistan to teach what Lyndon Johnson would have called a "pissant country" not to defy the will of a superpower. Brezhnev and his colleagues underestimated the reaction of the Americans and the international community to steps they considered vital to their security.

Carter responded vigorously. With striking hyperbole, he called the Soviet action the greatest danger to peace since World War II. He imposed a grain embargo against the Soviet Union, infuriating American farmers. He decided to have American athletes boycott the summer Olympics scheduled for Moscow, outraging the athletes and those who considered athletics more important than politics. He declared the Carter Doctrine, warning the Soviets that the United States considered the Persian Gulf a vital interest and would not tolerate a Soviet advance toward the Gulf. Of greatest consequence, he called for an arms buildup to meet the new Soviet threat.

The Soviets were shocked by the forcefulness of Carter's response and put on the defensive in the court of world opinion. They surrendered hope of cooperating with the Carter administration and hunkered down for a new era of confrontation. The war in Afghanistan drained resources from their already troubled economy. The glorious achievement of parity with the United States had hardly been savored before the foundations of the Soviet empire began to crumble. The army, no matter how brutally it acted, could not crush Afghan guerrilla forces, supplied primarily by the Chinese and Americans. The weak economy could not stand the strain of subsidies to allies such as Cuba and Vietnam, the price of empire. And now there was likely to be a costly arms race with the United States.

Fearful of Soviet communism, Americans had long exaggerated the threat posed by the Soviet Union. In 1980 many Americans perceived the Soviet Union as on the offensive, poised to achieve its goal of world domination. Brezhnev and the other party ancients reveled in that vision, but the reality was a regime everywhere on the defensive.

The years 1969 through 1980 were years of halting steps by the superpowers toward the end of the Cold War. The euphoria of Nixon's openings to Moscow and Beijing in 1972, the hopes for peace, were dashed in the closing months of the Carter administration. But the forces propelling the superpowers toward accommodation remained powerful. Foremost were the economic realities from which no American or Soviet leader could escape. The empires built at such great cost in the years since World War II had placed unacceptable burdens on both societies. America's relative decline had begun in the 1960s, but the agricultural and industrial foundation of American power remained stronger than anything the Soviet system could construct. The Soviets kept straining to equal, to surpass the United States, but what they succeeded in doing militarily, they could not accomplish in their consumer economy. The United States might be in decline, but the Soviet Union could not overtake it.

Neither Soviet nor American leaders surrendered hegemonic visions, and the structure of their respective societies continued to erode. The competition continued into the 1980s. Advocates of the "new thinking" in the Soviet Union knew the race could not go on much longer; their country could not withstand the strain. The American system was stronger, its people living farther from the edge. Under the leadership of Ronald Reagan, Americans were prepared to mortgage the future of their children in a renewed effort to win the Cold War. Brezhnev's successors had nothing to mortgage.

16

THE REAGAN
SURPRISE—ENTER GORBACHEV

E LECTING A ONETIME movie actor to lead them in a world of extraordinary complexity, with nuclear holocaust a hair's breath away, was the ultimate act of faith by the American people. Their faith did not go unrewarded.

Ronald Reagan was a man of unusual charm, a likeable man who shared the nostalgia many Americans felt for the days of American hegemony. In 1980 their economy was a shambles, and they were still heartsick from defeat in Vietnam and from the humiliation of the Iranian hostage crisis. He was the charismatic leader his people wanted, and he restored the nation's confidence. His impact was reminiscent of that of his early idol, Franklin Delano Roosevelt, who had assured Americans oppressed by the misery of the Great Depression that they had "nothing to fear, but fear itself," that they had "a rendezvous with destiny."

Unlike Roosevelt, Reagan knew little about world affairs and was not terribly interested. He ignored briefing books and the efforts of foreign policy specialists to explain issues. He was generally uncritical of stories that fit his presuppositions. And yet most of those who worked with him as governor of California or president of the United States insisted he was not stupid.

More troubling than the peculiarities of his mind was his disinterest in governing. He had wanted to be president, to provide his vision to

Americans, to ride into Washington on his white horse and rescue his country. Once there, he had little interest in how things were done. On most issues, he was quite content to delegate authority, to let others make decisions and determine how they would be implemented. Once the script had been prepared by his advisers, he would perform for the public.

Reagan was not without ideas relevant to foreign affairs. He perceived a world in which the forces of good led by the United States were pitted against the "evil empire"—the Soviet Union. Opposition to the Soviets was central to his thinking about foreign policy. He contended that they had achieved military superiority in the 1970s as a consequence of détente and was critical of arms control agreements. He argued that the Soviets had cheated on all of them. Confronted by such an opponent, the United States could depend only on military power. He was determined to rebuild that power, to regain the nation's status as the world's dominant military force. Not until then could the Soviets be expected to keep their agreements. He despised the Soviet political system and doubted the United States could ever reach an accommodation with it.

Despite the military buildup and his confrontational rhetoric, Reagan had an intense emotional horror of nuclear weapons. He was appalled when he realized American security rested on the concept of Mutual Assured Destruction: a fraction of each superpower's strategic force would survive a first strike and destroy the other, making an attack pointless. Deterrence had been central to American defense strategy since the Soviets developed a credible strategic force in the 1960s, but it was not good enough for Ronald Reagan. He wanted nuclear weapons eliminated rather than merely controlled. Short of their elimination, he wanted some means to prevent them from being used against Americans—a weapon capable of destroying enemy planes before they could reach their targets, a strategic defense system. That desire surfaced in a plan he announced in 1983.

In 1981, however, the United States was slipping into the worst economic decline since the Great Depression. The president and his aides, like Herbert Hoover and Franklin Roosevelt in the early 1930s, were preoccupied with the domestic crisis. The Soviets and the rest of the world could wait.

In the interim, the president's rhetoric was inflammatory, but American actions were contradictory. Despite Reagan's vow to be tougher on

Moscow, his first foreign policy act was to lift Jimmy Carter's embargo on grain sales to the Soviet Union. Rewarding American farmers who had voted for him proved more important than punishing the Soviets for sending troops into Afghanistan. For all his ideological rigidity, Reagan had little trouble rationalizing compromises dictated by political exigencies, foreign or domestic. His determination to abandon Carter's SALT II agreement evaporated when he discovered the Joint Chiefs of Staff were content with its provisions and angered by his charges of American military inferiority.

Similarly, the president found he could not dispense with arms control negotiations. Carter, responding to European anxieties over Soviet missile deployments in the late 1970s, had agreed to station a new generation of American missiles in Europe in the 1980s. The Soviets were outraged by the threat the proposed American deployment posed and organized a major propaganda campaign against it. To protect themselves from antimissile political activists, the European host governments needed to demonstrate a good-faith effort to achieve security through arms reduction: they needed to have the United States negotiate with the Soviets for the removal or reduction of intermediate missiles from Europe before accepting the necessity of deploying new weapons. Reagan had to send negotiators to meet with the Soviets in what were known as the intermediate-range nuclear force (INF) talks. Soon afterward Congress forced him to resume strategic arms limitation talks (SALT). He disguised his retreat by calling these strategic arms *reduction* talks (START).

A crisis in Poland in 1981 also forced Reagan to retreat under pressure from European allies. As the Solidarity movement of workers and intellectuals threatened the Communist regime, Soviet pressures prompted the Polish Army to seize power. The United States responded with economic sanctions against Poland and insisted that its NATO allies follow suit. In particular, the Reagan administration demanded that Europeans stop assisting the Soviet construction of a gas pipeline to carry Soviet natural gas to Western Europe. When the Europeans failed to respond to Reagan's satisfaction, Washington ordered American firms licensed in Europe to withhold essential parts, infuriating host governments. The United States retreated again and the pipeline construction resumed.

Reagan seemed content to accelerate the arms race and bash the Soviets verbally. Alexander Haig, his volatile secretary of state, wanted to demonstrate American resolve by striking at Soviet friends around the world, particularly in Central America. He focused his attention on El Salvador, where murderous right-wing army officers contended with leftist guerillas, both ignoring a would-be democratic government. The leftists were receiving aid from the Sandinistas—who had wrested power from the Somoza dictatorship in Nicaragua—and Cuba. The rightists, despite their responsibility for murdering the politically moderate Archbishop Romero and their complicity in the murder of American nuns, received aid from the United States. It was not a happy choice of fields for liberal democracy to contend against authoritarian socialism, but it was accessible and risk-free.

Further comfort for those whose mistrust of the Soviets knew no bounds came when the administration repudiated an informal arms control agreement reached in July 1982, negotiated by Paul Nitze. Nitze had long since established his anticommunist credentials as principal author of NSC-68 in the Truman era and as the driving force behind the Committee on the Present Danger, created to alert Americans to the threat Carter's arms control programs posed to their security. He and his Soviet counterpart went for a walk in the woods in Switzerland and worked out a compromise on intermediate missiles, to the chagrin of a White House that wanted no agreement. Repudiation upset European leaders, but Reagan was spared embarrassment by Soviet rejection of the arrangement.

Reagan sent another message to the world early in his administration. In a "don't tread on me" signature gesture, U.S. Navy pilots destroyed two Soviet-built Libyan jets that dared to challenge them over the Gulf of Sidra, an area claimed by Libya. Carter might have turned the other cheek, inviting disrespect; Reagan most definitely would not. "Let friend and foe alike know that America has the muscle to back up its words," the president warned. Additional evidence of Reagan's willingness to project American power came in 1982, when, against the advice of his secretary of defense, he ordered U.S. Marines to Lebanon to create order out of the chaos resulting from an Israeli invasion.

Despite Reagan's campaign rhetoric and anti-Soviet reputation, Soviet anger at Carter had been so great that Soviet leaders had welcomed Reagan's election. They assumed that, once in office, Reagan, like Nixon, would stop Red-baiting and work toward détente. Brezhnev died in 1982, however, without seeing a glimmer of hope that Reagan would accept accommodation with the Soviet Union.

Surviving Soviet leaders recognized Reagan's intransigence and could only hope that dissatisfaction with his belligerence, in both Europe and the United States, would bring a new, more reasonable president in 1984. Of greater long-term consequence was evidence that the people to whom Yuri Andropov, Brezhnev's successor, looked for advice had begun to recognize that Soviet actions contributed to American militancy; that the United States might perceive the Soviet military buildup in the 1970s and expansionist policies in the Third World as threatening; that changes in Soviet behavior might be necessary to obtain the desired changes in American policy. And Andropov and his advisers, reviewing the strains on the Soviet economy, began to realize that their empire was overextended.

Nonetheless, Andropov, slowly dying of kidney failure, presided over the worst year in Soviet-American relations since the Cuban missile crisis of 1962. Moscow's diplomatic offensive to prevent the deployment of new American intermediate-range missiles resulted in a humiliating failure. European governments overcame internal opposition and approved installation of the missiles. In November 1983, hoping to place blame on the United States, the Soviets walked out of the INF talks, accomplishing nothing.

Most threatening to the Soviet leadership was the apparent intention of the Americans to begin a new high-tech race for defensive weapons. In March 1983 Reagan suddenly announced—with minimal warning to his secretaries of state and defense—that the United States would seek to create a strategic defense system (SDI, or "Star Wars"). He imagined a shield that would prevent any missiles from striking American territory. His conception may have been pure science fiction, but SDI came to be the critical element in arms negotiations for the remainder of his administration. Soviet scientists, like most American scientists, thought the idea preposterous, but Soviet leaders could not take the risk of ignoring it. SDI had to be stopped or the Soviets would have to compete in its development, a task for which they were ill-equipped.

The worst political disaster of the year, the incident that probably had the most adverse effect on any movement toward Soviet-American accommodation, came at the end of August, when a Soviet plane shot down a Korean jetliner, KAL 007, en route from Alaska to Seoul. The crew and all passengers, including several Americans, were killed. The Soviets initially denied downing the plane, then charged that it was spying. American intelligence intercepts determined that the plane had indeed strayed into Soviet airspace and been mistaken for a spy plane. Reagan falsely alleged that the Soviets had knowingly fired on a civilian plane. Foolishly, Andropov refused to accept Soviet responsibility, to express regret for the tragedy. Similarly, Reagan's deliberate abuse of the evidence to belabor the Soviets—who persisted in believing that American intelligence was using KAL 007—was needlessly inflammatory. So tense was the relationship that, in November, Able Archer, a routine NATO exercise, panicked the Soviet military into preparing for a nuclear attack.

The principal American setback of the year came in Lebanon. In June 1981 the Israelis had invaded Lebanon, with the acquiescence of Al Haig, who saw Israel as a surrogate against the Soviets and their friends. The Israelis were determined to eliminate the Palestine Liberation Organization (PLO) sanctuaries and to turn southern Lebanon into a buffer zone to shield Israel against Arab attacks.

Reagan was appalled by Israeli aggression and unmoved by Israel's insistence it was acting defensively, clearing out terrorists. When the Israelis failed to prevent their Lebanese Christian allies from massacring Palestinian refugees, Reagan sent the marines to attempt to maintain order in Beirut. Slowly the Americans were drawn into the civil strife as Lebanese factions backed variously by Syria, Israel, and Iran struggled to control the country. In October 1983 a terrorist with a truckload of explosives attacked the marine barracks, killing 241 Americans. The president then withdrew the survivors to ships offshore.

American forces had been put in an untenable position and lives had been lost. Intervention had accomplished nothing. The Soviets had avoided direct involvement but resupplied the Syrians, who became the dominant force in Lebanese politics. The Israelis were trapped in a quagmire and spent many lives, Israeli as well as Arab, before extricating themselves. Lebanon ceased to exist as a viable country.

Two days after the U.S. Marines were withdrawn from Beirut, American forces attacked the Caribbean nation of Grenada, ostensibly to rescue American medical students trapped between rival Marxist factions vying for control of the island. Vastly superior American forces overwhelmed local resistance, including that of several hundred Cubans and a handful of North Korean advisers. The Soviets, suspicious of the self-styled Marxists of Grenada, did not attempt to counter the display of American force. But Reagan's message was clear: the eagle was screaming. American pressures on the periphery of the Soviet empire would increase.

SDI, the aftermath of the KAL 007 incident, the American use of force in Lebanon and Grenada, and the deployment of new missiles in Europe all suggested to Soviet leaders that a sharply increased level of confrontation was ahead for them. In fact, as Soviet apprehensions began to crystallize, George Shultz, who replaced Haig as secretary of state in mid-1982, had already begun moving Reagan toward a less apocalyptic vision of how to cope with adversaries.

Shultz discovered that the president was interested in traveling to China and the Soviet Union. He explained that an improvement in relations would have to precede a visit to either nation. Reagan remarked that he was not unwilling to reduce tensions and indicated to the Soviet ambassador that he was interested in a more constructive relationship. The Soviets responded by allowing a group of Pentecostal Christians who had taken refuge in the American Embassy in Moscow—and for whom Reagan had expressed concern—to leave the country. Shultz pushed for conciliatory moves, arguing that the United States had recovered economically, was rebuilding militarily, and was in a strong position to negotiate. And polling data showed that foreign policy was Reagan's one weak point with the electorate. In January 1984 Reagan gave a relatively amiable speech about future Soviet-American relations, and Shultz persuaded the Soviets that the president was in earnest. Andropov responded with a secret letter manifesting interest in developing communications between the two leaders.

The death of Andropov and his replacement by the ailing Konstantin Chernenko precluded any dramatic moves by Moscow. Reagan continued to offer friendly gestures, but no significant change in the relationship was likely until the Soviets had a leader as strong as the American president. Shultz and Reagan turned their attention to the other corner of the strategic triangle: China.

Tensions with China were partly the result of the inability of Reagan, prior to taking office, to understand that China had become a strategic asset. Chiang and "Free China" (the Republic of China on Taiwan) were important symbols to the American Right, and candidate Reagan was surrounded by advisers who saw Nixon's rapprochement with the People's Republic as a betrayal. He talked of restoring recognition of the Taiwan regime, withdrawn when Carter recognized Beijing in 1979. He frequently offered remarks and gestures offensive to the government of Deng Xiaoping. His behavior aggravated disagreements over the continued American sales of weapons to Taiwan. The advantages his predecessors had gained by drawing China closer in opposition to the Soviet Union were evaporating.

Vice President George H. W. Bush and Secretary Haig had traveled to Beijing to reassure Chinese leaders of American interest in a cooperative relationship, but the Chinese were unconvinced and distanced themselves from the United States. An agreement on arms sales to Taiwan in August 1982 merely papered over unresolved differences. Shultz never shared the Kissinger-Brzezinski estimate of China's strategic importance but recognized the importance of good relations. Gradually he brought Reagan to an understanding of the value of Chinese-American collaboration, especially in gathering intelligence about the Soviets. In April 1984 Reagan visited China, his first foray into a Communist country. The Chinese greeted him with the extraordinary hospitality for which they were renowned—and they never had any trouble with him again. He enjoyed the trip enormously and came away with a view of life in China more sanguine than justified. Trade and cultural relations prospered. The political relationship never regained the closeness of the late 1970s, but with the resurgence of American power it did not seem as important.

In November 1984 the American people once again chose Ronald Reagan to lead them. At the peak of his popularity and power, he turned to the Soviet Union to look for possible accommodation as the centerpiece of his second administration. Arms control negotiations, begun in January 1985, stalled when Chernenko died. Enter Mikhail Gorbachev, destined to become one of the most important political figures of the twentieth century.

Soviet leaders had realized since Brezhnev's dying days that their economy was in trouble, that their society was on the verge of crisis. Andropov had begun the process of reform, but his failing health precluded significant progress. Chernenko was less active. By March 1985 the Politburo was ready to select a young, vigorous leader to modernize the Soviet economy.

Gorbachev understood radical change was necessary, but his support in the Politburo was fragile and the military and the civilian bureaucracy were resistant. The support of Soviet intellectuals was enormously helpful, but the Soviet Union of 1985 was not a state in which the power of the pen seemed likely to prevail. He would have to move slowly.

Gorbachev had traveled in the West and had no illusions about the superiority of the Soviet model of development. He knew that apart from its great military power, conditions in the Soviet Union were like those of a Third World country. It was "Upper Volta with missiles." He understood that to modernize, the Soviet Union could not just buy technology; it would have to accept some Western ideas and values as well. He would have to dismantle the Stalinist obstacles to Western civil society, to complete the task Nikita Khrushchev had begun. The job would have to be done with extraordinary care to avoid a conservative backlash or to undermine the Communist Party, the source of his power.

Modernizing and strengthening the Soviet Union would also be costly. Virtually the entire infrastructure would have to be replaced. Gorbachev's colleagues, especially in the military, were greatly troubled by Reagan's SDI program and by high-tech defensive equipment already part of NATO's force structure. Where would they find the assets, material or intellectual, with which to compete? Gorbachev could ill afford to increase military expenditures.

Then there were Soviet commitments to the Third World, a tremendous drain on the country's resources. They were not only an extravagance; they were also a major irritant in Soviet-American relations. Not least of his problems was Afghanistan, expensive in both blood and rubles and increasingly unpopular at home. The Soviets had learned little from the American experience in Vietnam, but Afghanistan was teaching them firsthand how difficult it was to win or extricate themselves from a civil war in an undeveloped country.

In brief, Gorbachev needed a respite from the Cold War to enable him to devote his energies and his nation's resources to building a modern, efficient Soviet state. He was persuaded that his country was safe from external threat. More nuclear weapons were unnecessary. More was not better: Soviet accumulation of missiles aroused apprehension in the United States and triggered a new cycle in the arms race. He was the first Soviet leader to understand the security dilemma, to understand that there could be no security for the Soviet Union without security for the United States. He was aware also that Reagan's military expenditures had resulted in an intolerable deficit in the American budget. The Americans would probably be receptive to overtures for an arms control agreement, for a mutual reduction of military spending. Finally, Gorbachev recognized that the Soviet obsession with secrecy, initially born of the need to hide weakness, created anxieties abroad. It allowed for exaggerations of Soviet military capabilities and misperception of Soviet intentions. He was ready to open the society a little, even to consider the on-site inspections the Americans demanded.

Reagan and the rest of the world were not quite ready for the extraordinary course Gorbachev contemplated. Nor were Americans sure that it was in their interest to help him build a modern Soviet economy, a stronger Soviet Union. Reagan persisted in his efforts to roll back Soviet influence. The Reagan Doctrine, American assistance to forces attempting to overthrow Communist or pro-Soviet regimes in the Third World, intensified. The CIA had gone to war against the Sandinista government in Nicaragua in 1982, beginning with the training and equipping of "contras," who Reagan described as "freedom fighters." Nicaragua was the central front in the campaign, but aid in various forms went to opponents of the Soviet-backed governments of Afghanistan, Angola, Cambodia, and untold other distant lands. When Congress tried to restrain the executive branch, the president's aides raised money in the private sector and from wealthy friends abroad, such as the Saudis and the sultan of Brunei. The Israelis and Iranians became involved as zealots in the National Security Council decided to sell arms secretly and illegally, with Israeli collusion, to the Iranians. The proceeds were used to support the contras, subverting the intent of Congress and the Constitution. Reagan seemed only vaguely aware of what was being done in his name but was weakened gravely when the Iran-Contra scandal became public knowledge in 1986.

The Soviets continued the struggle in Afghanistan, supported the Vietnamese takeover of Cambodia and the Angolan government against its enemies, but backed away from sending fighter jets (MIGs) to Nicaragua and urged Cuban restraint. Gorbachev had higher priorities. He wanted an arms control agreement, and he wanted to meet with Reagan to try to persuade him to give up the expensive fantasy of SDI. In November 1985 Reagan and Gorbachev traveled to Geneva for the first meeting between Reagan and a Soviet leader.

Reagan despised and mistrusted Communists and hated the "evil empire" in the abstract. But he responded differently to contact with people, with individual Soviet citizens. In Gorbachev he found a man as personable and confident, as determined to protect his nation's interests—and to avoid nuclear holocaust—as he was. At Geneva and in the meetings that followed, the two men found common ground. From time to time each grew angry or impatient with the stubbornness of the other, but the antagonism between them and their countries gradually diminished. Summitry, often derided by diplomats and scholars, proved remarkably useful. Reagan could not have come to trust Gorbachev had he not met him, argued with him, shared his hopes and fears.

Little besides the establishment of a personal relationship resulted from the first meeting between the leaders. The Americans did not take the dramatic Soviet proposals seriously, and Reagan left no doubt of his commitment to SDI. In the months that followed, however, Gorbachev electrified the world with the changes he began to institute in the Soviet

Union and his ideas for ending the arms race. He professed willingness to sign an INF agreement on American terms, to accept limits on the intercontinental ballistic missiles so worrisome to Americans, and he indicated he was ready to redeploy Soviet forces in Europe from their traditional offensive posture to a defensive one. Gorbachev was prepared to take risks that appalled his military. He was determined to end the Western perception of a Soviet threat, to obtain an arms control agreement, and to avoid a struggle for advantage in strategic defense.

The American response had to be disappointing. In April American planes attacked Libya with the intention of killing Muammar al-Qaddafi, the Libyan leader with whom the Soviets had ties. At approximately the same time, Reagan authorized the CIA to provide the Afghan resistance with shoulder-fired antiaircraft missiles, with which the Afghans promptly began downing Soviet helicopters. The United States was increasing the pressure on Soviet friends in the Third World. And in May Reagan announced that the United States would no longer be bound by the terms of the unratified SALT II agreement. As the Soviet leader waved the olive branch, the United States became more threatening.

At virtually the same time, late April 1986, the Soviet Union was devastated by a nuclear catastrophe, an explosion at the Chernobyl nuclear power plant. Gorbachev and his colleagues handled the crisis badly. Most Soviet citizens learned of the explosion and of the danger to them from foreign broadcasts. It took Gorbachev nearly three weeks to issue a statement—in which he rejected Western estimates of the magnitude of the disaster. The episode did little to encourage Western faith in the Soviet leader's promise to open his society.

By October the two superpower leaders were in need of a dramatic breakthrough to enhance their domestic political fortunes. Gorbachev had little to show, at home or abroad, for his efforts. Reagan was beginning to lose his magic. The American people still loved him, but Congress cut his defense budget sharply and then overrode his veto of sanctions against the racist regime of South Africa. Both leaders stood to gain politically from a major agreement at their meeting in Reykjavik, Iceland.

Gorbachev had asked for the meeting, hoping to reach a deal on limiting SDI. He was prepared to offer major concessions. He suggested 50 percent reductions in strategic missiles over a five-year period, the removal of American and Soviet intermediate missiles from Europe, and the elimination of all ballistic missiles in ten years. He dropped a number of previous Soviet conditions for an agreement and even accepted SDI laboratory research. Reagan indicated his willingness to accept Gorbachev's proposals—until he understood that SDI testing would be limited to the laboratory.

The Reykjavik summit collapsed over SDI, but it was clear that SDI had motivated the Soviets to take the initiative in arms control. It was evident they were ready to move forward. Reagan's obstinacy on SDI and his inability to comprehend some of the issues—as when he agreed to surrender the missiles on which European security arguably depended—muddied the waters, but the American negotiators sensed that historic agreements were within reach.

The next few months were difficult for Reagan. The Republicans lost control of the Senate and the Iran-Contra scandal broke, revealing his willingness to deal with terrorists, the disregard of his aides for the law, and the extent of his detachment from the operations of his government. His presidency lost its moorings in the early days of 1987. The president was adrift.

Gorbachev was struggling to stay in control of the apparatus of power in the Soviet Union. He had failed to achieve anything by insisting on halting Reagan's SDI program as a price for Soviet concessions. In February he proposed the elimination of intermediate-range missiles *without* mentioning SDI. Those of Reagan's advisers *least* amenable to an agreement had the president respond favorably, contingent on the Soviets accepting highly intrusive verification procedures, which the Soviets always rejected. They were astonished when the Soviets agreed. It took several months of haggling, with Gorbachev fighting off opposition in Moscow, but in November Shultz and Eduard Shevardnadze, Gorbachev's foreign minister, reached agreement. In December Gorbachev went to Washington, where he and Reagan signed a momentous INF agreement to destroy more than 2,500 intermediate-range missiles. The arrangements for verification were so through that American officials feared Soviet inspectors might learn too much about what was going on in the United States.

Signs that the Soviet Union was on a radically new course multiplied. At home, human rights abuses declined and political dissidents were released from exile or prison. Criticism of the Soviet system became more acceptable. Gorbachev won approval for reforms that pointed toward a less centralized economy. And in foreign policy, the Soviets began pulling troops out of Afghanistan. In May they began withdrawing from Mongolia, and there was even talk of the Red Army leaving Eastern Europe. Polls showed that only 30 percent of the American people still perceived the Soviet Union as an enemy. Reagan readily acknowledged it was no longer an "evil empire."

Gorbachev had found the path to ending the Cold War. His initiatives astonished his Western interlocutors. Indeed many American leaders— Richard Nixon and Henry Kissinger foremost among them—and most of Reagan's advisers remained mistrustful. Prominent conservatives charged Reagan with appeasement. But Reagan was convinced the Soviet Union was changing. He had faith in his own judgment and found in Gorbachev a man willing to meet him more than halfway. Prominent American scholars such as Melvyn Leffler and James Mann credit Reagan with the good sense to allow Gorbachev to succeed in ending Soviet-American tensions.

In December, after George H. W. Bush was elected to succeed Reagan, Gorbachev flew to New York and announced at the United Nations that he would reduce Soviet forces by 500,000, *unilaterally*, and would eliminate units stationed in Germany, Czechoslovakia, and Hungary. The remainder of the Red Army in Eastern Europe would be shifted to a defensive posture, eliminating the threat to the West. As he explained to President-elect Bush, the crisis within the Soviet Union left him no choice. The Soviets could no longer afford an empire.

The collapse of the Soviet empire came faster than anyone had imagined. The United States had little to do with conditions in Eastern Europe or the Soviet Union as the dominoes toppled on the Kremlin. Events the world's leading analysts considered inconceivable occurred one after another. Freedom came to much of Eastern Europe, the two Germanys were reunited—and one day, the Soviet Union disappeared. The Cold War was over, and the United States, greatly weakened, staggering, but still on its feet, claimed victory.

Gorbachev's domestic policies heartened reformers throughout the Communist world. The old-line Stalinists trembled as the Kremlin encouraged emulation of Gorbachev's policies. In March 1989 the Soviet Union conducted the freest elections in its history. Many Communist Party regulars were defeated in the competition for seats in the Congress of People's Deputies. In April Andrei Sakharov, the great Soviet physicist and Nobel Prize–winning symbol of the fight for human rights in the Soviet Union, freed from exile by Gorbachev, was chosen to sit in the Chamber of Deputies. It was not democracy, nor was democracy Gorbachev's goal, but the Soviet Union was changing. Soviet troops and tanks began to pull back from Poland, Hungary, and East Germany.

In May Gorbachev traveled to Beijing to deepen the rapprochement he had effected with China. He was upstaged, however, by thousands of Chinese demonstrators, who, chanting his name, demanded political reform from their own leaders. They had assembled in the vast Tiananmen Square and ignored government demands that they disperse. The world, watching the demonstrations on satellite television, imagined that Chinese leaders might yield, that China, too, might be verging on a democratic revolution. But on June 4 the aging Chinese leaders sent the People's Liberation Army to crush the people. Hundreds, perhaps thousands, died, and many more were imprisoned. China, the Communist nation whose successful economic reforms had won widespread admiration in the 1980s, would not join the march to freedom. Instead, the "Chinese solution" came to signify the choice of repression in response to the cries of the people.

The Communist governments of Eastern Europe were also forced to choose. Gorbachev indicated that the Soviet Union would not interfere in Poland, where a resurgent Solidarity movement was on the verge of overwhelming the Communist regime, or in Hungary, where reform Communists were moving the economy away from socialism and opening the political system to opposition parties. When the Communists of Poland reached out to Gorbachev for help in salvaging their power, he advised them to let go.

Astonishing as the events in Poland were, East Germany provided yet greater drama. In September 1989 Hungarian authorities decided to allow East German refugees to cross their borders to flee to the West. A German appeal to Moscow was brushed aside. No new wall was built to contain freedom-seeking Germans. The Soviets would not challenge the

Hungarian decision. Massive demonstrations swept East Germany. Hundreds of thousands of Germans took to the streets demanding democracy, freedom, and unification with West Germany. The German Communist leader chose to emulate Deng Xiaoping, to replicate Tiananmen in Leipzig, but his subordinates refused to turn their guns on their own people. The regime was forced to open the gates of the Berlin Wall in November, and that hated symbol of the Cold War, of the division of Germany and Europe, came tumbling down.

Soon the Czech people were back in the streets and the dissident playwright Vaclav Havel, released from prison only months earlier, was elected president. In Bulgaria and Romania, the people rose against their Communist rulers. The Romanian dictator attempted the Chinese solution but was ousted and executed by the party apparatus. The Soviet sphere of influence in Eastern Europe, conceded by Roosevelt at Yalta, long perceived as Moscow's most vital interest, had vanished. In Poland, Hungary, Germany, and Czechoslovakia, the people had freed themselves, but it was Gorbachev who opened the door to freedom by signaling willingness to see the old party leaders replaced. He had not anticipated the utter rejection of the Communists, but he made no effort to resist radical change until it began to threaten the survival of the Soviet Union.

As Gorbachev attempted to open Soviet society, to give a degree of legitimacy to pluralism, long-smoldering separatist movements and interethnic violence erupted. The Baltic republics—Estonia, Latvia, and Lithuania—constituted a special problem. They had enjoyed independence between world wars but were annexed by Stalin as part of the notorious Nazi-Soviet nonaggression pact of 1939. By 1989, discussion of the pact was no longer forbidden and the Soviet government admitted its culpability. The Baltic republics then denounced the pact and demanded their independence. Here Gorbachev drew the line: if the Baltic republics were allowed to become independent, how could other republics such as Ukraine and Georgia, with strong separatist movements, be denied?

When Gorbachev attempted to threaten and cajole the Baltic republics into remaining part of the Soviet Union, complications with the United States arose. There were vocal Lithuanian, Latvian, and Estonian populations in the United States. There were still Americans who mistrusted the

Soviet Union. The use of force against the Baltic republics would undermine much of the goodwill Gorbachev had generated and bring considerable anti-Soviet pressure to bear on Bush, who was less confident than Reagan about the "new" directions the Soviets were taking. Given the intransigence of the Lithuanian independence movement and the anti-Lithuanian belligerence of the Russian elements in the Soviet military, there was probably no way Gorbachev could hold on to the Baltics without alienating the United States.

For a year, amid this incredible turmoil, amid the dissolution of the Soviet empire and the unraveling of the Soviet Union, Gorbachev tried with minimal success to reach out to Bush. He indicated his willingness to make huge cuts in Soviet conventional forces to highlight the absence of hostile intent. He expressed the desire to integrate the Soviet Union in the world economy, to accept the offers Stalin had rejected in 1945. Bush temporized. Finally, in December 1989, the two men met in Malta.

Bush seized the initiative and assured Gorbachev of American support. He indicated his readiness to negotiate a Soviet-American trade agreement without restrictions on most-favored-nation (MFN) treatment. The United States would support Soviet efforts to participate in the international economic order. And the United States was ready to respond to Gorbachev's desire for rapid progress in arms control and force reductions. In turn, Gorbachev stressed his desire for partnership with the United States. The Soviets now *wanted* an American presence in Europe, most likely to contain the Germans. It was not quite a resurrection of the grand alliance of World War II, but the United States and the Soviet Union had ceased to be enemies.

Tensions over Germany and the Baltics continued into 1990. Neither the United States nor the Soviet Union was eager to confront a united Germany, but they lacked the power to prevent the *Anschluss*. The economic and political power of West Germany dictated the timing and terms of unification. Helmut Kohl, West Germany's chancellor, dominated the process and forced the pace. He assured the Soviets and his allies that Germany was satisfied with its existing borders and promised the Soviets desperately needed economic assistance. Reluctantly, Gorbachev accepted first reunification and then participation of a united Germany in

NATO. The Baltic issue remained troubling, but both Bush and Gorbachev did what they could to minimize the irritation.

The decisive test came in the confrontation with Iraq that began in August 1990 with Iraq's invasion of Kuwait. The Soviet Union abandoned its longtime ally and aligned itself with the United States. The Soviet-armed and -trained Iraqi Army was left to be decimated by the United States and its European and Arab allies. Even Bush, who prided himself on his lack of the "vision thing," was inspired to promise a New World Order.

For Gorbachev, the end of the Cold War brought a well-deserved Nobel Prize, but the great statesman won little honor at home. Neither his diplomatic exploits nor his end to repression put food on the plates of his people nor did anything to alleviate the miserable economic condition of the Soviet Union. In August 1991 he was deposed in a coup led by conservatives and held prisoner in the Crimea. A few days later the coup leaders found the military unwilling to crush a few thousand demonstrators who had rallied around Boris Yeltsin, a one-time Gorbachev supporter who now personified the demand for more radical change. Gorbachev returned to Moscow, but events had passed him by. Communism, however reformist, was finished in the Soviet Union. Indeed, the Soviet Union was finished. One after another, the constituent republics declared their independence, the Communist Party was outlawed, and Gorbachev had no empire, no country, and then no government to rule. Before the end of the year, Yeltsin, popularly elected president of the Russian Republic, moved into the Kremlin and Gorbachev was forced into early retirement. On December 31, 1991, the Soviet Union officially ceased to exist.

The United States was the only superpower to survive the Cold War. It had triumphed economically, ideologically, and politically. Curiously, few Americans stopped to celebrate. They found, in fact, that the quality of their lives was declining rather than improving. They were confronted with an industrial infrastructure and transportation system in decay, a corrupt banking system that had cost thousands of people their life's savings, massive unemployment, and widespread homelessness. The Reagan administration, in its effort to expand American military power without asking the people to pay for it, had run up an incredible deficit, leaving the government without the means to respond to the nation's domestic crisis. Once the country on which the world depended for investment capital, it had become in 1985 the world's leading debtor, dependent on Japan, Germany, and the Arab oil-producing states. It had to solicit donations from foreign governments to finance the war against Iraq in 1991. It could no longer provide sufficient aid to needy countries abroad or necessary services for its own people. Voter apathy eroded the value of its electoral system, and racism simmered and boiled up with painful frequency.

Some analysts, most notably the historian Paul Kennedy, suggested that the United States was in decline, that it suffered from imperial overreach and a lack among its leaders of the political will or courage to ask the people to rebuild the nation for their children and their children's children. But the United States had won the Cold War: it was still number one.

17

THE NEW WORLD ORDER

F OR MORE THAN four decades, the lodestar of American foreign policy had been opposition to the Soviet Union and its allies. With the end of the Cold War and the disintegration of the Soviet Union, the men and women in Washington who were responsible for shaping relations with the rest of the world, with ensuring the nation's security, scoured the compass in search of a new guiding principle. They never found it.

George H. W. Bush, although more experienced in world affairs than most American presidents, never had a vision of the role the United States would play in the years ahead. He and James Baker, his secretary of state, were superb problem solvers, not given to long-range planning. Several midlevel officials, most notably Paul Wolfowitz, undersecretary of defense, foresaw an opportunity for the United States to hasten what they imagined to be the inevitable process of creating a liberal democratic world order. But Brent Scowcroft, Bush's national security adviser, perceived himself as a Kissinger-style "realist" and concentrated on relations with major powers, minimally interested in events in the rest of the world. Dick Cheney, secretary of defense, was an old-fashioned nationalist who favored exercising presidential and state power without restraint.

The earliest test had come in 1989 when Deng Xiaoping ordered the brutal suppression of protestors in China's Tiananmen Square, crushing the reform movement. Bush considered China to be an important strategic partner, and he determined not to allow the massacres to disrupt the relationship. Forced by public outrage to impose sanctions on China, Bush sent Scowcroft on a secret mission to assure Deng of Washington's continued friendship. Not wholly persuaded of Gorbachev's good intentions, Bush discerned a need to avoid antagonizing Beijing. The atrocities perpetrated by the People's Liberation Army in the vicinity of Tiananmen and elsewhere occurred several months before Eastern Europeans liberated themselves, before the Berlin Wall came down. And the United States had condoned comparable brutality by friendly states throughout the Cold War.

Before the year was out, *after* the Wall had been breached, Bush did appear to strike a blow for democracy. In Panama, Manuel Noriega was no longer useful to the CIA. Kept on the payroll despite the objections of the Department of State and the National Security Council, despite indications he was guilty of drug trafficking, money laundering, and murder, the Agency protected him. His assistance against the Sandinistas in Nicaragua had been his "get-out-of-jail-free card," but Baker was preparing to disband the contras in exchange for a Sandinista pledge to hold elections. Noriega resisted suggestions he allow democracy to prevail in Panama, and his men began harassing Americans.

A few days before Christmas in 1989, Bush sent twenty-seven thousand troops to eliminate the regime and capture Noriega. Noriega had defied Bush, leader of the free world, and American inaction had prompted questions about Bush's resolve—the "wimp factor." There was nothing like a major and successful military operation to dispel concerns about the president's manhood or willingness to use deadly force.

Since the hostage crisis in 1979, the United States had been openly hostile to the Iranian government. Unfortunately it could not be disposed of as readily as Noriega's regime or as easily as the Eisenhower administration helped dispose of the Tehran government in 1954. Washington settled for efforts to contain its influence, and Reagan ordered assistance to the vicious Iraqi dictatorship of Saddam Hussein when it fought Iran in the 1980s. But when that war ended in 1988, Saddam's actions became increasingly irritating. His belligerence toward Israel and Kuwait worried the National Security Council.

In July 1990 Saddam massed troops along the Kuwait border. Assuming Saddam was bluffing, the United States did not indicate to Baghdad how it would respond if the Iraqis invaded Kuwait. Bush was shocked by the invasion and determined not to allow the aggression to go unpunished. He equated it with unchecked German and Japanese actions in the 1930s. If Saddam succeeded, he would seek dominance over the entire Arab world and its oil. Bush prepared for a crusade against evil—and to preserve the flow of oil. Many Americans, including Colin Powell, chairman of the Joint Chiefs, saw no compelling reason for the United States to ride to the rescue.

Once the president decided to act, he and Secretary Baker managed affairs magnificently. They succeeded in persuading the Saudis to allow American troops to be stationed on their sacred soil to deter an attack. They won UN Security Council approval for an economic embargo against Iraq. They won the support of the Soviets—despite objections from the Soviet military. Bush personally contacted leaders of other countries to gain support for American military action. But he also needed money. The Reagan era deficits had left the country unable to finance a war. Bush wrung the money he needed out of Germany, Japan, and Saudi Arabia.

Congress proved more difficult. Bush wanted congressional approval, but there was strong opposition, especially from Democrats. Secretary of Defense Cheney argued against seeking either UN or congressional backing, insisting the president needed neither. Bush, however, followed Baker's advice to obtain a UN-supported coalition that would assuage congressional concerns about American unilateralism.

When Iraq failed to withdraw by the stipulated date of January 15, 1991, the United States commenced savage air attacks. Iraq's infrastructure was devastated, and tens of thousands of Iraqi civilians were killed despite the use of "smart bombs" designed to hit specified targets. Defiantly, Saddam promised his people victory in "the mother of all battles."

On February 23, 1991, coalition forces attacked. It took less than forty-eight hours to eliminate organized Iraqi resistance. Kuwait was liberated quickly, and Iraqi survivors fled toward Baghdad. Expecting Saddam to be overthrown as a result of his defeat, Bush called a halt to the fighting exactly one hundred hours after the ground offensive began. American forces had lost only 146 lives, and neither Bush nor any of his senior advisers saw any point in risking additional American lives by driving on to Baghdad. Mission accomplished.

Wolfowitz was dissatisfied. He thought the cease-fire had come too early, leaving Saddam in power and his elite forces intact. He still had his programs to create weapons of mass destruction, and his regime's human rights abuses and hostility to Israel were not likely to subside. When Shiites in the South and Kurds in the North rose against Saddam, Wolfowitz wanted to support them, to give democracy a chance in Iraq. His superiors, however, feared the rebellions would fragment the country to Iran's advantage. They allowed Saddam to crush the rebellions, establishing "no fly" zones against Saddam's air force only after thousands of rebels had been killed. American leaders had no interest in occupying Iraq and bearing the burden of nation building. The president and his advisers were content to bask in the glory of their impressive victory.

If democracy was going to spread, there seemed little likelihood of the United States serving as its handmaiden. The overthrow of democratically elected President Jean-Bertrand Aristide in Haiti in September 1991 provided further evidence that the administration would do little to further Wolfowitz's vision. Baker and his colleagues preferred the military junta to the restoration of Aristide, viewed by conservatives as a dangerous radical. More embarrassing for the moral standing of the United States, it forcibly returned Haitian refugees—or interned them at Guantanamo, a U.S. naval base in Cuba.

Of greater consequence was the administration's unwillingness to cope with the crisis in the Balkans as Yugoslavia disintegrated. By spring 1991 it was evident that Croatia and Slovenia, two of the six republics of the federation, were preparing to secede. It was equally clear that Serbia, led by the demagogue Slobodan Milosevic, would attack both if they declared independence. Bush and Baker decided that Yugoslavia was a problem best left to the Europeans.

Serb behavior began to trouble European observers. There were indications of "ethnic cleansing," the killing and deportation of non-Serbs in territory that came under Serb control. Men and women who had admired the historic city of Dubrovnik were appalled when the Serbs shelled it needlessly. And then came the horrors of Serb atrocities in Bosnia.

Bosnia-Herzegovina, the most ethnically diverse of the Yugoslav republics—with a Muslim plurality—also chose to withdraw from the federation. Hoping to preserve the territorial integrity of Bosnia, the United States joined the European Community in recognizing its independence in April 1992, and the United Nations sent a peacekeeping force. Milosevic, however, was determined to seize control of Bosnia and used Bosnian Serb fighters, supported by irregulars from his own forces, to achieve his end. The Serbs launched major offensives against majority Muslim towns, raping and murdering innocent civilians everywhere they went. The UN peacekeepers proved hopelessly inadequate, and Bosnia became a humanitarian nightmare.

In Washington, there was a growing sense that the United States, the world's greatest power, had a moral responsibility to stop the Serbs. Wolfowitz pressed hard for intervention to stop what he perceived as genocide. Scowcroft was equally troubled, but Baker, Powell, and Cheney argued there was no threat to national interests. As Baker famously framed their conclusion, the United States "had no dog in this fight."

Throughout the country, however, Americans who followed world affairs called for action against Serbia. Over the objections of Cheney and Powell, Bush approved the use of force to deliver humanitarian relief to the besieged Bosnian capital of Sarajevo. The Serbs backed off, allowing the relief supplies to be delivered. But as evidence of Serb atrocities against Muslims mounted, support grew for a more robust response. The most popular proposal was for lifting the arms embargo to allow the Bosnians to obtain weapons to defend themselves and to bomb Serb positions to level the playing field. But Bush would do no more against the advice of Cheney and Powell. The horrors in Bosnia intensified.

The administration had decided initially to stand clear of the Arab-Israeli tangle. One president after another had failed to persuade the Israelis to abide by UN resolution 242, which called on them to surrender the land occupied after the Six-Day War in exchange for peace treaties that would constitute Arab recognition of Israel's right to exist—the "land for peace" formula. Bush and Baker were angered, however, by Israel's persistent building of settlements in Arab East Jerusalem and amid Arab populations of the West Bank and Gaza. Nonetheless they saw no point to arousing the hostility of pro-Israel groups in the United States if nothing could be accomplished. They would have left matters alone but for a promise made to Gorbachev in return for his support during the run-up to the Gulf War offering him a role in the search for peace in the Middle East.

Working together, perhaps the United States and the Soviet Union could bring an end to the hatred their Cold War rivalry had exacerbated in the region. To honor the commitment, Baker began discussions with Arab and Israeli leaders in the spring of 1991. Skillfully, he managed to get all the players to a conference in Madrid in October 1991. Agreement after agreement unraveled, but he stayed with it and prevailed. It was an extraordinary performance. For a brief moment, there was hope of peace as Palestinians and Israelis sat together and negotiated for the first time. Although no settlement was reached, there were signs of flexibility on both the Israeli and Palestinian sides. And renewed pressure by the Bush administration led to the demise of the right-wing Likud coalition and the rise of Yitzhak Rabin, who agreed to stop building settlements and proved open to territorial compromise.

Across the Pacific there was North Korea, a problem that persisted even with the end of the Cold War. In the mid-1980s intelligence analysts reported that Pyongyang was attempting to develop nuclear weapons. Bush and Baker inherited the situation and hoped to win assistance from China and the Soviet Union to persuade Kim Il Sung to cease his efforts. Beijing was not interested in dealing with the issue. The Soviets were more responsive, but when Gorbachev established diplomatic relations with South Korea in September 1990, Moscow lost what little leverage it had with Kim.

North Korea had signed the Nuclear Nonproliferation Treaty (NPT) in 1985. It had failed, however, to sign a required safeguard agreement with the International Atomic Energy Agency (IAEA). Pyongyang insisted there could be no inspections while it was threatened by American nuclear weapons, especially those in South Korea. The American ambassador in Seoul, the commander of U.S. forces in Korea, and the Department of Defense recommended removal of the weapons to facilitate negotiations, but Scowcroft was unwilling. He persuaded Bush that removal would give the North Koreans something for nothing. The intelligence community warned that Kim might have his weapons by the mid-1990s, but the administration, divided on the issue and preoccupied with Soviet, Chinese, and Iraqi affairs, initially did nothing.

In a different context, in an attempt to gain an important arms control objective before Gorbachev lost control, Bush announced the United States would remove all its overseas tactical nuclear weapons. At the same time, he quietly approved removal of all nuclear weapons from South Korea, allowing the president of South Korea to declare his country nuclear-free in December 1991. The Bush administration simultaneously indicated its willingness to have the high-level meeting Kim wanted.

Kim's regime was in economic trouble. The Soviets had abandoned it. The Chinese, eager to expand ties with Seoul, might withhold aid if Kim was inflexible. Desperate, he looked to South Korea and the United States as well as China for possible economic assistance. His representatives met with their South Korean counterparts and quickly agreed to a nonaggression pact and a ban on the processing of uranium. After persuading the South Koreans to cancel the intimidating U.S.-ROK Team Spirit military exercise, the North Koreans made the concession most important to Washington: they agreed to sign the safeguards agreement with the IAEA and to allow inspections of their nuclear facility. But the Americans offered no aid in return, merely insisting on an end to North Korea's nuclear program.

The situation deteriorated rapidly. IAEA inspectors found discrepancies between what Pyongyang declared and what they found on the ground. South Korea urged the United States to stiffen its approach to the North. Its military asked to resume the Team Spirit exercise, and Cheney authorized the operation without consulting the Department of State.

Kim's overtures had gained nothing, and his nuclear ambitions had been exposed. He had gambled on his ability to deceive the inspectors—and lost. He broke off talks with the South, refused to allow further inspections, and waited to see how the Bush administration would react. Focused on his campaign for reelection, Bush chose not to respond. Tensions between the IAEA and Pyongyang intensified in November 1992, but having failed in his bid to remain in the White House, Bush left the problem to his successor.

The Bush administration presided over the beginning of the post–Cold War world. The Cold War ended, the Soviet Union collapsed, and Germany reunified. The administration played a secondary role in these great events but played it well. Richard Nixon, in particular, criticized Bush for not giving more aid to Gorbachev and Boris Yeltsin, but Reagan had emptied the Treasury and Bush had little leeway. Helmut Kohl needed no help and managed German unification brilliantly, on terms with which Washington was quite content.

The two interventions the president ordered—Panama and Iraq—went well. Its basic goals, elimination of Noriega and the liberation of Kuwait, were attained with minimal American casualties—the sine qua non for public approval. Panama disappeared from Washington's horizons. Unfortunately, Saddam Hussein did not. But criticism of Bush's decision not to send troops on to Baghdad, not to rescue rebellious Shiites and Kurds, struck no chord with the American people.

Bush's handling of other issues was more contentious. His response to the Tiananmen massacres outraged Americans who demanded that their country's policies reflect its ideals as well as its interests. Similarly, his unwillingness to stop Serb atrocities disappointed millions who believed the United States was obligated to stop genocide.

Nevertheless, the president scored well with his people for his leadership in foreign affairs. They faulted him, however, for his failure to bring the country out of economic recession—and his campaign was hurt by the third-party candidacy of Ross Perot, a wealthy Texas businessman who condemned Bush's efforts to bring Mexico into the North American Free Trade Agreement (NAFTA), alleging it was causing the loss of jobs to the cheap labor market south of the Rio Grande. Even a desperation move to provide jobs in Texas and California by selling fighter planes to Taiwan failed to save

Bush. He doubted the wisdom of the sale but took the risk. As he antici-pated, he infuriated the Chinese—and lost the election anyway.

After the election, Bush made a foreign policy decision that had un-imaginable consequences. He sent American troops into Somalia where hundreds of thousands of Somalis were dying amid civil strife. Strategically located, the country had interested both superpowers during the Cold War. After the collapse of the Soviet Union, few in Washington or Moscow thought the country of much importance. But American television showed images of starving Somalis, producing what came to be known as the "CNN effect," the ability of television reporters to force Washington to at-tend to crises it preferred to ignore. Bush authorized the airlift of food un-der UN auspices.

Supplies proved insufficient to alleviate the misery of Somalis. Despite the opposition of the CIA, the Pentagon, and the State Department, Bush sent American troops as part of a multilateral operation to stop theft and oversee the distribution of food. Neither Cheney nor Scowcroft liked the plan, but the president was being pushed by Congress and public opinion. He assumed the troops would be withdrawn in a matter of weeks and sending them would—and did—save tens of thousands of lives. Unfortu-nately, intervention did not stop clan warfare, and the troops were still on the ground when Bush's successor took the oath of office.

And Washington still lacked a vision for foreign policy in the post–Cold War world. Toward the end of the administration of George Herbert Walker Bush, there were no imminent threats to the security of the United States. Its apparent victory in the Cold War allowed its people to conclude that foreign affairs were no longer important, that they were entitled to a "peace dividend." The country no longer needed a president focused on external events. It could afford to elect a small-state governor who prom-ised to focus on domestic affairs. Arkansas's William Jefferson ("It's the economy, stupid") Clinton was the man they chose.

Clinton had little interest in foreign policy. He once remarked that only a handful of journalists cared about foreign relations. For the next several years, his inattention frustrated those of his advisers with foreign policy responsibilities. He never developed a useful working relationship with Warren Christopher or Lee Aspin, respectively his first secretaries of state and defense—and neither provided strong enough leadership to compensate. He ended the practice of receiving daily briefings from the director of the CIA. At the urging of Tony Lake, his national security adviser, he agreed to have weekly meetings with these senior officials but postponed them as often as not. Other than on trade issues, his staff found it difficult to engage him.

Clinton's relations with the Pentagon were especially poor. He was often derided as a "draft dodger" for avoiding service in Vietnam. His desire to allow gays to serve openly in the military was opposed by Colin Powell, his inherited chairman of the Joint Chiefs. Aspin proved to be an incompetent administrator, and it was only when William Perry replaced him that military-civilian relations functioned effectively again.

There were three men who, sharing his priorities, had easy access to the president: Samuel "Sandy" Berger, Lake's deputy and ultimate successor at the National Security Council; Ron Brown, secretary of commerce; and Mickey Kantor, who served as U.S. trade representative (USTR). All were intensely concerned with trade issues, opening foreign markets, and facilitating corporate access to cheap labor and natural resources in less-developed countries.

Three others were able to gain Clinton's attention through personal ties and force of personality. Strobe Talbott, a journalist with exceptional knowledge of Russian affairs, had been close to Clinton for many years. He won the president's support for efforts to assist the Russians toward developing a democratic government and a market economy. The other two—Madeline Albright and Richard Holbrooke—were enormously successful at attracting media attention, overshadowing Christopher and Lake. Albright, before succeeding Christopher at State, served as ambassador to the United Nations and worked to invigorate the organization. Her banner line was "assertive multilateralism"—which did not prevent her from referring to the United States as the "indispensible nation." The notoriously aggressive Holbrooke served briefly as ambassador to Germany and then as assistant secretary of state for European and Canadian affairs. He was unquestionably the right person to handle Slobodan Milosevic when Clinton finally decided to take on the Serb leader.

And then there was Winston Lord, a Kissinger protégé who had served as Bush's ambassador to China. Lord was disappointed by Bush's management of Chinese-American relations, especially on issues of human rights. He was troubled sufficiently to advise Clinton on policy toward China in the election campaign of 1992 and was rewarded with appointment as assistant secretary of state for East Asia and the Pacific. Aware of Lord's outrage at the Tiananmen massacre, Chinese leaders were uneasy about his presence in the administration. They need not have worried. Although there was no longer a strategic reason for appeasing China, for Clinton the expansion of trade took precedence over human rights—and Ron Brown rather than Lord had Clinton's ear on policy toward China. Moral imagination was in short supply in the White House.

Clinton was no less determined to maintain American preeminence in world affairs than his predecessors. He differed from them in devaluing military power and perceiving the principal threat in economic terms. This was most evident in his approach to Japanese-American relations. In addition to Ezra Vogel's classic *Japan as Number One*, Samuel Huntington, his influential Harvard colleague, argued that the Japanese were practicing economic warfare, attempting to use economic power to replace American influence in the world. Should they prevail, he warned, the world would be more violent with less democracy and economic growth.

Clinton minimized the Japanese-American security relationship, considered the keystone of American strategy across the Pacific, and took the offensive in trade relations. Kantor threatened and cajoled the Japanese in a modestly successful effort to get them to liberalize their trade practices. Putting economic concerns first, Clinton worried American specialists concerned with maintaining the strength of the alliance in the face of an unfriendly China and North Korean provocations.

If additional evidence of Clinton's priorities was necessary, he offered it in his willingness to challenge major interests in the Democratic Party by fighting for ratification of NAFTA. He was enamored of the concept of "globalization." To him it meant the spread of "market democracy." To the labor unions it meant the loss of American jobs, specifically to Mexico in the case of NAFTA. Most congressional Democrats opposed NAFTA, but Clinton pushed on, winning only because of strong support from Republicans. No other foreign policy issue engaged him comparably in the early years of his presidency.

There were other situations to which the president had to respond, such as the presence of 30,000 American troops in Somalia. As president-elect, Clinton had defended Bush's humanitarian intervention, but once in office, his attention was elsewhere. In the absence of presidential leadership, his foreign policy apparatus functioned poorly.

The initial success of the UN mission to Somalia had led to mission creep. Having saved hundreds of thousands of lives by establishing order sufficient to allow food distribution, the United Nations determined to pacify the warlords and reconstruct the failed state. In June, however, the forces of Mohammed Farah Aidid, the most powerful Somali warlord, ambushed a UN patrol and killed twenty-four Pakistani peacekeepers. UN forces proved inadequate to capture Aidid, and Albright persuaded the president to send in Rangers and Delta Force commandos. The efforts of the former American ambassador to Somalia, Robert Oakley, to negotiate with Aidid were brushed aside by the UN secretary-general, who was determined to punish the warlord.

The president and his national security adviser offered no direction, leaving control of the Somali venture to the troops in the field—until disaster struck in October, when Aidid's forces downed two American Black Hawk helicopters. Eighteen U.S. soldiers were killed in the disaster, a captured pilot was mistreated by the Somalis, and the body of one casualty was dragged in front of television cameras. Suddenly a horrified American public found Somalia on the map and a president, awakened to realities there, demanded that his aides clean up the mess. He wanted out of Somalia as quickly as possible short of further humiliation. Congress and the media agreed: if the people the United States and the United Nations were trying to help were shooting at their would-be saviors, it was time to get out.

The American retreat was disguised by first reinforcing American troops in Somalia. Clinton's advisers hoped this action would demonstrate to the world the United States could not be intimidated by some tin-pot warlord. Oakley resumed negotiations with Aidid and won release of the captured pilot. Then Clinton ordered the withdrawal of American forces, and Somalia ceased to be of interest to the public or the media in the United States.

To adversaries of the United States, the retreat from Somalia suggested that the sole remaining superpower could be outmaneuvered simply by killing or threatening to kill a few American soldiers. This was quickly apparent in Haiti. Clinton had criticized Bush's policy of forced repatriation of Haitian refugees but reneged on his promise to reverse Bush's policies. There was no interest in the United States in accepting tens, perhaps hundreds of thousands of Haitians alleged to be preparing a mass exodus to celebrate Clinton's election.

Officially, Washington continued to demand the restoration of Aristide to his presidential office, but the reality was different. Powerful elements in the U.S. government, including the CIA, the Pentagon, and the chair of the Senate Foreign Relations Committee, preferred the military junta that had overthrown him in 1991. Aristide was a defrocked priest, a preacher of liberation theology, who outraged American investors by threatening to double the minimum wage in Haiti.

Lake, Talbott, and Albright, on the other hand, stressed the fact that Aristide had won an overwhelming victory in a fair election. The junta was thwarting the will of the Haitian people. Diplomatic efforts to arrange for Aristide's return failed. The junta had no intention of relinquishing power and reneged on a deal.

In October the Haitian generals demonstrated what they had learned from events in Somalia. They had agreed to allow a small number of American and Canadian military trainers to land in Haiti to work with local security forces. When the American ship carrying the troops attempted to dock, it was challenged by an armed mob chanting "Somalia." Unprepared to land under fire, the ship sailed away. Unwilling to risk the lives of its troops, the United States retreated—and did nothing to relieve the humiliation.

Human rights groups and the Congressional Black Caucus intensified their efforts on behalf of Haitians. Lake and Talbott called for an invasion, unsettling a risk-averse Pentagon. In July the Organization of American States called for the use of force to restore Aristide, and the UN Security

Council, prompted by Albright, authorized a "coalition of the willing" to invade Haiti.

Polls showed the American people opposed the operation, and Congress followed the people. Clinton insisted he had authority to send in troops. In September, when the operation was ready, the junta blinked. The generals invited Jimmy Carter, accompanied by Colin Powell and former Georgia senator Sam Nunn, to come to Haiti to find a peaceful resolution. Clinton gave them one day, accepted several brief delays as the junta stalled, and then told Carter the invasion would commence in thirty minutes. The junta folded and coalition forces landed unopposed. In the absence of casualties, debate over the wisdom and constitutionality of Clinton's decision evaporated.

Humanitarian interventions had limited popular appeal in the United States. Clinton, ever attuned to public opinion, grew more resistant to the use of force, even less interested in foreign policy problems unrelated to economic issues. He vacillated in response to the crisis in Bosnia and refused to intervene when confronted with genocide in Rwanda. In what was the most reprehensible moment of his administration, the United States obstructed UN efforts to save hundreds of thousands of lives in Rwanda. Somalia was doubtless in his thoughts.

Like Bush, Clinton was content to leave peacekeeping in the former Yugoslavia to the European Union (EU) and the United Nations. But neither organization was prepared to intervene forcibly to stop the fighting and ethnic cleansing. Their mediators had failed to halt the bloody test of wills between Serbs and Croats, but in 1992 they came up with a peace plan that preserved a semblance of Bosnian independence but left Serbs in control of two-thirds of the country. It was the best the Bosnian Muslims could obtain in the absence of foreign intervention. Clinton was not willing to send troops to drive the Serbs out of Bosnia, nor was he willing to endorse the EU-UN plan, which clearly rewarded the aggressor.

Lake was eager to intervene on humanitarian grounds and pressed Clinton, who was troubled by the atrocities and spoke out against ethnic cleansing but remained unwilling to act. The Pentagon provided the principal opposition to involvement, its leaders convinced that airpower alone would not stop the Serbs. Fearing a Vietnam-like quagmire, the Joint

Chiefs were adamantly opposed to sending in ground troops. Albright outraged Powell by voicing her contempt for generals who claimed to have a superb military but were averse to using it and risking casualties.

While Clinton dithered and hoped the war in Bosnia would be forgotten, the story was kept alive by the extraordinary efforts of Christiane Amanpour, a CNN television journalist. Appalled by the atrocities, she was convinced that stopping the Serbs was a moral duty. Many other reporters picked up on her stories. Several Foreign Service officers resigned in protest against inaction. The continuing horrors in the Balkans could not be ignored. But there seemed no way to engage the president or awaken the Pentagon from its Vietnam-inspired nightmares. In desperation, Talbott arranged to bring the abrasive and overbearing Holbrooke back to Washington to take charge of European and specifically Balkan affairs, to the dismay of the leadership of the Pentagon, the State Department, and the National Security Council.

Returning to Washington in September 1994, Holbrooke demanded that NATO bomb the Serb "fuckers." Neither Clinton nor European leaders were ready. The Serbs murdered and raped thousands more, harassed UN peacekeepers, and concluded no one had the will to stop them. In July 1995 they pushed aside a handful of Dutch peacekeepers at Srebrenica and systematically murdered seven thousand Muslims who had taken refuge there. At last the monstrous behavior of the Bosnian Serb military forced a NATO response. Clinton would still not send troops, but he agreed to Holbrooke's demand, and NATO carried out a massive three-week bombing campaign that won the attention of Serb leaders. At almost the same time, encouraged by Holbrooke and the American ambassador, Croatia began a ground offensive, driving the Bosnian Serbs out of territory they had taken from Croats and Muslims.

Flying to Yugoslavia, Holbrooke took charge. Milosevoic stopped pretending he had no influence with Bosnian Serbs. Aware that the tide had turned against him, he agreed to negotiate. Holbrooke won a cease-fire in September and arranged a meeting in Dayton, Ohio, where he bullied Milosevic and the Croatian and Bosnian leaders into accepting a settlement. The Holbrooke plan called for a division of Bosnia on de facto ethnic and religious lines, similar to the UN-EU plan Clinton had rejected in

1993—although the Serb share of Bosnia was reduced significantly and a semblance of a unified Bosnian state retained.

Only the presence of NATO troops in Bosnia, including twenty thousand American peacekeepers, kept the Bosnian Serbs from overturning the Dayton agreement. But the NATO commanders failed to arrest those Bosnian Serb leaders who had been indicted as war criminals. It was not until General Wesley Clark, who had been with Holbrooke in Bosnia in 1995, took over the NATO command in 1997 that vigorous efforts to enforce the Dayton accords began.

Unfortunately, the United States was not quite free of Milosevic and Yugoslavia. Milosevic had revoked the autonomy of Kosovo, a Yugoslav republic inhabited primarily by Albanian Muslims and a territory of great historical significance to Orthodox Christian Serbs. Kosovo had been relatively quiet during the Bosnian crisis. In the late 1990s, however, the Kosovo Liberation Army (KLA) emerged as the dominant force in the Muslim community and attacked Serb police and vandalized Orthodox churches and cemeteries, deliberately provoking Milosevic. KLA leaders anticipated NATO support, but Washington considered the KLA a terrorist organization and was unsympathetic to its goal of an independent Kosovo.

Inevitably, the Serbs retaliated. Albright, now secretary of state, warned Milosevic against ethnic cleansing, to no avail. In early 1998 the president was coping with revelations about his affair with a White House intern and was even more removed from foreign policy concerns than usual. It was a job for Holbrooke, who in October succeeded once more in reining in Milosevic, however briefly.

The respite lasted only a few months. In January 1999 Serb irregulars and police massacred dozens of Kosovar villagers. Clinton and his advisers could not escape memories of Rwanda and Srebrenica. The United States could not stand aside again. Once again the Pentagon resisted intervention, and once again Albright led the demand for action. She staged a conference in which the KLA was forced to agree to disarm if the Serbs withdrew most of their forces from Kosovo, restored a degree of autonomy, and accepted NATO peacekeepers. But Milosevic rejected the terms, and in March NATO began to bomb Serbia.

Clinton undermined the effort to restrain the Serbs by declaring he would send no ground troops. Undeterred by the bombing, buoyed by indications no NATO troops would intervene, and anticipating Russian support, Milosevic ordered a massive offensive that drove more than a million Kosovar Muslims from their homes to seek refuge in Albania or Macedonia. The humanitarian crisis had begun.

General Clark angered his superiors by calling for the use of attack helicopters, even ground troops if necessary to stop the Serbs. Permission was denied. Instead he intensified bombing of Serbia, inflicting immense suffering on Serbian civilians. It took eleven weeks of devastating attacks and evidence the Russians were not riding to the rescue before Milosevic abandoned his offensive and accepted the terms he had been offered in February. Thousands of Kosovars and Serbs had died—but not a single American.

American reluctance to use its power in Somalia, Rwanda, Haiti, Bosnia, and Kosovo reflected what the air force historian Jeffrey Record called "force protection fetishism," wherein the military's mission is subordinated to the avoidance of casualties. Based on lessons drawn from the war in Vietnam, senior military officers mistrusted civilian leaders generally—and Clinton in particular. But it was clear that if the United States did not act forcefully, no other state would. In Bosnia, where the European Union might have been expected to lead, all the European states abdicated responsibility, tolerating atrocity after atrocity. Perhaps the United States was in fact "the indispensible power."

Largely due to Talbott's influence, Clinton focused frequently on relations with Russia. Efforts to continue Gorbachev's reforms accelerated under the mercurial Boris Yeltsin. But Yeltsin faced opposition at home, where many people were hurt by the changes being implemented. The Russian parliament, the Duma, proved recalcitrant, and when Yeltsin tired of legislative restrictions on his power, he sent in tanks to fire on the parliamentary building—an act that might have been considered undemocratic and excessive.

Nonetheless, the Clinton administration continued to support Yeltsin, convinced that he alone of potential Russian leaders was committed to the reforms necessary to Russia's liberalization and integration into Europe. Yeltsin's Russia promised to be friendly to the United States and supportive of American foreign policy. His transgressions would have to be tolerated.

A critical question for American officials in the 1990s was what to with NATO, an organization once viewed as a means of containing German as well as Soviet power. Some advocated expansion to protect the new democracies of Central and Eastern Europe from a resurgent Russia; others, to prevent a united Germany from dominating Europe again. For Clinton there were potential domestic political advantages to NATO expansion: bipartisan support in Congress and the votes of Americans of Czech, Hungarian, Polish, and Slovak ancestry.

There was also a powerful argument against NATO expansion: the strong probability that it would anger Russia and undermine Russian-American cooperation. Talbott, wanting to build a strong relationship between NATO and Russia first, opposed expansion. George Kennan called expansion the most fateful error of the post–Cold War world. The Pentagon resisted, fearful of being called on to defend a region beyond the traditional scope of American power. The secretary of defense considered resigning.

Clinton's new chairman of the Joint Chiefs, General John Shalikashvili, proposed creating a Partnership for Peace, a relationship with NATO that every nation in Central and Eastern Europe—*and* Russia—would be invited to join. NATO would not be required to defend these partners. Yeltsin seemed pleased by the concept.

Suddenly, in November, Yeltsin reversed course, denouncing the Partnership for Peace and the expansion of NATO as a threat to Russia. His political advisers warned that NATO expansion was angering the Russian people. Even those most supportive of the new Russian-American relationship perceived the United States as taking advantage of Russia's weakness. It was time for Yeltsin to play to his domestic audience, to force the Americans to treat Russia with a little more respect.

In fact, Washington no longer felt any need to defer to Russian sensibilities. As the sole remaining superpower, acting in what the commentator

Charles Krauthammer called the "unipolar moment," the United States was prepared to act unilaterally. When Clinton and his advisers asked for Russian cooperation, they were looking for a compliant junior partner.

Mounting pressure from nationalists led Yeltsin to a disastrous decision in 1994 to use force in an attempt to crush a separatist movement that emerged in Chechnya, a primarily Muslim Russian republic in the Caucuses. Long hostile to the Russians, Chechens sought greater autonomy after the collapse of the Soviet Union. In 1994 their provocations were met by an invasion of Russian troops and the bombing of Chechen cities. Clinton called the war an internal Russian affair, hoping the rebellion would be suppressed quickly.

Within a month it was evident that the Chechens were not going to collapse. It was also apparent that Russian troops were poorly trained and led and were behaving brutally toward people who were still Russian citizens. The war in Chechnya continued until casualties among their children fighting there led the Russian people to demand an end. An agreement was reached in August 1996, although Russian troops did not withdraw until mid-1997.

Yeltsin continued to try to win support from both the United States and the Russian people. He fought his war in Chechnya and made anti-Western speeches at home. Privately he assured Clinton of his continuing intention to cooperate, to integrate Russia into Europe. Polling in the single digits, Yeltsin faced a grim future, but Clinton's advisers, fearing a return to power of the Communists, could muster no alternative to backing him. Supported by the West and the "oligarchs"—the robber barons who accumulated great wealth in the privatization of Soviet state-owned assets—Yeltsin won an easy second-round victory in the presidential election of 1996, which some observers suspected was rigged.

Less than a year later, Russia signed an agreement with NATO that all but made it an honorary member of the Western alliance. Two months later, the Czech Republic, Hungary, and Poland were invited to join NATO, to the dismay of the Russian military establishment. Russian officials were not willing to accept a unipolar world in which Russia was expected to play by Washington's rules while the United States did as it pleased. They were angered by U.S. intrusions into Russia's sphere of influence. The

Russian foreign policy elite insisted on a multipolar world in which Russia remained a great power.

In August 1998 the Russian economy collapsed, and Moscow defaulted on loan repayments to the International Monetary Fund. The last of the liberal reformers considered responsible were fired, and Yeltsin's new administration rejected the so-called Washington Consensus. Rapidly privatizing state-owned property, abolishing price controls, lowering trade barriers, and counting on the market to solve all problems and provide economic growth had not worked. The results brought misery to millions through the undermining of social welfare while jobs were lost and wages declined. Analysts in Europe and the United States questioned whether Russia would stay on the path to democracy and cooperation with the West.

Yeltsin remained determined to integrate Russia with the West, but it was apparent he was weakening, physically as well as politically. Trying to retain power, he fired his prime minister in August 1999 and replaced him with Vladimir Putin, an unknown former KGB agent. Putin had no interest in political democracy. He demonstrated distaste for opposition politicians and a free press. He resumed brutal military operations against Chechnya. And the Russian public responded favorably. Putin appealed to Russian nationalism, and the people were willing to accept deterioration of their new freedoms in exchange for a sense of security. Four months later Yeltsin astonished the world by stepping aside and naming Putin as his successor. And Putin wasted little time setting a course to counter American influence everywhere.

And then there was China, ruled by the "butchers of Beijing." Clinton and Lord had promised a stiffening of sanctions against China, but it was not to be. Those eager to punish China called for withdrawing most-favored-nation status for its exports to the United States, subjecting Chinese goods to tariff rates higher than those of other nations, putting China at a competitive disadvantage. Bush had blocked such sanctions. Clinton was expected to approve them.

Clinton's ultimate concern, however, was reviving the American economy. A trade war with China would not stimulate economic growth or put Americans back to work. It might cost tens of thousands of jobs. So he temporized, persuading his supporters in Congress to delay legislation to eliminate MFN while he tried to get the Chinese to release political prisoners, respect Tibet's cultural heritage, stop jamming Voice of America broadcasts, and stop selling missiles to Pakistan. In May 1993 he renewed MFN conditionally: China would have one year to improve its behavior.

American corporations trading with China undertook a massive lobbying campaign to prevent conflict. In addition to the economic arguments they raised, "realists," most notably Henry Kissinger, argued that the strategic relationship with China was too important to jeopardize by pressing human rights matters. The issue crystallized in August 1993, when the administration denied licenses for the sale of satellites to China. The Chinese turned to European suppliers, and the affected American companies, including major donors to Clinton's political campaigns, demanded waivers. Clinton then made an extraordinary decision: he took authority on the licensing of technology to China away from the Departments of State and Defense and gave it to the Department of Commerce. Henceforth commercial rather than political or military considerations would be privileged.

Incredibly, lobbyists for the business community and other opponents of sanctions argued that the results China's critics desired—democracy and respect for human rights in China—would be brought about by increased trade, preaching what the foreign affairs analyst James Mann has called "The China Fantasy." Presumably trade would strengthen the private sector and China's nascent middle class, and one day China would be a middle-class democracy, just like America.

The claim that MFN would lead to democracy in China won few converts among human rights advocates or on the anticommunist right. But arguments for avoiding confrontation, for continued "engagement," had merit. Economic warfare would harm the American economy and reverberate throughout the world economy. And the strategic reasons for restoring a working relationship with Beijing could not be ignored. China could obstruct American efforts in the United Nations. It could help avoid a crisis over North Korea's nuclear program. Conceivably Beijing could be persuaded to cease its own contribution to nuclear and missile proliferation.

Deng Xiaoping and his advisers saw no need to make any concessions to the Americans. They were confident that American business leaders, eager for a larger share of the market in China, would force Clinton to renew

MFN. When Secretary of State Warren Christopher flew to China to see what concessions the Chinese would offer in return, he was treated with contempt. He was told that the Chinese Embassy in Washington reported that Clinton would renew MFN no matter what China did. Clinton offered Christopher no support and did not bother to attend the meeting at which his secretary of state reported on his mission. Few were surprised when Clinton abandoned his expressed concern for human rights and extended MFN to China without conditions in the spring of 1994.

In time, the memory of Tiananmen faded in the American imagination. The Chinese government continued to deny its people political, intellectual, and religious freedoms, continued to repress minorities and commit a myriad of other human rights abuses—with little impact on American policy. On the contrary, officials in Washington stressed the improvement in the quality of life of ordinary Chinese as a result of Deng's reforms.

Trade between the United States and China grew rapidly in the mid-1990s, and the PRC became an increasingly important trading partner. The Chinese, however, exported far more than they imported, creating a serious balance-of-trade problem for the United States. Tensions grew over Beijing's restrictive trade practices, use of prison labor, and currency manipulation, but these were trivial compared to those that exploded over Taiwan in 1995 and 1996.

Taiwan was evolving into a democratic state and in March 1996 was scheduled to hold the first direct election for president the Chinese people had ever known. The ruling Kuomintang, the party of Chiang Kai-shek, no longer exercised absolute power. Chiang's son, Ching-kuo, before his death, had allowed an opposition party, the Democratic Progressive Party (DPP), to emerge. Its popularity with the Taiwanese majority native to the island—and its call for independence from China—threatened the Kuomintang and Lee Teng-hui, Chiang Ching-kuo's designated successor. Lee, also a native Taiwanese, concluded that being more assertive internationally and hinting that he, too, favored independence would be good politics.

American specialists on Taiwan affairs recognized the changes and understood the desire of the island's political elite for an international role commensurate with Taiwan's de facto independence. Washington's dilemma was to find a way to adjust to these changes without provoking

Beijing, without negating the one-China policy, accepted by every administration beginning with that of Nixon. Only a few senior officials from Taiwan had been allowed to visit the United States after derecognition in 1978.

In 1994 President Lee forced the issue by requesting a visa to stop over in Hawaii en route to Central America. The request was denied, but he was offered a reception in a transit lounge. Angered, Lee commenced a successful lobbying effort with Congress. The Senate passed a resolution calling for the State Department to issue visas to Taiwan officials, and Lee's lobbyists demanded a visa to allow him to attend a reunion at Cornell, where he had earned his doctorate. The administration refused and assured Beijing that Lee would not be allowed to enter the United States.

But Lee prevailed. In May 1995 the House of Representatives voted 396–0 to demand a visa for Lee. And the vote in the Senate was 97–1. Taiwan's lobbyists had performed well, but the key to their success was the democratization of Taiwan, assuring support across the political spectrum. Delight in the political evolution of Taiwan combined with anger at Beijing's human rights abuses won support for Taiwan—and Lee's visa request. Clinton surrendered and allowed Lee to visit Cornell in June 1995.

Chinese leaders were outraged, and a major diplomatic crisis ensued. They recalled their ambassador and refused to accept the credentials of the newly appointed American ambassador. They broke off the "cross-strait" dialogue they had been having with Taipei, the most promising venue for peaceful reconciliation. To intimidate the people of Taiwan, the People's Liberation Army conducted operations in the Taiwan Strait, firing nuclear capable missiles into the sea north of Taiwan. Support for independence declined on the island and its stock market fell sharply, as did the value of its currency.

Rising tensions won Clinton's attention, and his advisers had him write to President Jiang Zemin, inviting him to Washington and assuring him the United States would oppose Taiwan's independence and admission to the United Nations. The letter ended the crisis. The American ambassador was received in Beijing, and the Chinese ambassador returned to Washington.

The Clinton administration also protested against the PLA exercises, reminding the Chinese of American insistence on the peaceful resolution of the issues between Taiwan and China. But relieving American concerns was not a high priority in Beijing. In February 1996 the PLA massed troops across the Strait from Taiwan. In March, just before the presidential election, the PLA bracketed the island with missiles, demonstrating its ability to devastate Taiwan without invading.

Clinton's advisers agreed that the United States had to respond to the challenge. Lake warned a senior Chinese diplomat of the "grave consequences" of military action, and Clinton ordered two carrier battle groups to the vicinity of the island. Taiwan went ahead with its election, and Lee Teng-hui won a decisive victory. The PLA troops returned to their barracks, and the American warships sailed away. No shots were fired, and another phase of an apparently unending crisis was over.

The Chinese-American partnership of the late Cold War era had ended with the Tiananmen massacres of 1989. Efforts to accommodate Chinese power, by Clinton as well as Bush, had not been reciprocated. Friendly relations were not likely, given the enormous gap between the values of the American people and of the Chinese leaders—and in the absence of a shared enemy. Nonetheless, China's ability to jeopardize American interests worldwide demanded that Washington find the path toward a decent working relationship. The two governments had to accept their differences, cooperate when possible—and avoid confrontation when it was not. Clinton and Jiang exchanged visits and achieved a modus vivendi that eased tensions between their countries for almost a year.

The quiet interlude in Chinese-American relations ended abruptly in May 1999 amid NATO bombing of Serbia to stop ethnic cleansing in Kosovo. The Chinese had opposed the bombing as an illegal sidestepping of the UN Security Council, where they had veto power. Sensitive about the possibility of foreign intervention to protect Tibetans or Uighurs from Chinese oppression, Beijing opposed Kosovo operations as interference in the internal affairs of a sovereign state. And then in May, NATO accidentally bombed the Chinese Embassy in Belgrade, killing three Chinese. The Chinese government rejected American explanations and encouraged its people to believe the attack had been deliberate. Outraged demonstrators besieged the American Embassy in Beijing and set fire to the home of the American consul general in Chengdu. The incident triggered an explosion of discontent with Jiang's policy of accommodation with the United States, but he resisted PLA pressure to end strategic cooperation with Washington.

The debate within the American foreign policy elite continued without resolution. On one side were those who perceived China as the next great threat to the nation's security, supported by those troubled by China's human rights record. They were unable to devise a policy that would force Chinese leaders to be more responsive to their concerns. On the other side were those whose eagerness to trade with China overrode any anxieties about security or human rights. They perceived no alternative to continued engagement with a government that frequently behaved reprehensibly. It would not be the first time American leaders chose strategic partnerships with distasteful regimes—Mao Zedong's China, for example.

One obvious hedge against a potentially hostile China was the alliance with Japan. In 1995, with the American economy booming and the Japanese economy weakening, the Clinton administration eased its trade pressures. Secretary of Defense Perry and Joseph Nye, serving as assistant secretary for international affairs, made the case for more attention to security affairs. The initial purpose of the alliance—defense of Japan and containment of the Soviet Union—was redirected toward maintaining peace and stability in the Asia-Pacific region. The principal American concerns were North Korean nuclear weapons and tensions in the Taiwan Strait. In 1997 Tokyo and Washington issued new Guidelines for U.S.-Japan Defense Cooperation. The new guidelines extended the range of cooperation from defense of Japan to undefined "surrounding areas," a deliberately ambiguous reference to North Korea and Taiwan. With the rise of Chinese power and the threat from North Korea, the Japanese were being forced to contemplate revision of article 9 of their constitution, in which they renounced any right to go to war.

There were a host of seemingly lesser issues that troubled Clinton's advisers and occasionally gained the president's attention as well. Saddam Hussein's Iraq continued to be an annoyance, with his ceaseless pinprick challenges to the United States. Iraq, a third-rate power at its peak, was significantly weaker than in 1990, but Saddam seemed irrepressible. In 1993 a report of an Iraqi plot to assassinate former president Bush induced Clinton to strike Baghdad with cruise missiles. The action had the virtue of avoiding American casualties, but Clinton's critics considered the response inadequate.

France and Russia, eager to resume trade and investment ties, did what they could to undermine international sanctions against Iraq. Saddam maneuvered ably along the fault lines between the United States and the others. Some of Clinton's advisors urged military action, but there was virtually no interest elsewhere in the country or abroad. Regime change was desirable, but containment seemed the only option. Paul Wolfowitz, however, had another idea. He persuaded a Republican-controlled Congress to give $97 million to the Iraqi opposition, which, presumably with American air support, could do the job. Clinton's foreign policy advisers ridiculed the idea, arguing that the Iraqi National Congress had more support in Washington than in Iraq, but his political advisers persuaded him to sign the bill.

In December 1998, as Saddam continued to obstruct UN inspectors and Clinton faced impeachment for lying about a sexual liaison at the White House, the administration launched an air and missile attack on Iraq. Critics suspected Clinton of trying to divert attention from his peccadilloes, to rally the public around the flag. The American action appeared to have no impact on the impeachment proceedings or Saddam.

Iraq was a threat to its neighbors, to American interests, and to the post–Cold War international system. But the United States, the greatest power the world had ever known, seemed unable to cope with a tin-pot dictator ruling a Third World country with a decrepit military force. Republican campaigners in the election of 2000, Wolfowitz prominent among them, vehemently criticized Clinton's failure to get rid of Saddam.

Clinton vacillated in his approach to Iran. Tehran continued to be hostile, and there was increasing evidence that it was seeking nuclear weapons—as well as supporting Hamas and Hezbollah, both frequently committing acts of terrorism. Lake, Christopher, and Albright pushed for a more aggressive sanctions regime, but the CIA insisted there were much greater threats to American interests, such as Iraq, Libya, North Korea, and China. Most analysts argued that Iran's economic difficulties indicated it was not likely to make trouble for its neighbors.

The Republican seizure of control of Congress after the midterm elections of 1994 precluded any effort to reach out to Iran. Republican congressional leaders demanded tougher policies toward "rogue" states. The American Israel Public Affairs Committee (AIPAC), the powerful pro-Israel lobby, called for a ban on all commercial contact. Clinton ran before the wind and endorsed a complete economic boycott. Congress followed with legislation mandating sanctions against foreign countries that contributed to the development of Iran or Libya, angering allies being coerced into supporting a policy they considered counterproductive.

In May 1997 the Iranian people elected Mohammad Khatami, a reformist cleric, as their new president. It was evident the Iranian people wanted to change course, and Clinton's advisers reconsidered rapprochement. Khatami had considerable success moderating Iran's behavior. Support for terrorism and assassination of exiled dissidents declined. Tehran ratified the Chemical Weapons Convention, ostensibly surrendering one option for weapons of mass destruction (WMD). Khatami expressed regret for the Carter era hostage crisis and called for cultural and educational exchanges with the United States. Clinton took several steps to ease tensions, including easing sanctions and recognizing the legitimacy of the Iranian government, but Khatami, restrained by Ayatollah Ali Khamenei, the nation's ultimate power, was unable to move any closer to the Americans.

State-supported terrorism was not the only kind confronting the United States after the Cold War. Increasingly, the threat came from nonstate actors with grievances rooted in the Middle East. American backing of Israel was one source of anger at the United States. Support for authoritarian Arab leaders such as the Saudi royal family or Egypt's Hosni Mubarak was another. Probably the strongest grievance was the perception in the Muslim world of a Western assault on Islamic values, presumably led by the United States.

U.S. forces were frequently sent abroad to protect American interests and those of the international community: peace, stability, the free flow of commerce, especially oil. In foreign cities and ports they became targets.

Reagan sent marines to Lebanon, and 241 were killed when a suicide bomber drove a truck into their barracks in 1983. In 1996 terrorists killed 19 and wounded 240 American troops sleeping in Khobar Towers in Saudi Arabia. In 2000 the USS *Cole* was attacked in Yemen, resulting in the deaths of 17 sailors.

Comparable dangers faced American diplomats. In the worst episode, in August 1998, the American Embassies in Kenya and Tanzania were struck by car bombs almost simultaneously, injuring 5,500 people, mostly Kenyans and Tanzanians, of whom 211 died.

But staying home was not adequate protection. In 1993 terrorists struck in New York City, exploding a car bomb under the World Trade Center, killing five and injuring hundreds. The World Trade Center survived the attack, and the terrorists responsible were captured before they could execute attacks planned on the UN building and the Lincoln Tunnel—but the vulnerability of ordinary Americans was evident.

All the men involved in the attack on the World Trade Center were Muslims from the Middle East, led by an Egyptian cleric. American officials learned that the group's activities had been financed by a multimillionaire Saudi businessman, Osama bin Laden. Bin Laden was probably also responsible for the attack on American forces in Saudi Arabia in 1996. He often raged against the presence of non-Muslims on Saudi soil, insisting their presence was an offense against Allah. In 1998 he called for a jihad against the Jews and the "crusaders," his pejorative term for Westerners in the Middle East.

Bin Laden considered all American actions in the region a declaration of war against Islam. Killing Americans and their allies, wherever they could be found, was the sacred duty of every Muslim. Few Muslims agreed that the Koran called for terrorism, for the murder of innocent bystanders, but implementation of bin Laden's vision did not require many. And no one in Washington could come up with a plan for deterring nonstate actors.

Inevitably, the United States tried to capture or kill bin Laden. American intelligence tracked him to Sudan, but a deal with a Sudanese government apparently willing to turn him over fell through. When the United Nations forced Sudan to expel him, he fled to Afghanistan, where he collaborated with the country's Taliban rulers and ran training camps for terrorists. Clinton authorized the launching of cruise missiles against one such camp, and the CIA ran a covert operation with Ahmed Shah Massoud, a famed Afghan guerilla, hoping to capture bin Laden, but he remained out of reach. Reports that his men were working with weapons of mass destruction worried counterterrorism specialists. Bin Laden had the initiative, and an attack on an American city could come at any time.

North Korea provided a very different threat. There was no doubt about the existence of its nuclear weapons program. The North Koreans attempted to conceal their plutonium holdings, and in March 1993 Pyongyang announced its intent to withdraw from the nonproliferation regime it had accepted in 1985. Neither Clinton's hints of economic aid to the famine-ravaged country nor efforts to negotiate with it brought satisfactory results. Pyongyang kept raising, then dashing, hopes of a resolution while continuing to develop nuclear weapons. By the end of 1993 the CIA estimated North Korea had sufficient plutonium for at least one bomb, possibly two.

The inability of the Clinton administration to resolve the issue prompted Brent Scowcroft and other former officials to demand military action. The U.S. Air Force was prepared to turn North Korea into a "parking lot." Some experts warned, however, that there was no certainty that airstrikes would destroy underground or unknown sites. Others worried about what North Korea would do to South Korea if attacked.

With the possibility of war increasing, in June 1994 Kim Il-sung, North Korea's "Great Leader," invited Jimmy Carter to Pyongyang. Carter persuaded Kim to agree to freeze his nuclear program before any negotiations began. The North Koreans pledged not to refuel their key reactor or to produce any more plutonium. In July, instead of sending bombers, Clinton sent a delegation to Pyongyang to negotiate.

Despite Kim's sudden death, negotiations continued, resulting in the "Agreed Framework." North Korea agreed to continue the freeze and dismantle its nuclear program in stages. In return, the United States pledged to assist Pyongyang to obtain light-water reactors, not easily used to produce weapons-grade plutonium—and to provide fuel oil to replace energy lost when the existing reactors were shut down. The crisis passed—for the moment.

When the Republicans gained control of Congress after the elections of 1994, implementation of the agreement was not assured. Republican leaders charged Clinton with having bribed a brutal and untrustworthy regime. The United States did not fulfill its end of the bargain, and there was no reason to doubt that the issue of North Korea's nuclear weapons would rise again.

After the struggle over NAFTA and despite Clinton's eloquence on the subject of globalization, there was a growing sense among many Americans—and others in the international community—that the world economic system benefited capitalists at the expense of workers and the environment. Trade unquestionably contributed an increasing percentage to the nation's gross national product, but that provided little gratification to the hundreds of thousands of Americans who lost well-paying jobs to low-wage workers abroad.

Skepticism about NAFTA intensified with the collapse of the Mexican peso in 1994. Richard Rubin, who became secretary of the treasury in 1995, concluded Mexico needed a $40 billion stabilization loan. His warning that inaction would result in millions of additional illegal immigrants did not move the Republican Congress, which refused the appropriation. Undeterred, he found the money elsewhere, and the loan succeeded in stabilizing the Mexican economy. Within a year, Mexico registered a trade surplus and began paying off its debt. Not coincidentally, Wall Street bankers, whose loans to Mexico had been speculative, were bailed out as well.

In 1997 an enormous financial crisis began in Asia, again revealing the dark side of globalization and raising questions about Washington's insistence on the free flow of capital. It started with a speculative run on Thailand's currency. The Thais allowed the baht to float against the dollar and it dropped sharply, leaving the country unable to pay off its short-term debt to foreign banks. The IMF came up with a stabilization package to which the United States did not contribute directly, angering the Thais and other Southeast Asian financial ministries affected. From Washington came disparaging remarks about "crony capitalism," while Indonesia and South Korea slipped into serious trouble. None of those countries had institutions capable of controlling the movement of capital in and out of their territories. The Americans stood by as the authoritarian Suharto government in Indonesia collapsed, but they did aid South Korea, where democracy seemed to be taking root.

Serious doubts about the wisdom of open capital markets were expressed by prominent economists, but the United States continued to push for greater openness in Asia, part of the American mission to re-create the world in its own image. Asia survived, but skepticism about Washington's approach intensified.

Ireland and Israel, in contrast to Thailand and Indonesia, were countries whose affairs were followed closely by millions of Americans and often affected domestic politics. Both had Clinton's attention: he recognized the importance of Jewish and Irish voters and believed they were committed to the goals of Irish nationalists in Northern Ireland and of Israeli expansionists.

In 1992 Clinton bid for Irish votes by promising a visa to Gerry Adams—leader of Sinn Fein, political arm of the Irish Republican Army—and by criticizing Britain's human rights record in Northern Ireland. Clinton promised to pursue peace between Catholics and Protestants in the troubled part of the British Empire. In 1994, after stalling, he yielded to pressure from senators Ted Kennedy (D-Mass.) and Pat Moynihan (D-NY) and approved the visa.

Adams met with senior White House officials, set up an office to raise funds in the United States, and was invited to the White House for St. Patrick's Day festivities. Of greater importance was the appointment of former senator George Mitchell as special representative on the Northern Ireland issue. Mitchell spent much of the next three years chairing talks between Sinn Fein and the Protestant Irish Unionists, and in 1998 his efforts contributed to an agreement between Irish nationalists and unionists on the governance of Northern Ireland. Clinton's Irish policy was clearly successful.

Coping with Israel and its neighbors proved a more daunting challenge. Christopher flew to Damascus more than twenty times in a vain effort to broker peace between Syria and Israel. Yitzhak Rabin, the Israeli war hero and prime minister, offered to return the Golan Heights, taken from Syria during the Six-Day War of 1967, but the Syrians were unresponsive.

At home Israel had to cope with the Palestinian intifada, an armed uprising in the occupied territories of Gaza and the West Bank that began in 1987. In 1993, in secret negotiations in Oslo, Israelis and Palestinians reached agreement on principles for the resolution of their differences on the basis of land for peace. In exchange for an end to the intifada, Israel would turn control of the West Bank and Gaza over to a Palestinian Authority. The agreement was signed in Washington. Optimism about a comprehensive Arab-Israeli peace grew. And then came one of those moments that force scholars to evaluate the role of the individual in history. In November 1995 Rabin, vilified by Israelis opposed to yielding any of the lands conquered in 1967, was murdered by a right-wing Israeli Jew, an enormous setback to the peace process. In 1996, despite American efforts to bring about a different outcome, Benjamin Netanyahu and his Likud Party, opponents of the Oslo Accords, won control of the Israeli government. Apprehension spread throughout the Arab world and in Washington. Determined to heighten tensions, Palestinian radicals, engaged in a symbiotic relationship with the Israeli Right, terrorized Israel with suicide bombings.

Netanyahu resisted pressure from Washington to continue on Rabin's course. He knew the Israeli lobby and supporters in Congress would prevent the Clinton administration from punishing him. The peace process came to a halt. To Netanyahu's surprise, Clinton pushed harder, risking alienation of the strong support he received from the American Jewish community. Unfortunately, cooperation from the principal parties was minimal. The Israelis continued to build settlements in the West Bank, and the Palestinians persisted in acts of violence.

Hope reemerged in May 1999, when the Israeli electorate turned against Likud and allowed Ehud Barak, the Labor Party candidate, to become prime minister. Barak seemed much like Rabin and Clinton, deciding peace in the Middle East would be his foreign policy legacy, intensified his efforts. It was evident that he was more eager for negotiations than either of the adversaries.

In July 2000 Clinton invited Barak and Yasser Arafat, the PLO leader, to Camp David. At great risk to himself, physically as well as politically, Barak grudgingly accepted an American proposal to give Palestinians authority over parts of East Jerusalem. It was not sufficient for Arafat, who needed much more to compensate for the concessions he was asked to offer on the Palestinian right of return—the right of those who fled or were driven out of Palestine in 1948 to reclaim land and homes in what was now Israel. The negotiations failed.

Clinton kept trying to achieve peace before he left office. But in September a second intifada began, provoked by Ariel Sharon, an Israeli politician even more belligerent than Netanyahu. Clinton persisted, but both Israelis and Palestinians rejected a fresh American proposal on December 30. For Clinton the game was over. A few weeks later Barak's Labor Party was badly defeated, and Sharon, the man most dreaded by Palestinians and most feared by peace advocates around the world, was Israel's new prime minister.

Clinton also tackled two remnants of the Cold War: relations with Vietnam and Cuba. One important success in his first term was the establishment of diplomatic relations with Hanoi. Carter had chosen to focus on rapprochement with China and Reagan had shown no interest. Bush had other priorities. There were, however, compelling economic and strategic reasons for Clinton to establish a working relationship with Vietnam.

Hanoi indicated a willingness to help resolve the POW/MIA issue by assisting in efforts to account for missing Americans. The business community in the United States pressed for trade opportunities, and Clinton lifted the trade embargo in 1994. With essential support from prominent Vietnam heroes, most important Senator John McCain (R-Ariz.), Clinton recognized Hanoi officially in July 1995. Vietnam was about to be incorporated into the global economic system.

Improved relations with Cuba proved elusive, not least because Castro was not interested. But Cuba was also a third rail of American politics because of the anti-Castro Cuban-American National Foundation (CANF) and the heavy concentration of Cuban-American voters in Miami. Clinton accepted the need to pander to them.

The American business community was eager to get into Cuba, offering the familiar argument that increased commerce would lead to a more open Cuban society, perhaps even democracy. The United Nations criticized the American embargo, and even Cuban Americans began drifting away from CANF's hard line. But hopes of reconciliation between Washington and Havana were blasted in February 1996, when Cuban fighter planes shot down two unarmed aircraft flown by members of Brothers to the Rescue, a Cuban exile group that tried to help Cubans risking their lives as they attempted to sail to the United States in makeshift boats. In response to the public outcry, Clinton, up for reelection, signed a bill stiffening sanctions.

It was evident that Fidel Castro and the hard-liners in America thrived on each other's belligerency. Owen Harries, a leading conservative analyst, noted that whenever Castro was in trouble, he manipulated a crisis that provoked a tough American response, enabling him to blame Cuba's troubles on Washington. He argued that ending efforts to isolate Cuba, depriving Castro of an American threat, would force him to open Cuban society. Clinton lacked the political courage to follow Harries's advice.

Clinton and his advisers did not lack a vision for the post–Cold War world. They were determined to expand the community of free-market democracies. But the president kept his promise to focus on domestic affairs, and his principal appointees for foreign affairs lacked the charismatic personalities essential to compensate for a disengaged president. There were no Achesons or Kissingers among them.

The American role in the world was further constricted by the election of a nativist Congress in 1994, riddled with people who boasted that they had no passports and had never traveled abroad. These were the legislators responsible for the U.S. failure to pay its UN dues, who delayed ratification of the Chemical Weapons Convention, prevented acceptance of an international ban on the use of antipersonnel mines that were killing and maiming thousands of innocent civilians in various parts of the world, defeated the Comprehensive Test Ban Treaty intended to end testing of nuclear weapons, and intimidated the Clinton administration to the point where it refused to sign the treaty establishing the International Criminal Court and did not submit the Kyoto Treaty on global warming to the Senate.

And the American people, never known for a deep interest in foreign affairs were content. With the end of the Cold War, there was little desire for an activist foreign policy.

18

THE VULCANS RISE—AND FALL

I N 2001 THE "Vulcans," a group of highly regarded Republican foreign affairs specialists, took charge, with their own sense of the role the United States would play in the world. The new president, George W. Bush, and his foreign policy team had been sharply critical of Bill Clinton, arguing that he was responsible for the alleged decline in American military power. They were contemptuous of humanitarian interventions and nation-building efforts. They ridiculed his "pin-prick" retaliations against Iraqi provocations. They rejected his labeling China a strategic partner, insisting it was a strategic "competitor." Most of all, they were contemptuous of efforts to work through the United Nations and unwilling to accept international agreements that limited American freedom of action.

The Bush team was aware of the threat posed by terrorists but focused on state-supported terrorism. It was determined to deal with "rogue" states, especially those such as Iraq that were suspected of possessing or developing weapons of mass destruction. Al Qaeda was not considered a high priority, despite the urgency perceived by specialists on counterterrorism at the NSC and the CIA.

Unlike his father, the younger Bush had a vision of his country's place in the post–Cold War age. Like Woodrow Wilson, he was determined to use the power of the United States to promote American values as well as interests, to spread democracy around the world. He, however, did not share Wilson's belief in the importance of international institutions. On the contrary, he was an assertive nationalist, determined to shed restraints on the use of American power. And he assembled a superb group of foreign policy advisers.

The central figure among the Vulcans was Condoleezza Rice, a specialist on Soviet affairs, much admired by Brent Scowcroft and George Shultz. It was Rice with whom Bush was most comfortable, and as national security adviser she had an office in the White House and easy access to the president. She was an exceptionally able analyst and articulator of administration policy but proved unable to harness the rest of the president's team, least of all Donald Rumsfeld, secretary of defense, and his protégé Dick Cheney, the vice president.

Another Vulcan was the widely admired Paul Wolfowitz, named deputy secretary of defense. Although he had been involved in East Asian affairs for much of his career, his writings in the 1990s suggested his focus would be the Middle East. He was determined to bring about regime change in Iraq, confident that deposing Saddam Hussein and replacing his tyranny with a democratic state would be the answer to the region's woes. Democracy would then spread to nearby states, serving the interests of the United States and its friends in the Middle East.

The appointment that gave the most credibility to the Bush team was that of the highly respected Colin Powell. Among the many important posts he had held were national security adviser to the president and chairman of the Joint Chiefs of Staff. Had he chosen to run for president, he might well have been a nominee of either party for president or vice president. Powell was not, however, part of Bush's inner circle. Unforeseen was his inability to direct the course of policy. Frustrated and unwanted, he resigned at the end of Bush's first term.

Ultimately, it was not Powell nor any of the Vulcans who dominated the policy process but rather Vice President Cheney, the consummate Washington insider. He had served in Congress, as White House chief of staff, and as secretary of defense. He knew where the levers of power were and how to use them. He was more involved in foreign policy than any prior vice president. He set up his own national security council, and key positions throughout the national security bureaucracy were filled with his people.

Soon after the Bush team settled into its office, the first crisis hit, a collision between an American spy plane and a Chinese interceptor off the coast of China on April 1, 2001. Confident they could manage relations with China better than Clinton had, they were determined to confront China at the first opportunity, to demonstrate that the United States would not tolerate a challenge to its influence in East Asia—or its preeminence in the world. They would remind Beijing that the United States looked to Japan and South Korea as its true strategic partners across the Pacific. Bush signaled the new approach by excluding Chinese president Jiang Zemin from the list of leaders to whom he placed courtesy calls when he took office.

In the collision the Chinese pilot was killed. The American plane made an emergency landing on China's Hainan Island, where the crew was detained. Beijing demanded an apology. Bush and Cheney reacted instinctively by trying to intimidate China. In Congress there was talk of war or other means of forcing the Chinese to release the crew and return the plane. The Chinese were unresponsive. No senior Chinese official would take calls from Washington or meet with the American ambassador.

A little of the humility Bush had promised during the election proved necessary. After a few days the Chinese accepted an expression of regret for their pilot's death and the American crew's failure to obtain clearance before landing on Chinese territory—short of the apology Beijing had demanded. The crisis passed, and Bush learned that China was too strong, too important to be ignored—and too proud to be dictated to.

Toward Russia, the Clinton administration had despaired when Boris Yeltsin self-destructed and was intensely wary of Vladimir Putin. Rice, most knowledgeable of the Bush team, still saw Russia as a potential threat. Cheney had only grudgingly conceded that the Cold War was over. The consensus among the president's advisers was that the United States should use its overwhelming power to force Moscow to accept decisions it would not like, including NATO expansion and the building of a national missile defense system.

Bush and Putin met in June 2001 and appeared to like each other. Powerless to stop the Americans from abrogating the ABM treaty or going forward with NATO enlargement, Putin yielded gracefully. He gave no ground, however, on the matter of Russian assistance to Iran's nuclear program, an important source of income. Overall, Bush was pleased, and Russia dropped off his agenda.

Having resolved problems with China and Russia, Bush turned to domestic affairs. His foreign policy team planned strategy for challenging rogue states, specifically Iraq, Iran, and North Korea—the "axis of evil." In August, however, Richard Clarke, the NSC's counterterrorism specialist, warned that Osama bin Laden and his al Qaeda operatives were planning to attack the United States. He failed to convince any of the president's advisers of the urgency of the threat. The president was more concerned with Saddam Hussein, who had tried to kill his father.

Much of that changed on September 11, 2001.

On that day, after the twin towers of New York's World Trade Center came crashing down, Americans could no longer be complacent about the outside world. Bin Laden's men, seizing control of commercial airliners, had flown suicide missions against the symbols of American financial power and against the Pentagon, symbol of the nation's military might. More than three thousand Americans died in the attacks. Bin Laden had demonstrated that the lone remaining superpower was not invulnerable.

When Bush met with his advisers to determine his response, Wolfowitz, certain Iraq was involved, urged him to invade that country. But Bush couldn't wait the months until an invasion could be readied. He had to act immediately, and the intelligence community pointed to bin Laden, operating out of Afghanistan, under the protection of the Taliban, a radical Islamist force that controlled most of the country. Iraq could wait while the Taliban and bin Laden received a demonstration of American power.

When the Taliban refused to turn over bin Laden, Americans went to war against the Taliban, with a mandate from the United Nations and British troops alongside. Powell gained the critical support of Pakistan, the principal backer of the Taliban. But in general, offers of assistance were brushed aside. Rumsfeld wanted complete freedom of action: there should be no expectations of consultation with other nations—or of the multilateralism he despised.

Given the military's aversion to risking casualties, the Pentagon's war plan stressed technology over combat troops. When airpower and high-tech devices proved insufficient, the United States recruited the troops of the Northern Alliance, Afghan forces hostile to the Taliban. Victory came quickly, but al Qaeda and Taliban leaders escaped into the mountains. American commanders were reluctant to assign their troops the dangerous task of pursuing Taliban and al Qaeda fighters into the caves they had chosen for their last stand. The Afghan warlords on whose troops the Americans depended gave up the chase as soon as they drove the Taliban out of territories they coveted.

Victory over the Taliban had been easy, but nothing enduring had been accomplished. Disdainful of nation building, the Bush administration all but abandoned Afghanistan, returning its attention to Iraq. The American-backed regime of Hamid Karzai proved unable to assert its authority outside of Kabul. Regional warlords ruled much of the country, and gradually Taliban fighters returned to attack American and allied troops and foreign aid workers. Little progress had been made in the war against terrorism.

In the months that followed the 9/11 attacks, the Bush administration alienated a world that had been largely sympathetic and supportive in response to the attacks. It perceived the battle in Afghanistan as an American war when it could have assembled a broad coalition of states that recognized that terrorism was a threat to all societies, not only American. The administration's refusal to treat captives as prisoners of war, entitled to the safeguards of the Geneva Conventions, troubled people everywhere. Many were shipped to the American naval base at Guantanamo, Cuba, where they were denied legal counsel and some were tortured. In the view of the president and his advisers, national security concerns freed them from observing international obligations.

Bush's first State of the Union address to Congress in January 2002 redirected the country's focus from al Qaeda to the need for regime change in rogue states, specifically Iraq, Iran, and North Korea. He warned they were seeking weapons of mass destruction that they might make available to terrorists. At West Point a few months later, the president declared his intent to take preemptive action if necessary to prevent another terrorist attack. He told his audience that the world's most powerful nation intended to remain most powerful in perpetuity, acting as necessary to stifle any challenge.

In September the administration issued its statement on *National Security Strategy*. Echoing the words of Woodrow Wilson, the document declared that the United States would use its power to promote democratic values worldwide. Unlike Wilson, the Bush administration contemplated using unilateral military force to remake the world. The document was perceived widely as a revolution in American foreign policy.

Bush's principal target was Iraq. Most of his advisers assumed that lesser threats in the region would be mitigated as soon as the United States demonstrated its resolve in the Middle East. Iran and North Korea posed far more complex problems—and neither was as vulnerable to American power as was Iraq. Presumably they, too, would be chastened by a demonstration of American military prowess.

In fact, Iran had already signaled its interest in rapprochement, and both Powell and Rice favored engagement with the reformist Mohammad Khatami government. Tehran was at least as eager as Washington to destroy Saddam Hussein. When al Qaeda struck the United States on 9/11, Iranian leaders condemned the attacks and facilitated American-led operations in Afghanistan. Talks between Iranian and American diplomats suggested that the years of enmity that had begun with the Islamic revolutionaries' seizure of the American Embassy in 1979 might end.

Cheney and Rumsfeld, however, insisted that the United States seek regime change in Tehran. They received strong support from neoconservatives (mostly hawkish one-time liberal Democrats, appalled by perceived cultural excesses of the 1960s) with ties to the Israeli Right. The Israeli government considered Iran a major threat to the peace and security of the Middle East—and no one denied that Iran supported anti-Israeli terrorists. When Bush declared Iran to be a member of the axis of evil, he undermined Iranian reformers and prompted Tehran to intensify its efforts to obtain a nuclear deterrent.

The administration was similarly conflicted over policy toward North Korea. Cheney and Rumsfeld opposed engagement and urged the use of force if Pyongyang failed to comply with American demands. Powell urged continuation of Clinton's policy, but Bush was not persuaded, openly expressing his contempt for Kim Jong Il, who had succeeded his father as leader of the North Korean regime.

Specialists in Korean affairs insisted on the urgency of resuming dialogue with Pyongyang. Its nuclear program threatened American interests in East Asia, and it was feared that it would sell nuclear weapons to bin Laden or other terrorists. How could the administration justify its plan to attack Iraq on the grounds that it *might* have a nuclear weapons program when it was doing nothing about North Korea, which had an advanced program—and possibly already had several bombs?

The option of a preventive war against North Korea was discounted as too risky. North Korea had an enormous army and countless missile launchers within range of Seoul. If attacked, it could devastate South Korea, strike Japan, and, conceivably, the United States. Cheney and Rumsfeld, occupied by planning the invasion of Iraq, acquiesced to a diplomatic effort to persuade Pyongyang to back down. When that failed, Bush signaled a major policy shift. In January 2003, on the eve of war with Iraq, he declared that the United States had no intention of attacking North Korea and would consider offering economic assistance and a security agreement if Pyongyang would dismantle its nuclear program. Critics accused the Bush team of adopting a Clintonesque policy of doing nothing and hoping Kim's evil regime would fade away. But the president was determined to keep the focus on Iraq and was supported by like-minded neoconservatives.

There was another issue that begged resolution before the United States invaded a Muslim nation: the Arab-Israeli conflict. Whatever progress had been made during the closing days of the Clinton administration vanished with the election of Ariel Sharon as Israel premier in February 2001. No Israeli was feared and hated more by the Palestinians. No Israeli was perceived as more hostile to their aspirations, more ruthless in his determination to crush them. Terrorist attacks against Israel increased. Neither Sharon nor Yasser Arafat seemed interested in working toward a peaceful settlement. Bush saw no point to an effort to resolve the conflict.

The al Qaeda attacks forced the administration to reconsider. All Bush's advisers understood the Israeli-Palestinian struggle was an essential part of the politics of the Middle East but were uncertain as to how to proceed. Bush sympathized with the Israelis, equating terrorist attacks on Israel with those on the United States. Although he appealed to Arab opinion by becoming the first American president to support explicitly the creation of a Palestinian state, the U.S.-Israeli relationship grew stronger. Despite Sharon's ruthlessness, Bush labeled him a man of peace.

Cheney's efforts to win Arab support for regime change in Iraq foundered because of American support of Israel. Powell failed in his efforts with Sharon and Arafat, both aware he had no authority to put pressure on the Israelis. Bush abandoned Powell's attempt at being evenhanded. Planning for the war with Iraq continued.

Although Scowcroft and James Baker, the *elder* Bush's principal foreign policy advisers, opposed a new war with Iraq, Cheney, Wolfowitz and several prominent neoconservative public intellectuals pressed for action. Frustration with Saddam's games and erosion of the sanctions regime designed to contain him had made the idea of regime change popular across the American political spectrum. Atrocities committed against Iraqi Shiites and Kurds rallied human rights advocates to the cause of intervention. The Democratic Party opposition seemed cowed by the president's soaring popularity after 9/11 and fearful of being perceived as hindering the fight against terrorism.

Cheney emerged as the most strident advocate for war, contending that Saddam had weapons of mass destruction that he was preparing to use against the United States and its friends. The State Department's Bureau of Intelligence and Research (INR) was skeptical of Cheney's sources in the Iraqi exile community, but he and Rumsfeld brushed aside its doubts. Years later it became apparent that one Iraqi source, code-named Curveball, was utterly unreliable, and another, Ahmed Chalabi, leader of the exile group Cheney, Wolfowitz, and the neoconservatives most admired, had ties to Iran, the nation most likely to gain from an American defeat of Iraq's army. But they were telling the war hawks what they wanted to hear.

Within the administration, Cheney was also the strongest advocate of unilateral action and for ignoring Congress and the United Nations. His interpretation of presidential power precluded the necessity of legislative action in foreign affairs. He opposed seeking authorization for war from the Security Council, fearful of having restraints imposed on the exercise of American power. But Bush was persuaded that public support for the war would be stronger if Congress and the UN approved.

Cheney, Rumsfeld, and Wolfowitz were convinced that Saddam's forces could be defeated by relatively few Americans, perhaps half as many as the army chief of staff and outside analysts called for. They also assumed American troops would be welcomed as liberators by the Iraqi people and that Chalabi could install a democratic government quickly. They brushed aside elaborate State Department plans for postwar Iraq. Critics warned that the Pentagon was not prepared for victory.

Those of Bush's advisers who argued for preventive war against Iraq varied in their reasoning. Some were genuinely fearful of Saddam's alleged weapons of mass destruction. Some were eager to spread American power and values in the Middle East. Control of Iraqi oil does not appear to have been a high priority, but all were aware it would be a useful side benefit. Interest in Iraq and its neighbors had always been rooted in awareness of the importance of access to the region's oil.

Humanitarian concerns were also peripheral but unquestionably sincere. Saddam was a brutal tyrant, and his people would benefit enormously from his departure. Bush found the arguments persuasive, especially the Wilsonian vision of spreading democracy. Recognizing that many analysts and Republican conservatives preferred a policy more immediately related to national interest, the administration chose the WMD issue as the rationale for war that it presented to the public.

In September 2002 Bush appeared before the UN General Assembly to warn against Saddam's weapons of mass destruction. Next, he turned to Congress and requested authorization to use force against Iraq. Although there was strong opposition from Senate Democrats, those with presidential aspirations voted in favor of the resolution. The debate in the United States was over.

Throughout the fall, thousands of American troops were deployed to the vicinity of Iraq. Saddam determined that it was in his interest to invite the UN inspectors he had expelled to return. Coercive diplomacy had worked. French, German, and Russian leaders imagined there would be no need for military action. In November the Security Council unanimously demanded that Iraq surrender all weapons of mass destruction— without authorizing resort to force if he failed to comply. Bush, however, concluded that the UN resolution gave legitimacy to the invasion the Pentagon was planning.

In Baghdad, the inspectors found no evidence of WMDs or programs to produce them. In Washington there was palpable disappointment. The troops were in place, and the Pentagon was eager to invade before spring, before desert heat became a problem. But across Europe there was strong opposition to war. British prime minister Tony Blair urged Bush to try again for UN authorization. In February Powell, who had more credibility abroad than anyone else in the administration, was sent to the United Nations to obtain the necessary resolution.

Powell presented the case for the existence of WMDs in Iraq and won over many skeptics in the United States. He failed, however, to win the necessary support in the Security Council. Bush, Cheney, Rumsfeld, and Wolfowitz did not expect UN approval and saw no need for it. Rumsfeld dismissed America's longtime allies as "old Europe," where the will to fight had evaporated.

By the eve of the war, the administration had persuaded more than half the American people that Saddam had been involved in the 9/11 attacks. The time had come for vengeance. Undeterred by antiwar demonstrations across the globe, the world's most powerful nation, equipped with extraordinary military technology, invaded a Third World country possessed of a decrepit military armed with obsolete Soviet weapons. The outcome was never in doubt.

Great Britain provided major support, and a number of other states, including Australia, Spain, and Poland, sent token forces to join the U.S.-led "coalition of the willing." It took but three weeks for coalition forces to reach Baghdad and only three more before President Bush, standing on the deck of the USS *Abraham Lincoln*, declared victory.

It was quickly apparent, however, that defeat of the Iraqi Army had been easy compared to managing the postwar situation. American forces in Baghdad were unprepared for the chaos that followed the destruction of Saddam's regime. There were too few troops to stop widespread looting or provide security for the people of the city. Hospitals, museums, libraries, and public buildings generally were ransacked. Residents of Baghdad were left without basic necessities: water, electricity, jobs. The mood in the city turned ugly as the joy of those delivered from tyranny faded when confronted by the incompetence of their "liberators."

In the North, Kurds, who had enjoyed considerable independence before the war, established a state within a state. In the South, the power vacuum was filled by militia forces commanded by Shiite religious figures, eager to lead the country as soon as the coalition forces left. But in Baghdad and central Iraq, in the "Sunni Triangle," forces hostile to the United States, including some affiliated with al Qaeda, generated massive unrest.

Obviously, the assumption of quick victory, followed almost immediately by establishment of a friendly Iraqi government, was a fantasy. The United States would have to occupy Iraq until the security of its people could be assured and reconstruction was under way—precisely the nation building the Bush team abhorred.

To replace a retired general as civilian authority, the administration sent L. Paul Bremer, a former diplomat, who became the de facto dictator of Iraq—although his writ carried little weight outside the compound in which his Coalition Provisional Authority was housed. One Bremer decision proved disastrous: the precipitous disbanding of the Iraqi Army. Iraqi police and security forces vanished. The Pentagon had underestimated the number of troops necessary to maintain order and attacks on coalition forces occurred daily. Bush was contemptuous of the insurgents, but Americans in Iraq were being killed in increasing numbers, reminding many at home of the Vietnam quagmire.

The administration was also in trouble at home because of the failure to find weapons of mass destruction, the threat from which it had used to justify the war. Questions arose about the quality of intelligence reports used to justify the attack. There was a growing sense that the administration had "cherry-picked" intelligence to suit its preferred course of action. There were no WMDs in Iraq. They probably had been destroyed in compliance with UN demands. Apparently Saddam had chosen to maintain the charade that he still had WMDs to intimidate his enemies, especially Iran.

By the summer of 2003, as casualties mounted, it was evident that the U.S. military was facing intensified guerilla warfare. In addition to the ubiquitous improvised explosive devices (IEDs), rocket, mortar, and sniper fire, car bombs and suicide bombers appeared with increasing frequency. U.S. intelligence reported that non-Iraqi jihadis were streaming across the Muslim world, eager to confront the Americans readily accessible in Iraq.

Polls in the United States showed declining support for the war—and declining approval of the president's leadership. Neoconservatives criticized the administration for failing to devote adequate resources to the democratization of Iraq. In Great Britain, opposition to the war soared and Blair was castigated for supporting Bush. Nowhere could Washington find military, political, or financial assistance. In November the administration promised to end the occupation and transfer sovereignty to an Iraqi government on June 30, 2004, but the insurgency continued unabated.

Various Iraqi factions challenged the idea of creating a transitional government. The Kurds, having enjoyed virtual autonomy since 1991, declared they would not surrender their power and freedom to the proposed new government. Former exiles, operating in the Iraqi Governing Council, were insisting on retaining what little power they exercised. Grand Ayatollah Ali Sistani, the most widely respected Shiite cleric, demanded direct elections managed by the United Nations and mustered 100,000 supporters for a peaceful march in Baghdad. American authorities in Iraq yielded to Sistani's demands and hoped to finesse the challenges from the Kurds and the former exiles.

None of these maneuvers brought peace to Iraq. A year after the war began, Iraqi civilians were being killed almost daily by suicide bombers and assassins. Hundreds of thousands of Iraqis were out of work. Crime was rampant. The supply of electricity was uncertain. For all their tribulations, Iraqis blamed the United States. Most were grateful to be rid of Saddam, but they had no love for their new "oppressors" and were eager for them to be gone. Hundreds of American troops had been killed and thousands more wounded in the months *after* Bush declared victory.

In April 2004 the administration was shaken by revelations of the horrors inflicted on Iraqi prisoners at Abu Ghraib by American guards. Photos of prisoners being tormented and humiliated, beaten, forced to simulate sexual acts, attacked by dogs, piled naked in human pyramids, were aired by CBS and spread quickly around the world: American soldiers photographing each other grinning while abusing prisoners, bringing the blessings of democracy to the Middle East. The abuses had been reported months earlier, and nothing had been done to stop them. The administration had deliberately evaded the Geneva Conventions and allowed mistreatment of POWs in its quest for actionable intelligence.

By May an air of defeatism had settled over Washington. Some neoconservatives remained convinced the United States could prevail if it used sufficient power, but senior military officials warned the country was headed for defeat—and blamed Rumsfeld and Wolfowitz. The administration had no idea of how to get the violence in Iraq under control, no idea of how to achieve its goal of transforming Iraq into a democratic state with a free-market economy.

Despite the nominal transfer of power to an Iraqi regime on June 30, the insurgency intensified. Polls showed that only 2 percent of Iraqis had a favorable view of the occupation. In the United States, public approval for the war and the president's performance dropped sharply. William F. Buckley, doyen of American conservatives, declared, "If I knew then what I know now about what kind of situation we would be in, I would have opposed the war." Bush and his advisers had deluded themselves on the issue of WMDs and misled the American people on Saddam's ties to bin Laden. Defeat of Iraq had done nothing to diminish the threat of terrorism. Across the political spectrum, demand for an exit strategy grew.

Despite widespread unhappiness with the administration's foreign policies—the war in Iraq in particular—Bush was reelected in November 2004. There would be no change of course. The president was no longer looking for a graceful way out.

In January 2005 eight million Iraqis risked their lives to vote for a national assembly that would draft a new constitution. There could be no doubt that they had been inspired by the opportunity, and Bush claimed vindication. As expected, a religious Shia slate with ties to Iran won, but with only 48 percent of the vote, much less than anticipated. The party of a former CIA asset, a secular Shiite, received 14 percent—more than expected, thanks to covert support from the United States. But Sunnis, who dominated the insurgency, did not participate, a fact that boded ill for the future.

Sectarian divisions intensified and the rule of law was absent. Violence increased, as did calls for the withdrawal of the United States. But many analysts argued against withdrawal, some—especially neoconservatives—insisting *more* rather than fewer American ground forces were needed.

As Iraqi leaders of all religious and ethnic persuasions perceived the Americans eager to go home, fighting on the ground became more a struggle for power among Iraqis than an anti-American insurgency. There were indications some Sunnis were prepared to turn against the insurgency if assured of a long-term American presence as a hedge against Shiite domination. Most commentators contended that an American withdrawal would mean full-scale civil war, disastrous for the region as well as for Iraqis.

In November 2006 dissatisfaction with Bush and the situation in Iraq—where more than two thousand Americans had been killed—resulted in the Democrats winning control of both houses of Congress. At home and abroad, the vote was perceived as support for withdrawal. In December the Iraq Study Group, a bipartisan panel of respected elders appointed by Congress, issued its report. Much like the "Wise Men" who told Lyndon Johnson it was time to end the war in Vietnam, the group declared the situation in Iraq to be deteriorating and contended that the troops and resources dedicated to Iraq were needed in Afghanistan.

Support for maintaining the existing approach to Iraq was virtually nonexistent. The Shiite leaders were unable to rein in the Shia militias engaged in bloody ethnic cleansing. The ruling coalition was unwilling to make concessions to Kurds or Sunnis, concessions that might stabilize the situation. Many analysts argued for withdrawal if the Shia-dominated government failed to make progress toward reconciliation. But several neoconservatives continued to argue for more American ground forces. Senator John McCain of Arizona, a leading contender for the Republican presidential nomination, called on the administration to send 100,000 more troops to bring peace and order to Iraq. Even General Anthony Zinni, a highly respected critic of the decision to go to war, supported the idea of sending more troops over the next six months.

Bush, angered by the Iraq Study Group's account of his failures in Iraq, dismissed its recommendations as coming from people whose powers had peaked when they served his father more than ten years before. In January 2007 he announced plans to augment American forces by at least twenty thousand, the beginning of what came to be called the surge. General

David Petraeus, the army's leading authority on counterinsurgency, was appointed to command the Multi-National Force, Iraq.

To the relief of most Americans, the level of violence in Iraq declined over the next year. The additional troops provided more security for the people, but the key was Petraeus's skill at finding Iraqi allies, especially among the Sunnis. Al Qaeda fighters were concentrated in heavily Sunni Anbar province. The Iraqi Army, composed primarily of Shiites and Kurds, was neither welcome nor effective there. Failing to persuade Shiite leaders to reconcile with Sunnis, Petraeus won over Sunni sheiks in Anbar, providing them with money and training to turn against al Qaeda. Together, the Americans and the Sunnis of the "Awakening" produced order in Anbar, decimating al Qaeda forces—and the Sunnis no longer sought American withdrawal.

Combined with the decision of Muqtar al-Sadr—the Shiite cleric whose Mahdi Army had tormented Americans, Sunnis, and fellow Shiites—to call a truce in August 2007, the surge and the Sunni Awakening allowed the United States to withdraw troops at a measured pace. By the spring of 2008, although the number of Americans killed in Iraq hit four thousand, a Pew poll found 48 percent of Americans believed the military effort was satisfactory. The neoconservatives claimed success: Iraq, they contended, was now a stable country whose representative government controlled its territory and was oriented toward the West, an ally against militant Islamism.

But sectarian tensions did not disappear. Government forces began attacking members of the Sunni Awakening, and problems intensified along the Kurdish-Arab border where territory and oil rights were still disputed. Serious differences arose between Baghdad and Washington over a status-of-forces agreement to cover American troops in Iraq after the UN mandate expired in December 2008. And Barack Obama, leading in the polls as the American election loomed, was insisting that Iraq was not central to the war on terror and that if elected, he would withdraw American troops in sixteen months.

Shortly after Obama won the election, the Bush administration agreed to pull American troops out of Iraqi cities and towns by June 2009, and out of Iraq completely by December 31, 2011. For Bush and Cheney, however, time ran out in January 2009. Responsibility for managing the war in Iraq and the war against terror now belonged to Barack Obama.

After 9/11 Bush focused sharply on his "war against terrorism." By 2003 he had sent American forces to fight Islamic terrorists in approximately fifty countries around the world. The need for cooperation against terrorists led the United States to overlook the human rights transgressions of its friends in Central Asia, especially Uzbekistan, of the Russians in Chechnya, and of the Chinese in Tibet and Xinjiang. It had little choice but to cozy up to the Pakistani military, condemned by Washington when it overthrew a democratically elected government in 1999. Moral imagination had never been Cheney's long suit—and there were few foreign affairs specialists in the country who thought it a good time to indulge in moral righteousness.

While the administration struggled with the occupation of Iraq, it lost ground in its efforts to maintain pressure on North Korea and Iran. Both were determined to achieve nuclear weapons capability, perhaps for national status or as credible deterrents against an American preemptive strike. Cheney and other advocates of regime change prevented meaningful negotiations with Pyongyang, forcing Washington eventually to accept the fact that North Korea was a nuclear power. Iran made several overtures in the wake of 9/11, but Cheney and Rumsfeld prevailed over others such as Powell and Rice who were interested in engagement.

In April 2003 China stepped into the vacuum created by the unwillingness of the United States to address the nuclear crisis in Korea. Washington had given Beijing the opportunity to supplant American influence in Northeast Asia, and the Chinese seized it. Using their leverage with Pyongyang, which was reliant on China for food and fuel, they won North Korean assent to six-nation talks, an American demand, and obtained U.S. agreement to meet one-on-one, a North Korean demand. The initial talks failed, however, and further Chinese compromise proposals were rejected by the president at Cheney's insistence. And then both sides stalled to await the outcome of the American presidential election in 2004.

Rice took over as secretary of state in Bush's second administration and was immediately more assertive and more effective than she had been as national security adviser. Outmaneuvering Cheney and Rumsfeld, she worked out a tentative accord with Pyongyang in September 2005 but was undermined by Treasury Department sanctions against a Macao bank alleged to be laundering funds North Korea gained from illegal actions. Pyongyang used Treasury's action as an excuse to back away. Rice's support in the administration frayed when North Korea tested an underground nuclear device in October 2006, but she persisted. Finally, in February 2007, after Rumsfeld was gone and Cheney preoccupied with the criminal investigation of his chief of staff, she persuaded Pyongyang to freeze its principal reactor again and to readmit IAEA inspectors it had expelled. But by then North Korea was a declared nuclear power, with eight to ten more nuclear weapons than it had when Bush took office in 2001. North Korea was one more major unresolved issue to be left to his successor.

Similarly, the unwillingness to engage Iran precluded any improvement in relations. In May 2003, after the defeat of Saddam's forces but before it was evident that the aftermath would be disastrous, the Bush team was startled by a new Iranian initiative. Ayatollah Ali Khamenei representative proposed ending Iran's support of militant Palestinian groups such as Hamas and Islamic Jihad and converting Hezbollah into a strictly social and political organization. Tehran was willing to recognize Israel and a separate Palestinian state. In return, Khameni wanted the United States to guarantee Iran's security and remove economic sanctions. Once again, Cheney and Rumsfeld insisted on regime change. Flushed with victory in Afghanistan and Iraq, they were convinced of the imminent collapse of the Islamic Republic.

Iran grew stronger and more hostile to the United States in the remaining years of Bush's presidency. American forces had pushed aside the Taliban, a source of irritation to Iran, and eliminated Saddam Hussein's regime, the most immediate threat to Iran. In August 2005 Iranians elected Mahmoud Ahmadinejad president, and he proved to be exceptionally belligerent and provocative. Relations with the West deteriorated rapidly. He was a Holocaust denier who insisted Israel had to be destroyed, raising fears Israel would launch a preemptive strike. A controversial National

Intelligence Estimate in November 2007 suggested the Iranians had stopped development of nuclear weapons in 2003, but there was little doubt they were still progressing toward that capability. Ignoring sanctions and threats from the Bush administration, the Iranians had produced more than a ton of low-enriched uranium by the time the president left office. Another potential crisis left to his successor.

In addition, there was the perpetual Israeli-Palestinian conflict from which the administration preferred to remain disengaged. Neither Arafat nor Sharon was interested in a reasonable solution. Sharon was confident he could ignore American complaints. He knew Bush was running for reelection in 2004 and would not want to alienate Israel's American supporters—Christian evangelicals as well as Jewish Zionists.

Sharon surprised the world in December 2003 by announcing his intention to withdraw unilaterally from the Gaza strip and parts of the West Bank. Settlements on the other side of the line he drew would be abandoned, an idea that infuriated Israeli settlers and most members of his own party, the right-wing Likud. Part of the West Bank would be annexed to Israel, outraging many Palestinians and their supporters. But Sharon won the endorsement of President Bush, and Israel dismantled its settlements and withdrew from Gaza in 2005.

In April 2004 Bush announced a major shift in American policy. For the first time since the Six-Day War, the American government stated that it did not expect Israel to return to its pre-1967 borders and it approved Israel's policy of denying Palestinian refugees the right of return. The administration did urge Sharon to begin dismantling the West Bank settlements, to no avail. Few in the United States would press the point before the election. There was less questioning of Israeli policy in the United States than there was in Israel.

Nothing either Israel or the PLO said or did stopped harassment by Hamas from Gaza or Hezbollah from Lebanon. In 2006 Hamas kidnapped a young Israeli soldier and Hezbollah began rocket attacks on border towns. Israel struck back harshly and war ensued, with Hezbollah sustaining severe losses but able to deny the Israelis a decisive victory. Hamas, which seized control of Gaza on June 2007, began pummeling southern Israel with rockets in December 2008. After retaliating with air strikes that killed many civilians, Israel sent ground troops into Gaza in January 2009. It was too late for the Bush administration to act—had it wished to—and too soon for the incoming Obama administration.

As Bush and his foreign policy team prepared to leave office, the critical issue in Afghanistan remained the lack of security. Training of a national army proceeded slowly, suggesting it would be another decade before it would be ready to relieve coalition forces. It was outnumbered and outgunned by warlord forces and constantly attacked by the Taliban, both financing their forces by expanding the drug trade. Patience with Karzai and the war was evaporating in NATO capitals. Americans, exhausted by the war in Iraq, devastated at home by a severe recession, had little interest in pouring more blood and treasure into Afghanistan. What little hope remained for success there—and that would be defined far short of creation of a liberal democracy—depended on how long the United States and its allies stayed.

Much also depended on developments in Pakistan, whose security forces provided the principal support for the Taliban prior to 9/11 and remained reluctant to see it eliminated. The Pakistani military, focused on its unending struggle against India, imagined that having pawns in Afghanistan gave it strategic depth. Washington demanded that the Pakistani leader choose sides—and he chose to align Pakistan with the American cause, a decision unpopular with a majority of his people.

The greatest American fear was that the Pakistani government would lose control of its nuclear arsenal. Pakistan had never signed the Nuclear Nonproliferation Treaty and in 1998 had become a declared nuclear power. In 2004 the scientist Pakistanis considered a national hero for making their country a nuclear power confessed to having assisted Libya, Iran, and North Korea in their programs. The obvious point—that he could not have carried out his operations without the complicity of the Pakistani military—was not addressed. That terrorists might gain access to Pakistan's nuclear weapons led some analysts to argue that Pakistan—rather than Afghanistan or Iraq or Iran or North Korea—was the most dangerous country in the world.

Relations between Washington and New Delhi were among the few bright spots in American foreign affairs in the early years of the twenty-first century. Throughout the Cold War, India had been critical of the United States and had developed close ties to the Soviet Union. In the early 1990s, however, Indian leaders decided to liberalize their economy and open it to foreign investment, resulting in rapid growth. Gradually it became an important commercial partner of the United States, with trade soaring between 2004 and 2008.

In the closing years of the Clinton administration, American support for India against Pakistan had convinced New Delhi that rapprochement with the United States was in India's national interest. Improvement in relations between the world's two largest democracies was also facilitated by the existence of nearly three million Indian Americans and the lobbying activity of the U.S.-India Political Action Committee.

The Bush administration was no less interested in nurturing Indian-American relations. The two countries shared a common interest in fighting Islamic terrorism and anxiety about the rise of Chinese power—evidenced by India's participation in military exercises with the United States and Japan. Strengthening strategic ties with India may prove to be the most positive legacy of Bush's foreign policy.

The record in Latin America was mixed as that part of the world rarely succeeded in gaining Washington's attention. The administration pandered to the Cuban vote in Florida with actions hostile to the Castro regime and engaged in frequent unpleasantries with Hugo Chávez, a Venezuelan populist leader hostile to the United States. The principal activity in the region was in Colombia, source of most of the cocaine used in the United States, where Washington spent billions on what Congress called "the War on Drugs and Thugs," to little effect.

Problems with Haiti persisted long after the Clinton administration returned Jean-Bertrand Aristide to power. Aristide's presidency proved as disappointing as his American critics had anticipated. He was guilty of demagoguery and provided his people with neither good government nor satisfactory economic development. The Bush administration was unfriendly from the outset. When political violence increased, prompting fears of a flood of Haitian boat people, Powell flew to Haiti and persuaded Aristide to leave. A UN peacekeeping mission restored a semblance of order but with little promise that anything would be done to improve the lot of the Haitian people.

Most disappointing of the Bush administration's relationships in Latin America was that with Mexico. Although Mexico had become the second-largest trading partner of the United States, thanks to NAFTA, and there appeared to be a close personal tie between Bush and the Mexican president, disagreements over immigration proved impossible to transcend. Immigration reform was postponed indefinitely, the victim of popular anger in the United States at the presence of large numbers of illegal immigrants in the country. Relations were briefly quite chilly, but the two leaders papered over their differences in 2004.

In July 2003 Bush traveled to Africa, ostensibly to boost the fight against the AIDS epidemic there. Africa had little strategic value to the United States after the Cold War but provided 20 percent of American oil imports—a figure expected to rise. American businesses had invested billions in West Africa, and the president was persuaded it would be useful to show the flag, to demonstrate humanitarian as well as economic concerns.

While Bush was in Africa, a brutal civil war raged in Liberia, whose links to the United States dated back to the early nineteenth century, when American black nationalists had established a colony there. For much of its subsequent history, the country had been ruled by Liberians of American descent. During the Cold War, the United States had provided substantial aid, although the various regimes in Monrovia were undemocratic, often vicious. After the Cold War, Washington lost interest and withdrew support. In 2000 a rebellion took root.

By July 2003 Liberia was a humanitarian disaster, and pressure built for American intervention to stop the carnage. But U.S. forces were stretched thin in Iraq and Afghanistan, and the task was left to West African peacekeepers. Demonstrating concern, the Bush administration sent two thousand American marines to the coast of Liberia to support the peacekeepers. It would neither lead nor send troops ashore. Happily for all concerned, the war wound down in August.

Although the administration was similarly unwilling to use American power to stop ethnic cleansing in Sudan, its performance compared favorably to that of the rest of the developed world. Civil strife between the primarily Arab Muslim North and the largely black Christian South had begun on the eve of independence in 1955. By the 1990s nearly two million Christians had been killed, and American evangelicals worked desperately to help the victims and stop the fighting. Clinton was never engaged, but

Bush, obviously capable of moral imagination, took up the case on the eve of 9/11. He sent a representative who pressed successfully for peace talks late in 2003. But the government, as it eased its raids in the South, began bombing its people in Darfur, in western Sudan. It employed Arab tribesmen to raid villages, killing the men and raping the women. The people of Darfur were almost all Muslims, but they, too, were black and viewed with contempt by Arabs. The government was determined to drive them out of the country—and the rest of the world seemed unconcerned.

Bush quickly condemned what the United Nations declared to be "ethnic cleansing" and demanded that Khartoum stop the attacks. In the spring of 2004 the American media began to focus on the atrocities, and in July a congressional resolution called the killings "genocide." The Bush administration contributed $200 million in relief aid to Darfur refugees but received virtually no support from Europe. Hostile to the Bush team for its past unilateralism and self-righteousness, the other powers did not rally to America's side, even in so worthy a cause—and the people of Darfur were paying the price.

After 9/11 Russia faded from the view of the Bush administration until the brief war between Russia and Georgia in August 2008. Colin Powell expressed unhappiness with the fact that Putin and his comrades from the former KGB were eliminating opposition and silencing critics, but his colleagues had more immediate worries than the reversal of democratic reform in Russia.

Moscow had been uneasy about Washington's unilateralism and Bush's doctrine of preventive war. Putin and his colleagues were profoundly displeased by the continued eastward expansion of NATO. They perceived American promotion of democracy in Ukraine and Georgia as an attempt to undermine Russia's influence in its "near abroad." But Bush's foreign policy team dismissed Russia as a declining power whose complaints were unworthy of concern.

China, on the other hand, had to be treated with respect and, occasionally, even deference. It had become the engine of economic growth in East Asia, its military power surging, and it was poised to challenge American political and strategic influence in the region. Chinese foreign policy was becoming less passive, and its diplomats increasingly skillful. China's leaders and foreign policy intellectuals were beginning to accept their country's role as a great power.

Most of the issues between the two countries proved manageable. Knowledgeable Americans remained troubled by China's human rights violations, but the Bush administration privileged economic and strategic issues. Concerns about the erosion of freedoms promised to the people of Hong Kong were also expressed quietly, to the dismay of Bush's neoconservative supporters. The one major flashpoint—the Taiwan Strait—allowed for no complacency, if only because it was not a bilateral issue. As often as not, it was the Taipei government that stirred the pot.

Troubled by the PLA's preparations to attack Taiwan and the missile buildup in China across the Strait from Taiwan, Bush warned that the United States would defend the island against an unprovoked attack. "Unprovoked," however, was subject to interpretation, and Chen Shui-bian, Taiwan's president and leader of the pro-independence Democratic Progressive Party, kept trying Beijing's patience with gestures and rhetoric designed to win more international space for Taiwan. The Chinese contended that American arms sales encouraged Chen's troublesome behavior.

Although Bush was uneasy about being perceived as betraying democratic Taiwan, the United States needed a good working relationship with China. In December 2003 Bush publicly warned Taiwan against taking unilateral action toward independence. Most striking was the decision to issue the warning in the presence of the Chinese premier.

There was little doubt that Washington as well as Beijing hoped to see Chen defeated in Taiwan's March 2004 election. The Kuomintang Party of the late Chiang Kai-shek and Chiang Ching-kuo was perceived as less likely to be provocative. But Chen won a narrow, disputed victory and trimmed his sails a bit. Washington counseled China to be patient and did what it could to rein in Chen, but never enough to satisfy Beijing.

If the PLA attacked across the Strait, would the United States come to Taiwan's defense? For years American policy had stressed "strategic ambiguity," trying to keep both Beijing and Taipei guessing as to what the American response would be. If it was clear the United States would defend Taiwan, American leaders feared Chen or others might behave dangerously, sparking an attack. If it seemed certain the United States would not defend Taiwan, most analysts assumed there would be no restraints on the PLA. To the national security elites in both Beijing and Washington, the Taiwan Strait seemed the most dangerous place in the world—the only place where two great nuclear powers might stumble into war.

Despite their sharp differences over Taiwan, human rights, Chinese currency manipulation, and violations of intellectual property rights, leaders in both China and the United States desperately wanted a good working relationship. Their countries' economies were intertwined, and they recognized the enormous value, strategically as well as economically of cooperation. Differences had to be subordinated to joint management of the threats from terrorism and nuclear proliferation. Analysts in both countries wrote of maturing Chinese-American relations. In December 2006 Bush declared the relationship the "best ever."

In the United States, men and women troubled by China's continuing human rights violations, its repression of Tibetans and Uighurs, its support for the genocidal Sudanese government, the brutal Burmese junta, and Robert Mugabe's vicious regime in Zimbabwe, expected their government to press their concerns. But for the Bush administration—and the majority of the national security elite—these issues were negligible when weighed against the need for China's help in dealing with North Korea. "Realism" prevailed over "idealism." Moral imagination was in short supply. The consensus in Washington was that engagement had been a tremendous success.

The election of Ma Ying-cheou, the Kuomintang candidate, as president of the Republic of China in 2008 came as a tremendous relief to both the American and Chinese governments. Ma favored improved relations with Beijing, and tensions across the Strait were greatly reduced. American military analysts perceived the PLA relaxing its military posture, putting aside plans to invade Taiwan.

Bush began his presidency with a superb foreign policy team, comparable to John F. Kennedy's best and brightest. And like Kennedy's team, the Bush team advocated policies that took the nation to the brink of disaster.

In the course of their obsession with Iraq, they alienated many of America's friends in the world and mired the U.S. military in a quagmire of their own creation. When Bush left the White House in 2009, the United States was held in lower esteem by other nations than at any time in the twentieth century.

Also damaging to the security of the United States was the unwillingness of the Bush team to confront long-term threats to the environment. The administration catered to the interests of domestic constituencies that opposed regulation, even when based on international agreements premised on the assumption that clean air, clean water, and other environmental protection measures are a public good. The president was personally committed to using American wealth to stop the spread of AIDS, especially in Africa, but only a fraction of the funding he promised was forthcoming.

Across the world, the actions and rhetoric of the Bush administration turned public opinion against the United States. Resentment was strongest in Muslim countries because of policies deemed hostile to Islam, but polls nearly everywhere revealed a perception that the United States was the greatest threat to world peace. There appeared to be no force on earth capable of restraining Washington. There was an extraordinary erosion of "soft power," the admiration of American values and what America had once stood for. And then Bush went back to Texas, as the nation's economy collapsed.

19

THE OBAMA PROMISE

O N JANUARY 25, 2009, Barrack Hussein Obama, the Hawaii-born son of a white American mother and a black Kenyan father, was sworn in as president of the United States. The country was sliding into the worst recession since the Great Depression of the 1930s. The battle against al Qaeda and the Taliban in Afghanistan was going badly. Iraq appeared relatively stable but with little prospect of becoming the peaceful democracy Americans yearned to leave behind. North Korea continued to flex its nuclear muscles, and Iran continued on its devious path toward becoming a nuclear power, thwarting American efforts in Iraq as best it could. And these were only the more obvious problems the new administration would be forced to confront.

The Cold War was becoming a distant memory, but Russia and China continued to frustrate Washington in its effort to promote democracy and respect for human rights around the world—and the two countries undermined the sanctions the United States hoped would restrain Iran. The standoff between Israel and the Palestinians continued to fester, with Israeli settlers rivaling Hamas in Gaza and Hezbollah in Lebanon in provocations. Obama's supporters imagined he would make it all right. As testimony to worldwide expectations, he was awarded the Nobel Peace Prize in 2009, largely on the promise of his rhetoric, overflowing with moral imagination.

Two striking appointments headed Obama's foreign affairs team: Hillary Clinton as secretary of state and Robert Gates as secretary of defense. Clinton had been Obama's principal rival in the bitter battle for the Democratic nomination, and Gates had succeeded Donald Rumsfeld as George Bush's secretary of defense. Of the two, Gates had by far the most experience in foreign affairs, having served on the NSC and as director of the CIA. But neither person was part of Obama's inner circle in a White House determined to control policy.

In the election campaign, Obama had faulted Bush's war in Iraq and promised that as president he would reemphasize the battle against al Qaeda and the Taliban in Afghanistan. American combat forces would be withdrawn from Iraq in 2010. Once in office, Obama reached out to the Muslim world with a moving speech delivered in Cairo. He insisted that the United States was not hostile to Muslims, quoted from the Koran, and called for democracy and respect for human rights. He offered Iran and North Korea the opportunity to end their pariah status—and their nuclear weapons programs. He signaled to both Russia and China his desire to end adversarial relations and stepped into the morass of Israeli-Palestinian relations, eager to bring peace to the region. Not even the brutal regime in Burma was judged unworthy of an overture.

Although conditions in Iraq were far from optimal, the Obama administration withdrew most combat troops in 2010. Approximately forty-five thousand remained to provide training for the Iraqi Army and a modicum of security. A reasonably democratic election to the national legislature, held in January 2010, resulted in a near tie between the two leading parties and a stalemate that lasted months before the selection of a prime minister. Violence persisted, usually Shia attacks on Sunnis and vice versa, but also occasional warfare between the Iraqi Army and remnants of al Qaeda that eventually morphed into the even more horrific Islamic State in Iraq and Syria (ISIS). But American attention had shifted elsewhere.

"Elsewhere" was primarily to the domestic economy as the country was wracked with massive unemployment and a painfully slow recovery. Obama, like many of his predecessors, was far less interested in nation building abroad than in restoring the well-being of Americans. Clinton, Gates, and their colleagues remained focused on the president's foreign policy agenda, most obviously the war in Afghanistan, which had become "Obama's war."

American troop levels increased, efforts to win the support of the Afghan people intensified, but the resurgence of the Taliban continued. Dissatisfaction with Hamid Karzai's corrupt government soared, as did tensions between Karzai and the American diplomats who tried to work with him, including the redoubtable Richard Holbrooke, whose efforts received little support from the White House. In 2010 the highly respected General David Petraeus, who had overseen the surge in Iraq, took command of NATO forces in Afghanistan, allowing hope for a minimally acceptable outcome. Support for the effort was eroding in the United States and among NATO allies, who began to withdraw their troops. American troop reductions would begin before the next presidential election. Pakistani intelligence forces (ISI) continued to play a double game, providing some assistance to the NATO effort—and protecting Taliban leaders whom they saw as a strategic asset against India. Indeed, when Osama bin Laden was finally found—and killed by U.S. Navy SEALS in May 2011—he was living comfortably in a Pakistani military garrison town. Few doubted the ISI was complicit in sheltering him.

Many analysts argued that ending the Israeli-Palestinian standoff constituted the key to peace in the Middle East. Muslims throughout the world often pointed to U.S. support of Israel as the source of their anti-Americanism. The Obama administration committed itself to bringing the two sides together, appointing George Mitchell, who had brokered peace in Northern Ireland, to the lead role. Unfortunately, Hamas, controlling Gaza, demonstrated no interest, and the Palestinian Authority on the West Bank was too weak to make peace without concessions that the right-wing Likud government of Israel would not grant. Pressure on Israel to stop building settlements on Palestinian land merely convinced most Israelis that Obama was hostile to them.

Mitchell resigned in frustration. Israeli Prime Minister Benjamin Netanyahu, confident of support among the American people and their representatives in Congress, was openly dismissive of Obama's efforts. Neither man tried very hard to disguise his contempt for the other, and their relationship worsened in Obama's second term.

The most dramatic developments in the Middle East occurred without American agency, in some instances to the dismay of American policymakers. In 2011 the "Arab Spring," an apparent democracy movement, surprised the world, beginning with the overthrow of a dictatorial and corrupt Tunisian regime. Quickly the movement spread throughout the region to Egypt, Bahrain, Yemen, Libya, and Syria. Washington's Egyptian ally, Hosni Mubarak, found himself under pressure to resign. In Bahrain, headquarters of the U.S. Fifth Fleet, the ruling class was threatened, and in Yemen, where the unpopular president claimed to be assisting the United States against al Qaeda, protestors filled the streets. Hesitantly, Obama moved to support the demonstrators, uncertain as to who they were and how their success would affect American interests in the region. To the dismay of American allies in the Middle East, notably Saudi Arabia, Jordan, and Israel, he urged Mubarak to step aside, which he eventually did. In the democratic election that followed in Egypt, the Muslim Brotherhood came to power—and was pushed aside before long by a military coup, leaving Egypt under a regime perhaps more repressive than that of Mubarak. The Bahrain authorities were asked to refrain from violence: they did not. No one in the administration seemed to know what to do about Yemen, where al Qaeda was stronger than in Afghanistan or Pakistan.

Obama had less difficulty responding to the rebellion in Libya, where Muammar al-Qaddafi, long an irritant to the United States, ordered indiscriminate attacks on civilians as his forces attempted to crush the rebellion. U.S. planes destroyed Libyan air defenses and provided intelligence to facilitate British and French bombing of Qaddafi's positions. Libya was soon wracked by civil war. American, British, and French support enabled the rebels to withstand Qaddafi's onslaught, ultimately to kill him, but chaos ensued, allowing terrorists to establish a foothold in the country.

Syria prompted a more complicated and disastrously inadequate response, questioned more than any other of Obama's foreign policy decisions—even by Hillary Clinton and John Kerry, his secretaries of state, Samantha Power, his ambassador to the United Nations, and Susan Rice, his national security adviser. Only Robert Gates, his secretary of defense, suggested it might be best to conclude the two wars the country was already fighting in the region before it began another. If the regime of Bashar al-Assad were overthrown,

Syria's ties to Iran might be weakened and its threat to Lebanon lessened. But there might also be sectarian violence, and Assad's successors might be even more hostile to their neighbors. As Americans are wont to do, the administration called for reform, for an end to authoritarianism, some movement toward democracy. Assad offered verbal gestures toward a more open society, but his security forces began to kill the protestors. Belatedly, Obama concluded that the Syrian government, in its ruthless suppression of its people, had lost claim to legitimacy. He called for Assad to step aside. Instead the regime intensified its efforts to crush the revolt. Aware of Syria's stockpile of chemical weapons, Obama declared a "Red Line," warning that the United States would attack government forces if they used them. On August 21, 2013, Assad's troops used deadly sarin gas against rebel-held territory.

Obama did not want to go to war against Syria and resisted pressure from within his administration and from the foreign policy elite who feared a loss of credibility if he failed to respond to Assad's blatant disregard of his warning. He did not consider the Syrian civil war an existential threat to the United States or Israel. He imagined Assad could be overthrown without American intervention. He thought all the talk about "credibility" was overblown. He was not among the few who anticipated the rise of an entity such as ISIS—or who foresaw the incredible refugee crisis as hundreds of thousands of Syrians were killed and millions forced to leave their homes. As the horrors mounted and critics decried the absence of American leadership, Obama held firm.

Russian pressures on Assad appeared to persuade him to surrender his chemical weapons cache and spared Obama the need for action—which he correctly surmised neither the Congress nor the American people wanted. As he anticipated, Assad's grip on the country weakened as a variety of rebel forces, most prominently radical Islamists, some with links to al Qaeda, were strengthened by a flood of jihadi recruits from abroad. ISIS proclaimed a caliphate in June 2014, gained control of a large swath of Syrian and Iraqi territory, and proceeded to apply the most brutal interpretation of sharia law.

Gradually, destroying ISIS became a higher priority than ridding Syria of the murderous Assad regime. Obama authorized bombings, used drone strikes in an effort to kill ISIS leaders, supported Kurdish Peshmerga and the Iraqi Army. Slowly, too slowly for his critics, ISIS was contained and pushed back in 2015 and 2016—but its operatives were now spread across North Africa and committing acts of terrorism in Western Europe, especially France. ISIS sympathizers struck in the United States as well.

And then Vladimir Putin, proclaiming his opposition to ISIS, came to the rescue of Assad. Beginning at the end of September 2015, Russian bombers flew thousands of sorties against rebel groups fighting the Syrian government. Few of the attacks actually struck ISIS forces. Supported also by Iranian and Hezbollah troops, Syrian government forces were able to go on the offensive. In March 2016 Putin announced the recall of his air force—although Russian planes continued to support the Syrian government, including the bombing of hospitals in rebel-held areas. In November a Russian fleet, including an aircraft carrier, sailed into the Mediterranean to intensify the attack. Assad had the opportunity to negotiate from a position of strength.

In none of the uprisings in the Arab world was the role of the United States decisive—and only in Libya could it be called significant. Obama's hesitation to support the stated goals of the protestors did not go unnoticed. The enormous prestige he had won with his Cairo speech in 2009 quickly diminished. Faith in the American commitment to democracy all but vanished. And yet there was little the United States could do. Few Americans called for military action—and more thought he had gone too far in Libya. If democracy were to come to the Arab world, it would have to be fought for and won by Arabs.

Obama concluded that the problems of the Middle East were intractable—certainly beyond the capabilities of Americans to resolve. He concluded also that the area was no longer of critical importance to the United States, in large part because domestic oil production had reduced the need for oil from the Persian Gulf. Nation building at home, his domestic agenda, had first claim on the country's resources. In foreign affairs, he was convinced that East Asia had to be the primary focus for the future, as evidenced in the announcement in 2012 of a "pivot," a rebalancing of American military assets from the Middle East across the Pacific. And, with some success, he tried to persuade foreign leaders and the American people that climate change was *the* critical issue for the future. In December

2015 most of the world's nations agreed to take steps to slow global warning, and an accord to implement the agreement was signed at the United Nations in April 2016.

Obama's foreign policy team reached out to the Russians and Chinese with minimal success. Relations with Moscow were to be "reset." Obama and Dmitri Medvedev, Russia's new president, developed a relationship that offered some promise of cooperation. Russia and the United States signed a new strategic arms limitation treaty in 2010.

Putin, however, remained the most powerful force in Russian politics and resumed the presidency in 2012. He never wavered in his determination to resurrect his country's great power status and its influence in the former Soviet Republics. Cooperation with the United States was not high on his list of priorities.

Late in 2013 protests erupted in Ukraine after President Viktor Yanukovych, under pressure from Putin, abandoned an agreement on trade ties with the European Union, indicating that ties with Russia would strengthen. In January 2014 the protests turned violent, and before the end of February Yanukovych fled to Russia. The country, however, was divided between the majority who leaned toward Europe and a minority, mostly Russian speakers in eastern Ukraine, eager to remain close to Russia. Russian "irregulars" began to drift into eastern Ukraine and then quickly seized control of Crimea. A sham referendum in March indicated that 97 percent of the people in Crimea favored a return to Russia. By April a secession movement, supported by Russian troops and equipment, emerged in in eastern Ukraine and a civil war began. Obama and European leaders protested, but Putin was unmoved. Obama led the way to imposing painful economic sanctions on Russia, to no avail. The United States neither alone nor with NATO was going to go to war with Russia over Crimea or Ukraine. Policymakers in Washington understood that Ukraine was a core Russian interest and Moscow would always be prepared to outdo any American military escalation.

The Chinese were no more responsive. The men and women who oversaw relations with China in the Obama administration began by signaling they would not press Beijing on human rights and would defer to Chinese sensitivity on meetings with the Dalai Lama. Anticipating reciprocity, they were profoundly disappointed. Largely on the basis of their economy's faster recovery from the recession, Chinese analysts once again concluded that America was in decline. Chinese arrogance became increasingly blatant: China's rapid rise demonstrated that its form of government, its economic management, would provide a superior model for the future. Washington opposed the most constructive economic proposal from China, creation of the Asian Infrastructure Investment Bank. Beijing yielded little on any of the issues that divided it from Washington and became increasingly bellicose in its warnings to the United States on Taiwan and in its expansion of its "core" interests in East Asia.

In the Pentagon there was increasing unease about the rapid modernization and strengthening of the Chinese military and the threat it posed to American interests in the western Pacific. Chinese fishing boats were harassing American warships. Chinese claims to rocks and islands in the South China Sea and China's developing of military capabilities on these sites, contrary to assurances its leader, Xi Jinping, had given to Obama, troubled other claimants in the region, especially the Philippines and Vietnam, as well as Washington. Those countries fearful of Chinese assertions sought closer ties with the United States. Even Burmese leaders hedged against their overbearing Chinese neighbors and turned to the United States—including taking major steps toward democratization. And, as part of the "pivot," a small contingent of U.S. Marines was stationed in Australia.

Domestically, Xi's China grew more repressive. Xi demanded greater ideological conformity, clamped down on what little press freedom existed, intimidated nongovernmental organizations and lawyers struggling to extend the rule of law. Beijing proved indifferent to American protests, both quiet entreaties from the White House and public criticism in the media. Similarly, problems of cybersecurity mounted as Chinese military hackers were suspected of economic spying as well as attempting to glean U.S. military secrets. Washington had no leverage on the human rights issues, and awareness of them and the cyber threats turned the American public against China. Obama may have had some success pushing back on the cyber threats.

On the other hand, Obama found Xi to be more engaged, more substantive than his predecessor. There *were* some positive outcomes to their relationship. Xi did more than any previous Chinese leader to press Iran on its nuclear program. Perhaps Obama's greatest success was winning Xi's support on issues of climate change, of global warming, leading to the Paris Agreement of December 2015. Also worthy of note was the institutionalization of the relationship, the regularization of high level meetings such as the Strategic and Economic Dialogues and the U.S.-China Asia-Pacific Consultation.

The most controversial component of Obama's determination to focus on the Asia-Pacific region was his Trans-Pacific Partnership, best known as the TPP. Obama saw the TPP, ostensibly a trade pact, a "free trade" agreement among twelve countries with borders on the Pacific that together produced 40 percent of the world's economic output, as a means of strengthening the U.S. position in the region, providing the participating states with an alternative to Chinese influence. The agreement, signed in February 2016, was designed to lower trade barriers and increase economic growth for all the signatories. Some analysts foresaw the eventual emergence of a single market, something akin to the European Union. Many considered the agreement a remarkable achievement in the overall acceptance of American ideas of transparency, concern for the environment, and labor relations, including minimum wages. Vietnam even agreed to allow free labor unions. Economists differed as to the value to the economy of the United States, the majority arguing it would be useful but few contending it would be enormously significant. For Obama and his aides, the primary import of the TPP was strategic. Unfortunately, labor unions and the men and women who blamed their economic misfortunes, especially the loss of manufacturing jobs, on free trade agreements and "globalization" were easily rallied in opposition. In the American election campaigns of 2016, candidates of both major parties opposed and doomed the TPP.

Another high priority for Obama was the nonproliferation of nuclear weapons. The two countries of gravest concern were Iran and North Korea. The North Koreans already had nuclear weapons, had violated agreements to halt their programs, and were indifferent to sanctions. They were determined to be recognized as a nuclear power. Until the Chinese decided to enforce sanctions, to stop propping up Pyongyang's economy, there was no prospect for change. But Beijing, fearful of the collapse of the North Korean regime—and its probable ramifications, tens of thousands of refugees fleeing into China and a united Korea allied to the United States—was unlikely to act.

Iran did not yet have nuclear weapons, but its leaders had rejected Obama's overture to relieve tensions with the United States. Iran continued to work toward the development of weapons, insisting consistently—and falsely—that its nuclear program had no military purpose. Tehran continued to support terrorism, continued to support Hamas and Hezbollah attacks on Israel, continued to undermine American interests in Iraq and wherever else it could. In June 2009, in an apparently rigged election, the blustering Holocaust-denying president, Mahmoud Ahmadinejad, retained power, stirring protests in Iran that were suppressed violently. There appeared to be little the United States could do, but at approximately that time a cyberattack was launched against Iran's centrifuges that by 2010 had set back its nuclear program significantly. The attack was assumed widely to be a joint Israeli-American operation.

Surprisingly, Ahmadinejad, in his final months in office in 2013, indicated interest in some kind of deal with the United States and other interested powers that would halt Iran's nuclear weapons program—always denied—in exchange for relief from economic sanctions that were crippling Iran's economy and causing unrest. Ayatollah Ali Khamenei, the nation's "Supreme Leader," was contemptuous of dealing with Washington, "the Great Satan," and there was no progress. In June 2013, however, Hassan Rouhani, a relative moderate in Iranian politics, the man who had been Iran's nuclear power negotiator from 2003 to 2005—and who campaigned on a promise to resume negotiations—was elected president, with Khamenei's acquiescence. Rouhani and Obama ultimately agreed to negotiations that began almost immediately and by November had reached an interim agreement between Iran and the P5+1 (permanent members of the Security Council plus Germany).

Perhaps the principal obstacle to a final deal was the mistrust Washington and Tehran had for each other. A second significant obstacle was the adamant opposition of Israel. The Israelis perceived Iran's nuclear program as a grave threat to their security, to Israel's existence. In the past, Israel had attacked and destroyed Iraqi and Syrian nuclear facilities. Iran, because of distance and size, was a much more difficult target. Israeli leaders hoped the United States would do the job for them and were unaccepting of any agreement that left Iran with the ability to resume a weapons program. Despite fierce opposition from Netanyahu, the powerful Israeli lobby in the United States, and congressional Republicans—and comparable opposition in Tehran—a carefully crafted final agreement was reached in July 2015.

Iran would remain an adversary, would continue to support terrorism, but would do so without nuclear weapons. In the remaining months of the Obama administration, Iran complied completely with the terms of the agreement and sanctions were slowly lifted—with provision for an immediate "snap-back" should Iran renege on its commitments.

Obama had entered the White House determined to close the prison at Guantanamo Bay in Cuba, widely perceived as a symbol of American mistreatment of prisoners taken in Afghanistan during the Bush administration. Congress denied him authority to do that. But, requiring no Congressional approval, and with the aid of Pope Francis, he took the surprising step of reopening diplomatic relations with Cuba. His action was praised throughout Latin America and much of Europe. Cuban Americans, led by a younger generation, were generally accepting. In March 2016 Obama became the first American president since Calvin Coolidge to visit the island. On his own, however, he could not lift the congressionally mandated embargo, which remained an obstacle to the many American businesses eager to exploit a long-closed market. Nor did the Cuban regime demonstrate any greater respect for human rights on the island.

As Obama prepared to leave office, there were few foreign affairs specialists willing to praise his performance. His administration was responsible for no disasters such as those brought about by the Bush administration. There were no new wars. The operation that resulted in the death of Osama bin Laden was a striking success. Certainly the restoration of diplomatic relations with Burma and Cuba were worthy accomplishments. Most leading analysts thought the deal with Iran was important. But within the foreign policy establishment—of which he was disdainful—there were valid criticisms of the timing of troop reductions and withdrawals in Iraq and Afghanistan. His refusal to act more aggressively—and more rapidly—against the Assad regime in Syria was challenged across the American political spectrum.

Few denied that Obama's efforts to improve relations with China and Russia were worth a try, but there were not many who anticipated success. There *were* many who contended that his courtship of adversaries was matched by his failure to assure allies—although he was certainly more attentive to Japan in his second term, as evidenced by the new defense guidelines of 2015 and the relationship he established with Japan's prime minister, Shinzo Abe.

The strongest critique came from the many analysts who disparaged Obama's overall restraint, his "don't do stupid shit" mantra—what they perceived as an abdication of American leadership around the world. Ultimately, they were angered by what they concluded was his arrogance, his rejection of advice from specialists in and out of government, and his reliance on a small group of ill-informed White House loyalists. There was little doubt that the world had become a more dangerous place during his presidency—and there were some who held him responsible. Obviously, he was not, but his critics can be excused for being disappointed by the performance of a man in whom Americans—and others—had vested so much hope.

And then the unthinkable occurred. The American people elected as their president Donald Trump, a man with no governing experience and little if any knowledge of world affairs—a man who promised to destroy the liberal international order the United States had labored to create at least since 1945, who threatened to undermine the entire system of alliances that had served the nation's interests throughout the Cold War and after, who denied climate change, seemed uninterested in efforts to prevent the proliferation of nuclear weapons, and whose campaign was awash with bigotry, especially against Muslims and Mexicans. Those foreign leaders most fearful of evidence of moral imagination in the White House welcomed his victory. The twenty-first century does not appear likely to be remembered as the American Century.

LAST THOUGHTS

I N THE EIGHTY-ODD years of my life, I have often thought of how fortunate I was to have been born a citizen of the United States of America. I grew up with Franklin Delano Roosevelt's promise of the Four Freedoms: of speech and religion, from fear and from want—and with American leadership in the war against Nazi oppression and Japanese militarism. When I was old enough to read the Declaration of Independence, I understood it was aspirational, but as I explained in a July Fourth speech in Taipei in 1965, I believed almost every generation made some progress toward its promise of equality for all. But as an adult, especially in my study of history, I have been troubled by awareness of the many ways in which my beloved country and its people failed to live up to my vision of its exceptionalism, both at home and abroad.

At home, most obviously we have been guilty of racism and bigotry. Native Americans and African Americans endured horrors, massacres, and enslavement, such as we have not hesitated to condemn in other countries around the world. Native Americans had solemn agreements violated, their lands stolen, and they were herded into reservations where their suffering did not end. After slavery was abolished, African Americans faced lynchings and the miseries of segregation, much perpetuated to this day. I was proud when we elected Barack Obama to the presidency in 2008, an important symbol of how far we had advanced—and shocked by asinine claims that he was not an American, and by the response to the Black Lives Matter movement.

Bigotry in America has spared no Other in the course of our history. Our forefathers were hostile to Catholics generally, especially the Irish who came in large numbers in the mid-nineteenth century and the Italians and East Europeans who came later. In violation of treaty obligations we mistreated Chinese and then Japanese, many of whom had been recruited to ease labor shortages. And then, of course, there was anti-Semitism, which I experienced for the first time only in my early twenties, at Officer Candidate School, on the way to becoming an officer in the U.S. Navy— but I never forgot how incredibly different my experience likely would have been had I been born in Europe in 1934. As I write in March 2017, I am deeply saddened by the intensity of anti-Muslim feelings in my country, shaken by the way my president has fostered it, appalled by the bans he has attempted to impose on travel to our country from Muslim nations. What has become of Roosevelt's call for freedom of religion, of our national commitment to that freedom?

And yet we have transcended bigotry to some extent. The slaves were freed, Asian Americans and a Muslim have been elected to Congress. Americans elected a Catholic and an African American president. Americans nominated and a majority of voters supported a woman for president and an orthodox Jew for vice president. And homosexuals ceased to be persecuted. An optimist might see cyclical surges toward our expressed ideals.

My vision of American exceptionalism was also undermined by my study of how the American empire was created, so much like the Chinese empire thousands of years before: a people occupying a small territory gradually overpowering its neighbors and expanding as far as was feasible. We could go no further north, blocked by the power of the British Empire. We chose not to expand further south where the territory was heavily populated by a people deemed unsuitable to become Americans, despite southern interest in expanding slavery across the Rio Grande. To the east and west, we were slowed by the oceans and a temporary inability to exert sufficient power against competing nations. Before the end of the nineteenth century, however, the American empire included Hawaii, parts of

Samoa, Cuba, and the Philippines—where we denied the people their freedom and killed at least 200,000 Filipinos while suppressing them and introducing some to a form of torture called the "water cure." Even as Secretary of State John Hay urged the great powers not to carve up China, he explored the possibility of taking a slice for his country. The United States was late to the game, but its actions hardly differed from the imperialist practices of the other great powers.

Eventually, at the conclusion of the First World War, the United States became the greatest of the powers, and its president, Woodrow Wilson, attempted valiantly to create and lead a liberal international order, to create an environment in which democracies would thrive—and failed. The British, French, and Japanese were unwilling, and his own people were not ready for that role.

In the early 1950s Robert E. Osgood published an enormously important book, *Ideals and Self-Interest in America's Foreign Relations*. Reviewing the Spanish-American War and the intervention of the United States in World Wars I and II, he argued that a successful foreign policy required a balance between ideals and self-interest, that Theodore Roosevelt had failed because he failed to persuade the American people that the exercise of American power abroad was consistent with their ideals—and Wilson had failed because of his inability to persuade the people that his vision was consistent with the national interest. Franklin Roosevelt, on the other hand, had succeeded in achieving the necessary balance—even if he had to turn to Eleanor Roosevelt occasionally to reinforce his moral imagination.

In the years that followed World War II, Americans, Democrats and Republicans alike, were willing to lead the rest of the world toward the liberal international order that Wilson—and Franklin Roosevelt—had envisaged. The emergence of the Cold War, the threat posed by the Soviet Union and its allies, left no doubt that the national interest was involved—balancing the idealism of membership in the United Nations and concern for human rights. The U.S. role in the Cold War was not merely the beacon for democracy, refuge for the oppressed, the foundation of the liberal international order, but also, through *its* alliances, the protector of the "Free World."

Unfortunately, the perceived security needs of the Cold War forced the United States to ally itself with several unsavory governments and to play an imperial role, interfering in the internal affairs of others. Guatemala, Iran, Cuba, and Chile come quickly to mind. Dwight Eisenhower's penchant for covert operations led to the overthrow of democratically elected governments in Guatemala and Iran. Fidel Castro's threat to American interests in Cuba and his drift into the Soviet camp led to bizarre assassination attempts during the John F. Kennedy administration. Presidents Eisenhower, Kennedy, Lyndon Johnson, and Richard Nixon shared responsibility for the devastation of Vietnam—destroying a country to save it? Nixon and Henry Kissinger were complicit in the overthrow of the democratically elected government of Salvador Allende in Chile. And there was much more done—and that continues to be done—in the name of national security that is inconsistent with American ideals.

We have learned that the United States is a nation like all others; that when confronted with perceived threats to our interests—or obstacles to the expansion of our wealth and power—we act as other powers have throughout history. And yet I find much to be proud of, much our country has done to benefit other peoples: the liberation of Europe after both world wars—and of East Asia after the Second; the creation of a liberal international order after World War II that has benefited much of the world, as well as the United States. But as I study the Cold War era—through which I lived—and the years since the collapse of the Soviet Union, the moral leadership of my country is a little harder to pinpoint and praise. The "unipolar moment," America as the last standing superpower, was surely wasted.

Bill Clinton's only foreign policy concerns appear to have been economic, especially trade issues, unsurprising for a man whose election campaign mantra had been "the economy, stupid" and who was elected over George H. W. Bush, whose forte had been foreign affairs. He demonstrated little interest in human rights and had to be dragged into humanitarian interventions, as in Bosnia. To facilitate trade, he backed away from his campaign's charges against the "Butchers of Beijing," the men responsible for the Tiananmen massacres of 1989. Most shameful was his administration's failure to act to stop the genocide in Rwanda and its obstruction of UN efforts to act. But then, whatever his virtues, Clinton was never known for his moral imagination.

The rise of the self-styled "Vulcans" with the election of the younger Bush in 2000 facilitated the neoconservative drive to spread democracy, particularly in the Middle East. The destruction of the World Trade Center towers on September 11, 2001, sidetracked any vision Bush might have had for the humble American leadership he had promised in his election campaign. Policy was hijacked by Dick Cheney and Donald Rumsfeld, both old-fashioned nationalists eager to exploit American power without restraint by allies in "Old Europe" or the United Nations. The results were disastrous in Iraq but perhaps most tragically for the moral standing of the United States—not least because of the abuse of prisoners, from Abu Ghraib to waterboarding and other forms of torture.

The relief felt in much of the world with the transfer of American political power to Barack Obama in 2009 was epitomized by the award to him of the Nobel Peace Prize less than a year into his presidency. His efforts to reach out to hostile states such as Iran and North Korea, his appeal for friendship with Islam, his efforts to improve relations with China and Russia achieved little. His conviction that the United States could do little to ameliorate the suffering of the Syrian people, his aversion to humanitarian interventions, undermined faith in him among friends at home and abroad. Never lacking in moral imagination, he nonetheless failed to leave the world a better place.

And with Donald Trump as president of the United States, with the views he expresses, the policies he espouses, the tactics he uses, I, like most of my fellow countrymen and women, have little left of which to be proud. Who will appeal now, as did Abraham Lincoln in 1861 in *his* inaugural address, to the "better angels of our nature"?

I have to believe someone will.

INDEX